ASET Series

We often hear these days that the center of Christianity is moving toward the Global South and that Africa is a key player in that movement. This makes the study of African Christianity and African realities important – even more so when it is being done by Africans themselves and in their own context. The Africa Society of Evangelical Theology (ASET) was created to encourage research and sustained theological reflection on key issues facing Africa by and for African Christians and those working within African contexts. The volumes in this series constitute the best papers presented at the annual conferences of ASET and together they seek to fill this important gap in the literature of Christianity.

TITLES IN THIS SERIES

Christianity and Suffering: African Perspectives
2017 | 9781783683604

African Contextual Realities
2018 | 9781783684731

Because a nation is the sum total of its institutions, when these are in trouble, that nation is in trouble; when the institutions are well run, there is bound to be health and positive growth not just for those institutions but for the nation as a whole. *Governance and Christian Higher Education in the African Context* focuses on two key contributors to health and growth of a nation: governance and higher education. The topics discussed, in the light of Kenya and Africa, are contemporary and urgently relevant. Many of the perspectives are informed by research making the discussions inviting, interesting, often incisive, and worth reflecting on by any leader in similar contexts. The volume is a useful tool for anyone interested in sharpening and deepening their personal reflection, perspective and approach to a Christ-honouring leadership style.

Margaret Jepkirui Muthwii, PhD
Vice Chancellor,
Pan Africa Christian University, Nairobi, Kenya

Governance and Christian Higher Education in the African Context is one of the books that explores the commonalities and convergences of realities in Christian higher education in Africa. The critical views brought out by the researchers offer many aspects of the challenges affecting governance and education in general but specific examples also provide further understanding in Africa. By looking at themes such as authority and corruption, the volume evaluates the negative impact this has on education and governance. As well as these, the volume also explores other aspects such as the integration of Christian faith in higher education, especially the development of theological colleges to private chartered universities. The volume is based on biblical principles thus making it a significant book for researchers on the realities of education in Africa. I commend it to Christian institutions of higher learning and the churches that form the boards of those institutions. The book will also be of value for students as they endeavor to research and write and make thinking visible. It is both engaging and coherent, and it charts the important area of Christian higher education and it brings it into fruitful conversation in Christian theology.

Esther Mombo, PhD
Associate Professor, Faculty of Theology,
St Paul's University, Limuru, Kenya

ASET Series

Governance and Christian Higher Education in the African Context

Langham

GLOBAL LIBRARY

Governance and Christian Higher Education in the African Context

General Editors

David K. Ngaruiya
and
Rodney L. Reed

Langham

GLOBAL LIBRARY

Published 2019 by Langham Global Library
An imprint of Langham Publishing
www.langhampublishing.org

Langham Publishing and its imprints are a ministry of Langham Partnership
Langham Partnership
PO Box 296, Carlisle, Cumbria, CA3 9WZ, UK
www.langham.org

ISBNs:
978-1-78368-545-5 Print
978-1-78368-560-8 ePub
978-1-78368-561-5 Mobi
978-1-78368-562-2 PDF

British Library Cataloguing-in-Publication Data
A catalogue record for this book is available from the British Library

ISBN: 978-1-78368-545-5

Cover & Book Design: projectluz.com

CONTENTS

Preface

The world is only as good as the people that live in it and exercise responsibility over it. The degree of humanity's exercised responsibility both individual and collective is often reflected in contemporary happenings. In particular, such happenings require examination through contextual research. Among the issues that elicit much debate in our times regarding the degree of humanity's exercise of responsibility are Christians' relationship with secular authorities, the church, integration of faith, and Christian higher education.

The purpose of this book is to explore this range of issues in light of humanity's responsibility to be a good steward of the world, or more precisely, this God-given world. Debates on the relationship of the Christian to authority heighten when Christians don't so much question the legitimacy of authorities as hold such authorities accountable. Though sometimes neglected, such accountability is not only expected but should be the norm for a Christian. When Christians overlook the accountability of secular authorities, the opportunity to speak for the helpless and the prosperity of a nation is undermined.

Many metaphors have been used to describe the church. Some have referred to the church as a hospital where the socially and spiritually wounded find the care they need. Others have called the church a lifeboat, thus fronting the church as a place of rescue for all who run to God. The question addressed in this book regarding the church is how its desired growth impacts its administration.

It is not enough to consider the administration of the church while forgetting to address the question of governance. In our day and age, governance in some countries has led to devolution of power as a way to ensure that justice is served to all. Good governance is, however, enshrined in unchanging principles, and serving justice to all would be impossible without such unchanging principles – hence the need to examine principles of good governance.

It was Nelson Mandela who said, "Education is the most powerful tool you can use to change the world." So critical for Mandela was the education of citizens that, according to him, a nation could not develop without education. Important as it is, education, not only in Africa but around the world, has been constantly – and not without controversy – undergoing reform. In an increasingly pluralistic world, the integration of Christian faith into learning is vitally important.

That society invests much in the education of its members is undeniable. The question is often what philosophy to utilize in a given context. In the context of globalization, matters of education philosophy need an even greater articulation. This articulation has a bearing on the kind of workforce that the world calls for in this era of history.

The growth and reforms in Christian higher education have brought about the transition of some theological schools to universities. Such transitions have sometimes created a standoff between the church and the newly created universities, not to mention with governmental authorities in matters of education. While each of these parties raises issues about such reforms, the realities and implications of these reforms need to be articulated in light of serving the needs of the church and communities around those institutions.

To a considerable extent, it can be argued that universities are "liturgical spaces." This is because ritual and liturgy are part and parcel of the spiritual formation of students, particularly in Christian universities. Liturgy can be used as a lever to draw a close relationship between the devotee and the almighty God of all creation. As such, liturgy must be deliberately designed and used appropriately in the spiritual formation of university students and faculty.

This book addresses all the above-mentioned issues. The third publication of Africa Society of Evangelical Theology (ASET), it is the fruit of the ASET conference held in 2017 at Daystar University, Valley Road Campus, Nairobi, Kenya.

David K. Ngaruiya, PhD

Associate Professor,
School of Theology and Christian Ministry,
International Leadership University,
Nairobi, Kenya

Acknowledgments

Many thanks for this volume are due to a range of stakeholders. All the contributors have spent hours laboring over their work, allowing us to pester them to repeatedly make improvements. Their desire to transform Africa is celebrated. We also thank the reviewers who critiqued these papers and gave suggestions for improvements. We would not be where we are without a committed group of reviewers willing to undertake this task unconcerned as to whether they will be paid or not. Appreciation goes also to the leadership of Daystar University, where these papers were originally presented as part of an ASET conference. They were gracious hosts to the society. The good work of the Executive Committee of ASET must be acknowledged as well. The committee has given much-needed direction and support all along the way. Thanks also go to Vivian Doub and all the team at Langham Partnership, for their tireless support of this work and patience with us in this publishing endeavor. I extend a special word of gratitude to Professor David Ngaruiya, for joining me as General Editor of these works. When the work was getting too much, David stepped in to help lighten the load! Most of all, we thank our Lord Jesus Christ, without whose life, death, and resurrection the Africa Society of Evangelical Theology would have no "good news" to reflect upon and proclaim.

Rodney L. Reed

Associate Professor,
Deputy Vice Chancellor of Academic Affairs,
Africa Nazarene University,
Nairobi, Kenya

Part I

Christianity and Governance

1

Resisting Authority in Twenty-First-Century Kenya: An Analysis and Application of Romans 13:1–7

David Bawks

Minister, Nairobi Chapel

Abstract

Responding as Christians to oppression and corrupt systems of power has been a thorny subject from the very beginning of Christian history, and it continues to challenge Christians today. Romans 13:1–7 has proven a pivotal passage for Christians wrestling with their response to an oppressive government. What parameters are allowable for Christians in protesting a government that has violated the rights of the people and actively persecuted Christians and others of faith? What does Paul mean when he warns against "resisting authority" in a way displeasing to God? Christians certainly must pay their taxes and follow all laws that do not go against God's stated will. However, not all governments support God's will, and much of the polemic of the Old Testament prophets was directed against disobedient and evil governments, including those of Israel, Judah, and their neighbors. An important clarification is that governments only hold divine validity and God's sanction to the extent that they align with God's laws. Throughout the Bible, God makes it clear that he both appoints rulers and removes them from power.

A basic principle of biblical interpretation is that any passage must be interpreted in light of other passages on the same theme, and that it must be in line with the overall message of the Bible. Examples such as Daniel make it clear that not all laws are to be blindly obeyed. This paper argues that Romans 13 defends the status of government as an institution set up by God, but the passage does not preclude peaceful protest and attempts by Christians to fight corruption, improve systems, and advocate for the disenfranchised. The paper then explores some examples of how this passage can be lived out and applied in twenty-first-century Kenya.

Key words: Romans 13, Kenya, government, resisting authority, politics, protest, oppression

Introduction

Must Kenyans uncritically acquiesce to all government requirements, whether at a local or at national level? Does Paul require this obedience in the thirteenth chapter of his epistle to the Romans? The relationship between Christianity and politics has been hotly debated, with some Christians appealing to biblical principles as the foundation for their opposition to corruption and oppressive regimes, while many in power have done the opposite, citing passages such as Romans 13 as proof of their legitimacy. This paper will explore the background, literary setting, history of interpretation, and argument of Romans 13:1–7 to understand what Paul was communicating to the Roman Christians, and how this affects our relationship to civic duty and governance in Kenya today. These verses have been called "the most emphatic New Testament passage on relations with civil authority,"[1] and have resulted in intense controversy throughout Christian history as to their correct interpretation and application. Here is the passage:

> Let every person be subject to the governing authorities. For there is no authority except from God, and those that exist have been instituted by God. Therefore whoever resists the authorities resists what God has appointed, and those who resist will incur judgment. For rulers are not a terror to good conduct, but to bad. Would you have no fear of the one who is in authority? Then do what is good, and you will receive his approval, for he is God's

---

1. Ovidiu Hanc, "Paul and Empire: A Reframing of Romans 13:1–7 in the Context of the New Exodus," *Tyndale Bulletin* 65, no. 2 (2014): 313.

servant for your good. But if you do wrong, be afraid, for he does not bear the sword in vain. For he is the servant of God, an avenger who carries out God's wrath on the wrongdoer. Therefore one must be in subjection, not only to avoid God's wrath but also for the sake of conscience. For because of this you also pay taxes, for the authorities are ministers of God, attending to this very thing. Pay to all what is owed to them: taxes to whom taxes are owed, revenue to whom revenue is owed, respect to whom respect is owed, honor to whom honor is owed. (Rom 13:1–7)

Background of Romans

As Paul was preparing to travel to Spain, he wrote the epistle to the church in Rome, the center of the imperial network spanning the Mediterranean, for a few reasons, including, first, to strengthen, encourage, and proclaim the gospel to them.[2] Neil Elliott argues that "Paul intends this letter to Rome to serve as the medium of his 'evangelization' of the Romans."[3] Timothy Carter posits another overarching thread that holds the letter together: "Paul's pastoral response to the tensions between the weak and the strong in the Roman congregations."[4] Romans also serves other purposes: to introduce Paul to the Roman church community as an apostle of Jesus Christ, to detail the theological underpinning of his ministry, and to solicit support for his coming ministry journey to Spain, with Rome as a stopping point on the journey – a refueling pit stop.[5]

The health and continued vitality of the Roman church would have definite implications for Paul's future missionary endeavors. Jan Botha describes the purpose of Paul's letter to the Roman church, and of chapter 13 in particular, as follows: "Paul's text wanted to orientate a small Christian community

---

2. See Rom 1:9–15.

3. Neil Elliott, *The Rhetoric of Romans*, Journal for the Study of the New Testament Supplement Series 45 (Sheffield: Sheffield Academic Press, 1990), 84.

4. Timothy L. Carter, "The Irony of Romans 13," *Novum Testamentum* 46, no. 3 (2004): 217. He traces this theme throughout the letter: "In Rom 1–4, Paul seeks to establish the equality of the Jewish and Gentile congregations on the basis of faith in Christ, and in Rom 5–8 he argues that the ethnic boundary marker of the law has been effectively replaced by the eschatological boundary markers of baptism and the Spirit" (Carter, "Irony of Romans 13," 217). Dealing with the question this theological premise raises regarding the place of Israel, Paul argues that they will yet reach salvation because of God's faithfulness (Carter, 218).

5. See Rom 15:23–24. Moo writes that the verb used in 15:24, *propempō*, means "help on the way with material support" (Douglas Moo, *The Epistle to the Romans*, New International Commentary on the New Testament [Grand Rapids: Eerdmans, 1996], 17).

pragmatically in a specific situation for the sake of their continued existence and well-being."[6] For Paul's missionary purposes, compliance with the imperial powers had considerable advantages. Drawing upon these various themes, Paul composed the longest, densest, and most carefully reasoned of all his letters.

Historical Setting

The letter to the Romans is often dated in the late 50s, near the end of Paul's third missionary journey, as Paul was about to return to Jerusalem; it was perhaps written from the city of Corinth around AD 56 or 57.[7] In considering the situation of the original readers and hearers of the epistle, it is helpful to recreate as best as possible the significant events of that time. One major event affecting the Jewish community in Rome occurred about a decade prior to the composition of Romans, when the Emperor Claudius expelled Jews from Rome in AD 49.[8]

Significant debate has raged over the political environment at the time of Paul's writing, and to what extent this shaped the content and intent of what he sought to communicate to the Roman church. Pol Vonck writes that since Emperor Nero was still popular and had not yet descended to the depths of dictatorship for which he would become renowned, "we can hardly imagine any reason for critical political theology or rebellious tendencies among the Christians in the imperial capital at the time Romans was written."[9] Carter disagrees, highlighting a number of reasons why Christians would fear the imperial authorities, including the fallout from the Jewish expulsion by Emperor Claudius, and the treatment of poor Christians by the legal system.[10] Knowing the bloody and violent outcome for Roman Christians following the fire in AD

---

6. Jan Botha, "Creation of New Meaning: Rhetorical Situations and the Reception of Romans 13:1–7," *Journal of Theology for Southern Africa* 79 (June 1992): 35.

7. Moo, *Epistle to the Romans*, 2–3.

8. See Acts 18:2; Botha, "Creation of New Meaning," 31; Moo, *Epistle to the Romans*, 4–5. Gift Mtukwa explains the significance of this event for the interactions within the church: "The Jews were coming back to the city of Rome and finding Gentiles fully in charge of the church. Paul wrote to reconcile these two groups with the gospel" (Gift Mtukwa, "The People of God and Kingdom Political Ethics in Romans 13:1–7," *Didache: Faithful Teaching* 14, no. 1 (2014): 1.

9. Pol Vonck, "All Authority Comes from God: Romans 13:1–7 – A Tricky Text about Obedience to Political Power," *AFER* 26, no. 6 (December 1984): 339.

10. Carter, "Irony of Romans 13," 210–211. He writes, "One wonders how those who had been evicted from their homes, with the loss of property and business, would have responded to Paul's statement that those who do good need have no fear of the authorities" (Carter, 211). Carter postulates that the composition of the Roman church would likely have been "poor non-Latin citizens, who occupied no legal position and were of uncertain official status," making them easily taken advantage of by the rich and powerful.

64, not to mention the later brutality and persecution of countless Christians both in Rome and throughout the world, it would seem fair to conclude with Carter that the "apostle was misguided in his optimistic assessment of the goodness of the state," if indeed Romans 13 did reflect such a viewpoint.[11]

Ernst Käsemann argues for the presence of overly "enthusiastic" members within the Roman church who were so caught up with their newfound heavenly citizenship that they abandoned their earthly duties such as paying taxes.[12] Paul's intention in Romans 13, therefore, was to remind them that they still lived in the world and must comply with political realities. Botha connects features of Romans 12 and 13 with this possible scenario: "Against this background Paul warns in 12:3 against pompousness (a possible allusion to the enthusiasts) and urges his readers in 12:6 to humbleness. In 13:1–7 he explicitly warns them that they still have to live and function within earthly structures."[13] The reality of these "enthusiastic" Roman Christians has been questioned, but the point that all Christians do reside and operate within physical earthly systems is undeniable. Citizenship in heaven does not strip anyone of the citizenship they hold on earth.

Carter argues for a rhetorical strategy of irony in which the real meaning of Paul's words is hidden behind their literal meaning.[14] William Herzog supports the same interpretation, using the term "dissemble," writing, "[i]n a setting where power relations are asymmetrical, it will be much more likely that the political speech of the weak will dissemble, that is, it will feign obedience and loyalty to the colonial overlords while pursuing its own hidden agenda."[15] Thus, Herzog would ascribe a hidden meaning to the words of Paul in Romans, giving the impression of obedience to Rome without actually endorsing the

---

11. Carter, "Irony of Romans 13," 210. He says, "Given the social context of Paul's audience, it is hard to avoid the conclusion that his words might have sounded either naive or crass in the ears of those who were the victims of such oppression and injustice" (Carter, 211).

12. Ernst Käsemann, *Commentary on Romans*, trans. Geoffrey W. Bromiley (Grand Rapids: Eerdmans, 1980), 351. Corneliu Constantineanu agrees, saying, "It is probable that there were Christians who understood the lordship of Christ to mean a rejection of all human lordship and government authority. In response, Paul corrects this misunderstanding and offers the believers in Rome a framework for their Christian life in which the political powers are God's intention and therefore have divine legitimization" (Corneliu Constantineanu, "The Bible and the Public Arena: A Pauline Model for Christian Engagement in Society with Reference to Romans 13," *KAIROS: Evangelical Journal of Theology* 4, no. 2 (2010): 148.

13. Botha, "Creation of New Meaning," 31.

14. Carter, "Irony of Romans 13," 212–217.

15. William R. Herzog II, "Dissembling, a Weapon of the Weak: The Case of Christ and Caesar in Mark 12:13–17 and Romans 13:1–7," *Perspectives in Religious Studies* 21, no. 4 (1994): 341.

authorities' validity.[16] Throughout church history, this suggestion of irony has been a minority interpretation. Hanc strongly disagrees with the irony proposal, arguing that because Paul never suggested fighting for freedom in his letters, "believers are not only to submit to civil authority without engaging in subversive activities, but there is also a proactive exhortation of social implications (e.g. acts of euergetism)."[17] Far from having a hidden desire to subvert and undermine the Roman imperial establishment, Paul is instead submitting the Empire to God's ultimate authority.[18] Without knowing Paul's inner thoughts and intentions, it is difficult to prove which option is correct, but the middle ground between these two extremes provides the sturdiest exegetical footing. John Marshall argues for this median approach, insisting that we must recognize "the authenticity of his affiliation to Roman power *at the same time* as understanding his actions and strategies of resistance [emphasis his]."[19]

Some have questioned whether the contemporary political situation in Rome is even the right direction to take our theological investigation. Hanc argues against basing our interpretation on the Roman context: "His self-understanding as the Servant of the Lord, who seeks for a way of salvation not an escape from society, indicates that the original meaning of his theology is rooted in the Old Testament, not in the socio-political realities of first century Rome."[20] This point is surely overstated, and useful sources for grounding Paul's theological refection can be found both in the Old Testament and in the contemporary sociopolitical milieu.

Literary Context

Outlining the structure of Romans is helpful in setting the stage for chapter 13, but it also is not without controversy. Questions regarding the overarching theme and which parts of Romans should be considered the theological center

---

16. Herzog, "Dissembling," 342. He explains, "When writing to Christians at the heart of the empire, Paul calculates how to sound like an obedient Roman citizen while granting nothing to the actual Roman empire" (Herzog, 342).

17. Hanc, "Paul and Empire," 314.

18. Hanc, 314–315. He calls the idea of a subversive ideology in Paul's writing "presumptuous," concluding that "since Paul's theology of the state was shaped by his Jewish upbringing in light of the Christ event, an *intentional* covenantal- reading supersedes the *potential* political-reading" (Hanc, 316).

19. John W. Marshall, "Hybridity and Reading Romans 13," *Journal for the Study of the New Testament* 31, no. 2 (December 2008): 169.

20. Hanc, "Paul and Empire," 314.

have occupied tremendous academic debate and energy. Douglas Moo traces how the shift in focus has moved from chapters 1–5 by the Reformers, to Schweitzer and his followers who highlighted chapters 5–8, to scholars such as Stendahl who prioritized the treatment of chapters 9–11, to more recent figures who focus on Paul's exhortations in 14:1 – 15:13 as the letter's heart.[21] Moo also provides a helpful outline, unpacking Romans through the lens of what he identifies as its theme, namely, the gospel: the heart of the gospel in 1:18 – 4:25, the assurance provided by the gospel in 5:1 – 8:39, the defense of the gospel (the problem of Israel) in 9:1 – 11:36, and finally the transforming power of the gospel as lived out in Christian conduct in 12:1 – 15:13.[22]

The letters of Paul can often be divided into two major parts, the first section setting the theological stage and the second section then detailing the practical outcomes of our theological foundation.[23] While Romans is longer than most of Paul's other letters and doesn't break evenly into two parts, a significant shift does occur in Romans 12.[24] One of the terms used to describe Romans 13:1–7 is "paraenesis," or "ethical admonition."[25]

Within Romans 12–13, several ways of charting the thematic flow have been developed. Vonck identifies "doing good" as a dominant theme in Romans 12 and 13.[26] Romans 12 also encourages the Romans to live in humility and in love, and to bless those who are persecuting them.[27] In 12:18, Paul exhorts the Romans to "live peaceably with all" as far as possible. Corneliu Constantineanu argues that Romans 13 "should be interpreted in close association with the exhortation to love in 12:9–21, which, together with the similar exhortation in 13:8–10, brackets it."[28] Troels Engberg-Pedersen provides a helpful summary, distinguishing between features of this passage that relate to fellow believers

---

21. Moo, *Epistle to the Romans*, 33–35.

22. Moo, 33–35.

23. For example, Eph 1–3 lays the theological foundation, and chs. 4–6 detail the practical implications. First Thessalonians undergoes a similar shift in 4:1 with the use of "Finally"; and Paul also uses "Finally" in Phil 3:1, marking a distinction between Phil 1–2 and the second half in chs. 3–4.

24. Elliott writes that "one of the most evident structural features in the letter is the transition to formal paraenesis at 12:1" (Elliott, *Rhetoric of Romans*, 70).

25. Jon Nelson Bailey, "Paul's Political Paraenesis in Romans 13:1–7," *Restoration Quarterly* 46, no. 1 (2004): 11. See also Seyoon Kim, "Paul's Common Paraenesis (1 Thess 4–5; Phil 2–4; and Rom 12–13): The Correspondence between Romans 1:18–32 and 12:1–2, and the Unity of Romans 12–13," *Tyndale Bulletin* 62, no. 1 (2011): 109–139.

26. Vonck, "All Authority," 340.

27. Seyoon Kim argues for a connection between Rom 13 and the themes of "humility, non-retaliation, and enemy love in Romans 12:14–21" (Kim, "Paul's Common Paraenesis," 115).

28. Constantineanu, "Bible and the Public Arena," 145.

as an "in-group" and how we should behave toward outsiders, agreeing with Vonck's identification of "doing good."[29] Seyoon Kim argues for the cohesion of Romans 12 and 13: "Romans 12:14 – 13:10 is really a unit – a long unit in which Paul drills into the minds of his Roman readers the exhortation to 'live peaceably with all' by practicing humility, non-retaliation, and enemy love even in the situation of persecution."[30]

Exegetical Analysis

The primary thrust of Romans 13:1–7 comes in verse 1, with Paul's command that all people should be in subjection to the authorities in power, going beyond just Christians to include Romans and Gentiles. The Greek word for authority, ἐξουσία (*exousia*), is used in various forms four times in verses 1–3. The *Theological Dictionary of the New Testament* describes the word as follows:

> In the NT ἐξουσία denotes the power of God in nature and the spiritual world, the power which Satan exercises and imparts, and especially the power or freedom which is given to Jesus, and by Him to His disciples, and which includes, e.g., the right to support (570). . . . Here the sing. tends to assume the more general sense of "government," borrowing from the Rabb. רְשׁוּת, R. 13:2 f.; Mt. 8:9 and par.[31]

Some debate has taken place concerning whether ἐξουσία as used in Romans 13:2 indicates spiritual or purely human authority.[32] Those who argue in favor of a spiritual understanding, such as Oscar Cullmann, Karl Barth, and others, point out that angelic powers were a core aspect of New Testament concepts of authority structures. They argue two points in connection with

---

29. Troels Engberg-Pedersen, "Paul's Stoicizing Politics in Romans 12–13: The Role of 13.1–10 in the Argument," *Journal for the Study of the New Testament* 29, no. 2 (December 2006): 166. He explains, "In Rom. 12–13 Paul does not extend Christian αγάπη [love] to cover non-believers. Instead, he continues (in 12.15–16) to speak about behavior that falls under αγάπη in relation to the in-group. And when he then goes on to speak of relations outside the group (in 12.17–21), he employs a different terminology, which focuses on the basic contrast between good (αγαθόν) and bad (κακόν), that is, on what is objectively good or bad behavior with no implication that it springs from the subjective motivation of αγάπη. This point is of great importance since it also explains the transition from 12.21 to 13.1–7" (Engberg-Pedersen, "Paul's Stoicizing Politics," 166).

30. Kim, "Paul's Common Paraenesis," 117.

31. G. Kittel, G. W. Bromiley, and G. Friedrich, eds., *Theological Dictionary of the New Testament*, electronic edn, vol. 2 (Grand Rapids: Eerdmans, 1964), 565.

32. See Ray Barraclough, "Romans 13:1–7: Application in Context," *Colloquium* 17, no. 2 (May 1985): 16–17.

how authority should be understood: "both that a relationship was accepted in Judaism between angels and rulers between Satan and this world's governing authorities and that such thinking permeates Paul's understanding of rulers."[33] Paul's use of the term "authority" almost always carries this connotation.[34] However, along with Ray Barraclough, Douglas Moo, Robert Stein, and others, this paper argues that the meaning of ἐξουσία in Romans 13 refers only to human governments and authorities, not to angelic rulers behind them.[35] Stein points out that we are never asked elsewhere by Paul to submit to angelic powers, but rather to resist them, as in Romans 8:37–39.[36] The reference to paying taxes in Romans 13:6–7 also suggests human systems instead of spiritual ones.[37] Barraclough concludes that "only human rulers are designated in 13:1–7."[38]

Another significant term occurring in 13:1 is ὑποτάσσω (hupotassō), a middle/passive imperative meaning "subject yourselves" or "submit yourselves."[39] This word occurs numerous times throughout the New Testament, applying to the spirit of prophets as subject to the prophets, women in the church, all things as subject to God, wives to their husbands, and slaves to their masters.[40] John MacArthur notes that hupotassō is "a military term meaning to line up to take your orders."[41] Moo points out the potentially significant difference between a command to submit to versus a command to obey the governing authorities, pointing out that we are also ordered to submit to spiritual leaders,

33. Barraclough, "Romans 13:1–7," 16.

34. See Robert H. Stein, "The Argument of Romans 13:1–7," *Novum Testamentum* 31, no. 4 (October 1989): 328; Barraclough, "Romans 13:1–7," 16.

35. Cf. Alexander F. C. Webster, "St Paul's Political Advice to the Haughty Gentile Christians in Rome: An Exegesis of Romans 13:1–7," *St Vladimir's Theological Quarterly* 25, no. 4 (1981): 266; Stein, "Argument," 328.

36. Stein, "Argument," 328.

37. Stein, 328.

38. Barraclough, "Romans 13:1–7," 17.

39. See Herzog, "Dissembling," 352.

40. To be precise, it occurs thirty-eight times in thirty-one verses in twenty-five different grammatical forms. See 1 Cor 14:32; 14:34; 15:27; Eph 1:22; 5:24; Phil 3:21; and Titus 2:9. Alexander Webster describes the various nuances as follows: "In the NT this subordination seems sometimes to be compulsory and other times voluntary, and the range of material contexts entails marriage, parental relationships, slavery, ecclesiastical authority, God, Christ, the law and – in only three passages, namely Rm 13:1 and 5, Tt 3:1 and 1 Pt 2:13 – secular governing authorities" (Webster, "St Paul's Political Advice," 269).

41. John MacArthur, *The Christian and Government* (Panorama City, CA: Word of Grace Communications, 1986), 13.

and even to "one another."[42] Given the context of Romans 13 and the prevailing usage in the New Testament, I would argue that the focus of ὑποτάσσω in this passage is submission.

Verse 1 goes on to state that the underlying authority of all earthly governments and rulers is that of God himself, which is well attested throughout the Bible.[43] Thus, all earthly power is derived from the power of God – and is always subject to that greater power. Verses 2 through 7 then explain and unpack the implications of this theological premise. Because authority is ultimately derived from God, resisting authority is resisting God. The word for "resist" in 13:2 is ἀντιτάσσω (antitassō), a present middle participle that only occurs four other times in the New Testament: Acts 18:6; James 4:6; 5:6; and 1 Peter 5:5. Friberg, Friberg, and Miller define it as "*set in array against*; as setting oneself against, *oppose, resist, be hostile toward* (AC 18.6)."[44] In Acts 18:6, Jews in Corinth *opposed* and reviled Paul; James 4:6 and 1 Peter 5:5 both quote from Proverbs 3:34, which says that God *opposes* the proud but gives grace to the humble; and in James 5:6 the rich have condemned and murdered the righteous person, who does not *resist* the rich. It is this resistance and opposition that Paul forbids his readers to practice against the authorities.

Any such resistance will incur judgment (κρίμα, v. 2). Generally, κρίμα is used to refer to the judgment of God, such as the final judgment for sin, but within the context of Romans 13 it seems likely that this judgment is mediated through the state.[45] Verses 3 and 4 clearly refer to rulers being "a terror" to evil, "God's servant for . . . good," and bearing the sword for a purpose, all of which supports their role in mediating divine judgment. Judgment carried out properly both rewards obedience and punishes disobedience. To avoid living in fear and incurring judgment, we must do what is right, and obey.

---

42. Moo, *Epistle to the Romans*, 797. See 1 Cor 16:16 and Eph 5:21. Cf. Mtukwa, "People of God," 4; and James D. G. Dunn, *Romans 8–16*, Word Biblical Commentary 38B (Dallas: Word Books, 1988), 760–761.

43. God gives power to whomever he chooses, and all those in power owe their position ultimately to God. See Prov 8:15–16; Jer 27:5; and the words of Jesus to Pilate in John 19:11: "You would have no authority over me at all unless it had been given you from above." The book of Daniel elaborates a clear contrast between the permanency of the kingdom of God and the temporality of human kingdoms, and the power God exerts over the affairs and kingdoms of human beings (Dan 1:2; 2:21; and 4:34–35).

44. Barbara Friberg, Timothy Friberg, and Neva F. Miller, *Analytical Lexicon of the Greek New Testament*, electronic edn, Baker's Greek New Testament Library (Grand Rapids: Baker, 2000).

45. Stein argues that the final judgment at the end of history is in view, saying: "Of the eleven other instances in which this term appears in Paul, nine (or perhaps ten) clearly refer to God's judgment. More importantly still, in the other five instances in which the term is found in Romans all clearly refer to the divine judgment" (Stein, "Argument," 331).

This passage is structured around a command to submit to government authority, first given in verse 1 and then repeated in verse 5. The initial command is supported by the theological premise of God's underlying authority and the danger of punishment when doing wrong. Verse 5 recaps this argument, emphasizing the necessity of submission on two grounds: wrath and conscience, which correspond to the supporting reasons elaborated in verses 2, 3, and 4. It appears that Paul's appeal to conscience goes beyond just avoiding punishment to include the idea of doing right for the sake of internal consistency and peace of mind. Finally, a practical application is drawn in verses 6 and 7: we must pay taxes to the tax collectors, and provide honor, respect, and revenue to all who deserve them. Because the authorities are serving God, they deserve to receive taxes.

Theological Analysis

Having surveyed the historical context, literary features, and exegetical factors in Romans 13, we will shift to consider the theological meaning of these verses. If Romans 13 were the only source of a biblical theology of political submission and Christian responsibility, it might be possible to insist that Christians are required to submit fully to all forms of human governance. However, many other passages also address this topic, and to avoid being dragged off the straight course into the thicket of speculation by a single passage of Scripture, any responsible biblical theology must take into account the larger thematic portrayal. In addition to God's power over human governance, another consistent scriptural theme is disobedience of unjust laws. Exodus 1:17 relates: "the midwives feared God and did not do as the king of Egypt commanded them, but let the male children live." This disobedience of the midwives was rewarded by God, who treated them well and gave them families of their own.[46] Shadrach, Meshach, and Abednego refused to bow down to the image set up by King Nebuchadnezzar, choosing instead to be thrown into the fiery furnace.[47] Daniel himself refused to pray to King Darius, undergoing the punishment of spending a night in the lions' den.[48] Both stories end with miraculous deliverances. Perhaps the most famous declaration of civil disobedience comes

---

46. Exod 1:20–21.
47. Dan 3.
48. Dan 6.

from the mouth of Peter and the apostles: "We must obey God rather than men."[49]

Throughout Scripture, God's desire is always for justice and peace. The drumbeat of the prophetic voice pushes against oppression and in favor of righteous actions; as Micah declared: "He has told you, O man, what is good; and what does the LORD require of you but to do justice, and to love kindness, and to walk humbly with your God?"[50] As Jeremiah warned the king of Judah: "Thus says the LORD: Do justice and righteousness, and deliver from the hand of the oppressor him who has been robbed. And do no wrong or violence to the resident alien, the fatherless, and the widow, nor shed innocent blood in this place."[51] God's principles for an equitable and stable society are made abundantly clear through the Hebrew prophets.

Jewish nationalism, the Zealots, posed a strong theological challenge to a holistic Christian conception of civic duty and politics. The popular hope of a Messiah was for the deliverance of Israel from the tyranny of Rome, and of the reestablishment of the physical kingdom of David. Jesus did not accomplish this, however, but devoted his attention to setting up a far different kingdom. However, as we see from Paul, we cannot then dismiss the kingdoms of this world, but rather we must live within their framework.[52]

Paul's theology was deeply rooted in the themes and events of the Hebrew Scriptures. Hanc interprets Paul's theology in light of an exodus paradigm, arguing that Paul understood the deliverance of Israel from Egyptian bondage to be a foreshadowing of the true exodus performed by Jesus Christ on the cross.[53] This example of deliverance thus influenced and informed his entire political understanding. Moving even further back beyond the exodus to creation, Constantineanu notes the significance of creation in Paul's concept of authority and the rationale behind our submission to authority.[54] Daniel

---

49. Acts 5:29.

50. Mic 6:8.

51. Jer 22:3.

52. Hanc goes on to stress that "Paul commands the Church not to subvert the Empire, but to serve it in a Christ-like sacrificial manner. He is not a revolutionary figure but a servant who is willing to submit to civil authority as a servant of Christ" (Hanc, "Paul and Empire," 314). This point is almost certainly overstated, and we are not to serve governments, but to serve God.

53. Hanc, 315.

54. Constantineanu, "Bible and the Public Arena," 147. He breaks down the significance of creation for Paul's grounding of authority: "It is significant to observe that the first theological reason Paul gives for submission is not Christological (that Christ conquered the powers) or eschatological (that the end is near), but creational (God's order in creation), thus keeping in line with his Jewish theology of creation and order" (Constantineanu, 147).

would also have been a formative source of Paul's theological understanding, particularly of the Roman Empire. Carter expresses his understanding of Daniel as follows:

> As a Pharisee, he would hardly have been sympathetic to the Romans. Paul would have read Dan. 7 as a portrait of Rome as the "fourth beast, terrifying and dreadful and exceedingly strong. It had great iron teeth and was devouring, breaking in pieces, and stamping what was left with its feet" (7:7). Rome was the oppressor and enemy of God's people.[55]

As Christians, our political goal is not to set up a theocracy, or a "Christian" government. The Bible is not a handbook of political theory, advising on the details of the best structures to put in place for human governance. One of the principles that should be espoused by all, especially Christians, is the freedom of worship for any religion. A consistent application of religious freedom ensures that religious practice, and Christian presence, is not dependent on the changing religious inclination of those in power.

Christianity is not bound to any particular nation, culture, or region, and Christians retain their ethnic identity, culture, language, and civic obligations. Moo writes, "His [Paul's] purpose may be to stifle the kind of extremism that would pervert his emphasis on the coming of a new era and on the 'new creation' into a rejection of every human and societal convention – including the government."[56] Such a rejection of human conventions would isolate Christian communities and compromise their mission and witness.

History of Interpretation

In formulating an articulation of Romans 13, there is no shortage of historical options to draw from. Moo wryly notes that "it is only a slight exaggeration to say that history of the interpretation of Rom. 13:1–7 is the history of attempts to avoid what seems to be its plain meaning."[57] For example, Origen wrote,

---

55. Carter, "Irony of Romans 13," 212.

56. Moo, *Epistle to the Romans*, 791.

57. Moo, 806. Corneliu Constantineanu traces the variety of interpretive choices: "Opinions range all the way from removing it from the canon and treating it as an interpolation of non-Pauline origin, to assigning it extremely limited or no relevance for a theology of the state considering that it is a contextual piece of instruction addressed to a very specific situation in Rome, and to seeing it as a general statement that applies to all governments at all times as an expression of God's desire and purpose of God for order in society" (Constantineanu, "Bible and the Public Arena," 144).

"Is an authority which persecutes the children of God, which attacks the faith and which undermines our religion, from God? . . . Likewise, God's judgment against the authorities will be just, if they have used the powers they have received according to their own ungodliness and not according to the laws of God."[58] The question as to which parameters must be in place to qualify as divinely ordained authority has been raised by many other church fathers as well. Theodoret of Cyrrhus wrote:

> Even priests, bishops and monks must obey the commands of secular rulers. Of course, they must do so insofar as obedience is consistent with godliness. If the rulers demand something which is ungodly, then on no account are they allowed to do it. The holy apostle teaches us that both authorities and obedience depend entirely on God's providence, but he does not say that God has specifically appointed one person or another to exercise that authority. For it is not the wickedness of individual rulers which comes from God but the establishment of the ruling power itself. . . . Since God wants sinners to be punished, he is prepared to tolerate even bad rulers. (Interpretation of the Letter to the Romans IER, Migne PG 83 col. 193.)[59]

In formulating his monumental work *The City of God*, as well as other writings, St Augustine drew upon Paul in articulating his political theology. He believed that there are two cities, one of God and one of man, and they both exist in the world. These cities are difficult to describe precisely, but the city of God is generally considered to be the society of the elect, the church. The elect are members of both cities, at the same time, but their primary allegiance is to the city of God. The city of man can be thought of as secular society, the government, and the public square. This requires people to operate within the structures and expectations of secular society without abusing their Christian liberty.[60] Wilfrid Parsons describes how Augustine's conception of a "hierarchy of human affairs," with God at the top and all other authorities coming in layers underneath, solves the problem of reconciling disobedience with Paul's commands in Romans 13: "In an organic society, when an evil command is

---

58. Gerald Bray, ed., *Ancient Christian Commentary on Scripture* (Downers Grove, IL: InterVarsity Press, 1998), 324.

59. Bray, *Ancient Christian Commentary*, 325–326.

60. For more on this, see Wilfrid Parsons, "The Influence of Romans XIII on Christian Political Thought 2: Augustine to Hincmar," *Theological Studies* 2, no. 3 (September 1941): 326–329.

resisted, there is really no disobedience; there is merely obedience to the higher powers, as St. Paul enjoined. There is a unity in all being, from the bottom to the top, and at the top is God, above the emperor."[61] Augustine's understanding of power and obedience would be deeply influential throughout the Middle Ages.

Moving to more recent interpretations, Bernard Lategan examined scholarly responses to Romans 13 from 1989 to 2012, concluding that "the large majority of post-1989 readings of the passage are variations of resistant readings. The few affirmative readings are inevitable from readers who are in a position of power or who have an interest in maintaining the status quo."[62] Romans 13 continues to be actively unpacked and applied, increasingly from a post-colonial and anti-imperial perspective. Continuing political developments will no doubt lead to new perspectives on and approaches to Romans 13.

Application in Kenya

One of the key steps in formulating a responsible application of any biblical text is tracing the similarities and differences between the current situation and the situation of the original readers. The Roman church lived under the powerful and often brutal Roman Empire, which spanned the Mediterranean world and held control over all the areas traversed by Paul and the early apostles, as recorded in the New Testament. One of the most obvious differences between Kenya in the twenty-first century and first-century Rome is the system of governance: Kenyans live in a representative democracy, based upon popular input and voter selection.

Dunn expounds on the vast difference between the political potential experienced today versus the situation then: "our modern democratic traditions make it possible for individuals to exercise some political power and to pass judgment on whether rulers are operating for the good of their citizens."[63] Citizenship and civic responsibilities must be understood within an entirely different framework today. In Rome, the paths to power were few, basically by birth, connection, wealth, or self-promotion.[64] For the rest, especially ethnic

---

61. Parsons, "Influence of Romans XIII," 331.

62. Bernard Lategan, "Romans 13:1–7: A Review of Post-1989 Readings," *Scriptura* 110, no. 2 (2012): 266.

63. Dunn, *Romans 8–16*, 774.

64. Dunn, 770.

and religious minorities such as the Jews, their capacity to aspire to Roman political power was basically nonexistent.[65]

For a reader living in Kenya in the twenty-first century, there are definite similarities with believers in the first-century context: both have to reconcile their responsibilities as citizens of heaven with their responsibilities as citizens of their earthly country.[66] All Christians live within a political system that places demands upon their finances, behavior, and values. This, however, raises the question: What are the roles and responsibilities of Christians living in Kenya in the twenty-first century, especially as gleaned from this passage of Romans? In applying this passage, as argued above, it is helpful to keep a middle ground and avoid extreme interpretive paths.[67]

Positive Aspects of Governments

Just governance is greatly beneficial to human thriving and peace. Stein remarks, "That Paul saw the Roman government as being a positive force for good, a gift of common grace to humanity, is clear. In his personal experience he had already known the protection which the state could offer its citizenry, and in the future he would have occasion to experience this again and again."[68] Another positive aspect is what the government made possible in terms of missions, as explained by Mtukwa: "Paul was fully aware that good citizenship served the missionary enterprise (particularly his plans to evangelize Spain), which would result in the commendation of the gospel to those of good will."[69]

---

65. Dunn explains further, "It would not even have occurred to Paul and his readers that they could exercise political power in a Roman city, far less that they by their efforts might change its structures. All they could do was to live within the structures which existed, accommodate to them – as everyone had to – and seek to benefit from whatever rules or rights the governing authorities granted, such as Julius Caesar had granted the Jewish synagogues" (Dunn, 770).

66. As Constantineanu phrases it, "Since Christians have always had both an earthly and a heavenly citizenship, how are they to relate to the surrounding culture and society in a way that is true and authentic to both citizenships?" (Constantineanu, "Bible and the Public Arena," 136).

67. Our understanding of Paul should also avoid the extreme ends of the theological spectrum; in the words of Constantineanu: "a proper interpretation of Romans 13 would carefully consider Paul's complex understanding of the dynamic of the relationship of Christians to the powers that be, as well as his appeal for critical engagement in the life of the city, and would thus avoid a rigid categorization of Paul as either a radical critic or a blind supporter of the political powers" (Constantineanu, 153).

68. Stein, "Argument," 334. Hanc supports this point, writing that "in Paul's theology, Christology and imperialism are not mutually exclusive realities. The Roman Empire was often beneficial for Paul's mission. Paul wrote in a socio-political context that allowed him to present the governing authorities not as maleficent" (Hanc, "Paul and Empire," 316). This point should be received with caution, as it can easily be overstated.

69. Mtukwa, "People of God," 2.

Yet at the same time any government is imperfect, with weaknesses mixed with strengths. The challenge that Christians must engage in is to carefully evaluate and engage with their local government. Moo helpfully explains,

> To the degree that this age is dominated by Satan and sin, Christians must resolutely refuse to adopt its values. But the world in which Christians continue to live out their bodily existence (see 12:1) has not been wholly abandoned by God. As a manifestation of his common grace, God has established in this world certain institutions, such as marriage and government, which have a positive role to play even after the inauguration of the new age.[70]

Yet even within a functional system of governance, we must still be vigilant and careful as we evaluate the structures in which we live. Moo says that we must "refuse to give to government any absolute rights and should evaluate all its demands in the light of the gospel."[71] Our commitment to the commands and principles of God always supersedes that which we make to any other system or authority.

Negative Aspects of Governance

Examples of oppressive and corrupt governmental structures are so numerous that this point hardly needs extensive corroboration. As Herzog points out, "From the empires of the ancient world to the fascist states of the present, history has shown how often the state can become a ruthless and dominating force operating without regard for its so-called divinely ordained role."[72] Paul's words in Romans 13:1–7 would only truly apply in limited situations: "As far as Paul's readers were concerned, Paul's words would only have credibility if the authorities recognizably acted as God's servants for their benefit, if those who lived upright lives were commended for doing so and had no cause to fear those in authority."[73] Unfortunately, the relationship of Christians with authority is often much more complex.

One African country that has especially struggled with the significance and application of Romans 13 is South Africa. Jan Botha describes a particular instance in 1985:

---

70. Moo, *Epistle to the Romans*, 791.

71. Moo, 810.

72. Herzog, "Dissembling," 340.

73. Carter, "Irony of Romans 13," 220.

Addressing a gathering of a million members of the (mainly black and apolitical) Zion Christian Church near Pietersburg in April 1985, the former South African State President, P W Botha, praised his audience as people who "love and respect their Bishop," who have "a sincere and healthy lifestyle" and who "respect law, order and authority." Later on in his speech he said, "The Bible has a message for the governments and governed of the world. Thus we read in Romans 13 that every person be subject to the governing authorities."[74]

The original audience of Romans is highly significant in the application of chapter 13: as Botha points out, "the fact that Romans 13:1–7 was addressed to governed and not to those governing gives decisive motivation to rule out this type of abuse of the text by an authoritarian government."[75] Within Romans 13, especially as compared to the claims to divinity and absolute power made by the Roman emperors, there is actually a striking restriction on the power of human authorities in terming them "God's servant[s]" in 13:4 and those who have been appointed by God in 13:2.[76] All authority is ultimately subject and answerable to God, and must act according to God's desires and intentions for human interaction as revealed through the Scriptures.

Wright points out that Paul "is prepared to submit to the courts, but is also more than prepared to remind them of their business and to call them to account when they overstep their duty."[77] Barraclough highlights a significant gap in Romans 13:

So within the passages noted above a common silence on two important aspects of political authority is noticeable: firstly, there is no acknowledgement, much less any critical assessment, of the capacity of governing authorities to foster injustice and to live on oppression; secondly, there is no focus on the non-Christian neighbors who experience injustice and oppression. These silences must be noted and filled with the wider and deeper expression of compassion and the quest for justice sounded in the declaration and inauguration of the Kingdom of God.[78]

---

74. Botha, "Creation of New Meaning," 24.

75. Botha, 24.

76. See Constantineanu, "Bible and the Public Arena," 148–149; and Mtukwa, "People of God," 5.

77. N. T. Wright, *Paul in Fresh Perspective* (Minneapolis: Fortress, 2005), 70.

78. Barraclough, "Romans 13:1–7," 20.

Käsemann concurs with this idea, also arguing that Paul is "certainly not making exhaustive statements about the relation to authorities" and is "silent about possible conflicts and the limits of earthly authority."[79] It is to precisely these conflicts and limits that our attention will now turn, as we explore some specific scenarios and how this passage could be applied in each.

Specific Scenarios

What does resisting authority mean? Political activity should not seek to bring down the system and set ourselves up in power. On the other hand, in the words of James Moulder: "We cannot simply assume that Paul's command to the Christians at Rome is a plea for absolute obedience to one's government."[80] As Moo points outs, "perhaps our submission to government is compatible with disobedience to government in certain exceptional circumstances."[81] What types of exceptional circumstances would qualify? Let us dig into the following situations to see how the text speaks into each one.

Functional Democracy

Evaluating the political situation at the time of writing in 2017, most nations of the world currently operate within a democratic setup, of varying levels of effectiveness – especially in terms of how often elections are held, the strength of opposition parties, the freedom of the press, and the right of the people to assemble and demonstrate. In keeping with the arguments made against the Zealots of Jewish nationalism, setting up a theocracy or perfect utopian society should not be the rationale for Christian political activism. Hanc writes, "The fact that the Christian community and civil authority can coexist as God-appointed social entities, authenticates that the kingdom of God does not usurp the Roman Empire."[82] The kingdom of God also coexists with political systems today and does not require an alternative political system practiced by believers in Christ. An important consequence of this coexistence is that Christians must pay taxes, obey traffic laws, operate within business regulations, uphold building codes, and adhere to all nonoppressive government laws and requirements.

---

79. Käsemann, *Commentary on Romans*, 354.

80. James Moulder, "Romans 13 and Conscientious Disobedience," *Journal of Theology for Southern Africa* 21 (December 1977): 15.

81. Moo, *Epistle to the Romans*, 797.

82. Hanc, "Paul and Empire," 316.

Within a functional democracy, how should Romans 13:2 – "Therefore whoever resists the authorities resists what God has appointed, and those who resist will incur judgment" – be applied? If the system is operational – if elections are taking place, the court system is not wholly compromised, and political opposition is present – Christians should seek to further strengthen the system, not to weaken it. Christians seeking to live out this passage must reject violence as an answer to oppression or injustice. Anything that would lead to civil rebellion or anarchy must be avoided and disavowed. Rather, this passage calls for working for improvements within the system – in areas such as improving laws, adding stronger or new laws to fill in gaps of justice or equality, pushing to enforce laws consistently, ending corruption, and so on. These improvements can be sought in a variety of ways: demonstrations, advocacy campaigns, social media, and other avenues of political expression. Peaceful protests in Kenya and elsewhere are fully compatible with the spirit and underlying assumptions of Romans 13.

Leader Chooses to Illegally Remain in Office

Kenya, as of 2017, has established a tradition of term limits, with several living ex-presidents – a strong mark of a functional democracy. However, a number of nations in the Middle East and Africa have not consistently applied strict term limits, with several current national leaders having been in power for decades. When facing the situation of a long-serving national leader, one question must first be answered for each country: Who or what is the "authority"? Jonathan Draper explains three different foundations for a leader's claim to legitimacy, drawing from the sociological model developed by Max Weber: legal-rational (used by most democracies today), traditional-sacral, and charismatic-revolutionary.[83] If a national leader chooses to disregard the official constitution and law of a country in order to remain illegally in power beyond term limits, it is actually this leader who is resisting the authorities that are legally in place. The act of remaining in power itself undermines the power exercise of authority as intended. This interpretation is not new to the

---

83. Jonathan A. Draper, "'Humble Submission to Almighty God' and Its Biblical Foundation: Contextual Exegesis of Romans 13:1–7," *Journal of Theology for Southern Africa* 63 (June 1988): 31. He explains the meaning of the legal-rational claim to power: "Legal-rational authority structures are those based on the legality of normative rules and the right under rules to issue commands. A person commands deference only in his or her sphere of legal competence. This authority structure is normative, at least nominally, in most Western democracies today. Underlying it is the assumption of a 'social contract' between the rulers and the ruled. Authority is conditionally conferred on the rulers for the benefit of the ruled; it may also be removed" (Draper, "Humble Submission," 31).

twenty-first century and was found within the Elizabethan era in Britain, as described by Glen Bowman: "For example, John Ponet, in his *Short Treatise of Politic Power*, offered an unusual twist on the chapter. He argued that in the phrase 'Let every soul be subject unto the higher powers,' a 'soul' referred to an individual person. 'Higher powers' to him described not political rulers, but rather their authority. If leaders violate the real higher 'power' – divinely-ordained natural law – they should be removed, violently, if necessary."[84]

Thus, protesting a leader illegitimately remaining in power or pushing for elections is not resisting the authority – it is re-establishing it. Extenuating circumstances can render this decision more complex: What if the law or constitution is changed to allow a leader to remain in power? Each situation must be carefully evaluated on a case-by-case basis to determine if such a legal revision is justified, and how Christians should respond to such leadership. Still, even in a clearly illegal leadership scenario, violent resistance and anarchy must be avoided at all costs. Change within the system and restoration of fair, functional elections and democratic procedures must be the preferred route of seeking the reinstatement of appropriate authority.

Coup Attempt

This scenario is one of the most difficult and complex for Christians seeking to live out a twenty-first-century application of Paul's words to the Romans. Generally, the testimony of Romans 13 and parallel passages such as 1 Peter 2:13–17 would condemn coup attempts against the authority in power. Christians are not to achieve their political goals through the overthrow of the established order.

However, what about a successful coup attempt? If a new leader successfully revolts against the previous leader, is that new leader then worthy of respect and compliance? What markers would indicate a functional government worthy of support? Clearly this paper cannot explore all the various permutations and relevant details of regime change, but each situation should be carefully evaluated in order to remain as closely as possible within the spirit of conscientious conditional obedience.

Unjust Laws or Systematic Oppression

If one were to live during the regime of a dictator like Pol Pot, Hitler, Stalin, or Idi Amin and one was ordered to participate in genocide or elimination of

---

84. Glen Bowman, "Elizabethan Catholics and Romans 13: A Chapter in the History of Political Polemic," *Journal of Church and State* 47, no. 3 (2005): 533.

political opponents, Romans 13 could not be used to justify murder or any other violation of God's injunctions to live in peace. Commitment to God's stated commands in Scripture always takes precedence over commitment to any legal system. However, government actions and legal requirements are often not as demonstrably evil as murder and genocide, leaving the difficult work of discerning the ethical imperative for those within this system.

Another clear example of oppression is the former system of apartheid in South Africa. Such a system of oppression disregarded the overwhelming testimony of the Scriptures in relation to human relationships. The Bible is replete with instances of standing up for the marginalized and impoverished; and within a representative democracy, pursuing legal changes and just political systems is an important and central way of pursuing the goal of genuine *shalom* and justice.

Yet even within an unjust system, it is possible to comply within limits. Examine Paul's response after the earthquake in the jail in Philippi, when the magistrates sent officers to release them: "They beat us publicly without a trial, even though we are Roman citizens, and threw us into prison. And now do they want to get rid of us quietly? No! Let them come themselves and escort us out."[85] Paul is protesting a miscarriage of justice, and is seeking to strengthen the existing legal structures. He does not, however, uncritically accept whatever is spoken from any position of authority, and blindly obey any official request or command. Conscientious disobedience is a valid response to oppression, as Moulder concludes after his exploration of what he terms the "absolute obedience thesis" requiring total submission to any governmental imperative: "Paul's words do not undermine conscientious disobedience which is supported by Christ's example or by Christ's commands."[86] As Paul put it: "Do not be overcome by evil, but overcome evil with good."[87]

Conclusion

Following this survey of Romans 13, a few conclusions can be drawn. First of all, submitting to authorities is not an absolute command, but all human authority is ultimately subject to God. Second, unless circumstances demand

---

85. Acts 16:37 NIV. Moulder points out that Paul is acting out of "a moral conviction; namely, that government officials ought not to do what is illegal" (Moulder, "Romans 13 and Conscientious Disobedience," 16).

86. Moulder, 23. Another significant textual feature that becomes relevant at this point is Paul's appeal to conscience in Rom 13:5.

87. Rom 12:21.

resistance, our default position in regard to authority must be submission and compliance. Third, if the system in which we live goes against God's rule and the Scriptures, it is then incumbent upon Christians to resist that system as informed by our conscience, and seek to establish systems of justice and righteousness. Thus, we will "not be conformed to this world, but [will] be transformed by the renewal of [our] mind," seeking always to "love [our] neighbor as [ourselves]."[88]

Bibliography

Bailey, Jon Nelson. "Paul's Political Paraenesis in Romans 13:1–7." *Restoration Quarterly* 46, no. 1 (2004): 11–28.

Barraclough, Ray. "Romans 13:1–7: Application in Context." *Colloquium* 17, no. 2 (May 1985): 16–21.

Botha, Jan. "Creation of New Meaning: Rhetorical Situations and the Reception of Romans 13:1–7." *Journal of Theology for Southern Africa* 79 (June 1992): 24–37.

Bowman, Glen. "Elizabethan Catholics and Romans 13: A Chapter in the History of Political Polemic." *Journal of Church and State* 47, no. 3 (2005): 531–544.

Bray, Gerald, ed. *Ancient Christian Commentary on Scripture*. Downers Grove, IL: InterVarsity Press, 1998.

Carter, Timothy L. "The Irony of Romans 13." *Novum Testamentum* 46, no. 3 (2004): 209–228.

Constantineanu, Corneliu. "The Bible and the Public Arena: A Pauline Model for Christian Engagement in Society with Reference to Romans 13." *KAIROS: Evangelical Journal of Theology* 4, no. 2 (2010): 135–157.

Draper, Jonathan A. "'Humble Submission to Almighty God' and Its Biblical Foundation: Contextual Exegesis of Romans 13:1–7." *Journal of Theology for Southern Africa* 63 (June 1988): 30–38.

Dunn, James D. G. *Romans 8–16*. Word Biblical Commentary 38B. Dallas: Word Books, 1988.

Elliott, Neil. *The Rhetoric of Romans*. Journal for the Study of the New Testament Supplement Series 45. Sheffield: Sheffield Academic Press, 1990.

Engberg-Pedersen, Troels. "Paul's Stoicizing Politics in Romans 12–13: The Role of 13.1–10 in the Argument." *Journal for the Study of the New Testament* 29, no. 2 (December 2006): 163–172.

Friberg, Barbara, Timothy Friberg, and Neva F. Miller. *Analytical Lexicon of the Greek New Testament*. Electronic edition. Baker's Greek New Testament Library. Grand Rapids: Baker, 2000.

---

88. Rom 12:2; 13:9.

Hanc, Ovidiu. "Paul and Empire: A Reframing of Romans 13:1–7 in the Context of the New Exodus." *Tyndale Bulletin* 65, no. 2 (2014): 313–316.

Herzog, William R. II. "Dissembling, a Weapon of the Weak: The Case of Christ and Caesar in Mark 12:13–17 and Romans 13:1–7." *Perspectives in Religious Studies* 21, no. 4 (1994): 339–360.

Käsemann, Ernst. *Commentary on Romans*. Translated by Geoffrey W. Bromiley. Grand Rapids: Eerdmans, 1980.

Kim, Seyoon. "Paul's Common Paraenesis (1 Thess. 4–5; Phil. 2–4; and Rom. 12–13): The Correspondence between Romans 1:18–32 and 12:1–2, and the Unity of Romans 12–13." *Tyndale Bulletin* 62, no. 1 (2011): 109–139.

Kittel, G., G. W. Bromiley, and G. Friedrich, eds. *Theological Dictionary of the New Testament*. Electronic edn. Vol. 2. Grand Rapids: Eerdmans, 1964.

Lategan, Bernard. "Romans 13:1–7: A Review of Post-1989 Readings." *Scriptura* 110, no. 2 (2012): 259–272.

MacArthur, John. *The Christian and Government*. Panorama City, CA: Word of Grace Communications, 1986.

Marshall, John W. "Hybridity and Reading Romans 13." *Journal for the Study of the New Testament* 31, no. 2 (December 2008): 157–178.

Moo, Douglas. *The Epistle to the Romans*. New International Commentary on the New Testament. Grand Rapids: Eerdmans, 1996.

Moulder, James. "Romans 13 and Conscientious Disobedience." *Journal of Theology for Southern Africa* 21 (December 1977): 13–23.

Mtukwa, Gift. "The People of God and Kingdom Political Ethics in Romans 13:1–7." *Didache: Faithful Teaching* 14, no. 1 (2014): 1–11.

Parsons, Wilfrid. "The Influence of Romans XIII on Christian Political Thought 2: Augustine to Hincmar." *Theological Studies* 2, no. 3 (September 1941): 325–346.

Stein, Robert H. "The Argument of Romans 13:1–7." *Novum Testamentum* 31, no. 4 (October 1989): 325–343.

Vonck, Pol. "All Authority Comes from God: Romans 13:1–7 – A Tricky Text about Obedience to Political Power." *AFER* 26, no. 6 (December 1984): 338–347.

Webster, Alexander F. C. "St Paul's Political Advice to the Haughty Gentile Christians in Rome: An Exegesis of Romans 13:1–7." *St Vladimir's Theological Quarterly* 25, no. 4 (1981): 259–282.

Wright, N. T. *Paul in Fresh Perspective*. Minneapolis: Fortress, 2005.

2

The Corruption Menace in Kenya and How Christians Should Respond

Samuel Oketch

Coordinator, Nazarene Compassionate Ministries,
Church of the Nazarene East Africa Field

Abstract

Corruption is an element of African social, political, and even religious life that has terrible consequences. It hinders financial progress as well as growth needed for development by making a few people more wealthy while the majority get poorer. Since Kenya achieved independence from the British on 12 December 1963, corruption has continued to be a major hindrance to its development. Paying a bribe in Kenya can reduce one's taxes or one's water or electricity bill. Corruption perverts one's integrity and manifests itself through bribery, extortion, fraud, and nepotism. In political circles, it shows itself in vote-fixing, the vote-buying, and the distortion of election results. This is what led to the 2007 post-election violence in Kenya in which 1,133 people lost their lives and as a result of which over 600,000 were declared internally displaced persons. In this article the researcher looks at some of the dangerous ethical perceptions that give rise to corruption:

- One has the "right" to do something about one's interests if one's employer is not doing enough about them (e.g. small salary).
- The end justifies the means (corruption increases efficiency).

- There are worse "evils" in the world than corruption. It is simply a lesser evil compared to others.
- As long as there are other people involved in an action, it is justified.

A person responds to corruption according to his or her understanding of it. The Word of God serves as a primary resource for a Christian willing to act against the menace of corruption. This article refers to both the Old and the New Testaments for examples from which Christians can learn how to deal with corruption when confronted with it.

Key words: Corruption, ethics, Word of God, Christians, bribery, Kenya

Introduction

Kenya's history has not been one of war, the military principle, mass murder, or state failure; neither has it been one of enhancing expectations for everyday wellbeing, industrialization, developing national pride, and founding a major world economy. Rather it has been an account of continuing the political and monetary structures acquired from provincial days, when there were no proper accountability structures. It is a story that mixes government and financial aspects, a battle to make and expend assets that involved Western forces and Kenyans in a mind-boggling web of connections; a story of development hindered by political contemplation, of misuse of funds meant for development. This paper focuses on the menace of corruption that has hampered Kenya's development since independence on 12 December 1963, and how Christians should respond in order to eliminate corruption.

Corruption is a pervasive element of African social, political, and even religious life that has terrible consequences. It hinders financial improvement as well as much-needed development, making a few more wealthy while the majority get poorer. The BBC was not exaggerating when it observed that "Corruption is illegal everywhere in Africa, but everywhere it is woven deep into the fabric of everyday life. From the bottle of whisky slipped under the counter to speed a traveller's way through customs, to the presidents and ex-presidents living way beyond their declared means, it results in an assumption that no business will ever get done without a present changing hands."[1]

---

1. J. M. Vorster, "Managing Corruption in South Africa: The Ethical Responsibility of the Church," unpublished article, Faculty of Theology, North-West University, Potchefstroom, 2011, 24.

Although corruption in all its forms is illegal and generally viewed as undesirable, it seems to have a hold on us everywhere we go. Even mortuary attendants need to be bribed to provide services. Officials require bribes before they issue foreign exchange and import and production licenses. A bribe in Kenya can reduce one's taxes or one's water or electricity bill. "Even the police, who are supposed to be guardians of the law, also receive bribes to obstruct the administration of justice."[2] Recently, a senior pastor in the city of Nairobi was involved in a fatal accident in which his Range Rover hit a saloon car and killed a lady passenger while seriously injuring her husband. The police obstructed justice by substituting the name of his driver, who was even not present when the accident occurred, for that of the pastor. This serious case was referred to the office of the Director of Public Prosecutions because eyewitnesses said they had seen the pastor driving the Range Rover on the wrong side of the lane and that, following the accident, he quickly disappeared in another car (a Subaru) which arrived quickly at the scene of the accident. This incident shows that the web of corruption is so deeply entrenched in our society that even pastors, if they are not serious about their calling and putting their signature sins under control, can easily engage in it.

Defining Corruption

Corruption can be defined as the misuse of a public office or position of authority for private, material or social gain at the expense of other people.[3] It makes an individual morally corrupt. The following are some of the ways in which it seeks to pervert integrity:

- *Bribery* is giving cash or support to somebody who is in a position of trust with the end goal of corrupting that person's judgment or behavior. It is designed to make someone act wrongfully, treacherously, or improperly. The responsibility for bribery rests with both the giver and the taker (the briber and the person bribed).
- *Extortion* comes from a word that means "to squeeze," and refers to "the act of obtaining something, such as money, from an entity (whether a person, group, corporation or institution) through threats, violence or the misuse of authority."[4]

---

2. Stanley J. Grenz and Jay T. Smith, *Pocket Dictionary of Ethics* (Downers Grove, IL: InterVarsity Press, 2003), 38.

3. Otenyo, *Ethics and Public Service*, 59.

4. Grenz and Smith, *Pocket Dictionary of Ethics*, 15.

- *Fraud* comes from cheating somebody in order to get money or goods illegally; for example, producing checks and exaggerating expenses. It additionally happens when "assets raised for such exercises as alleviation of famine, bursary reserves for needy children, and supports to help the physically challenged in the society are not put to the expected use."[5]
- *Nepotism* happens when somebody raises relatives and companions to positions of power or gives them contracts. It regularly stimulates the predominance of one ethnic community over another, and has negative ramifications for the developing of the country.

Corruption also manifests itself in outright theft, match-fixing, examination fraud, kickbacks, illegal awarding of contracts, and the like. In the political circle, it shows itself in vote-fixing, vote-buying, and the distortion of final results. This is what led to the 2007 post-election violence in Kenya in which 1,133 lost their lives and over 600,000 were declared internally displaced persons.

Having defined different ways in which corruption can take place, we now focus primarily on bribery and extortion, investigating their links to traditional culture, their effects on Kenyan society, and what the Scriptures have to say about them.

Traditional Gifts and Bribes

Those who hold public office are expected to perform their duties without any external inducement. They should not have to be given gifts to persuade them to act. In some parts of the world, officials are even forbidden to accept any gifts. But in African traditional communities, offering endowments to those in authority was a common social custom. Were such gifts in effect bribes, extorted by those in authority before they would perform their duties, or were they intended to get them to do something illegal and immoral? In other words, was the giving of gifts in traditional communities equivalent to paying a bribe today? To answer this question, we need to examine the circumstances in which gifts were traditionally given:

- *At the point when drawing nearer to divine beings.* One needed to approach divine beings with a blessing to appease them for some wrongdoing or to express gratitude to them for such things as a decent harvest, the birth of a child, or a similar major event. Such

---

5. See Daniel Jordan Smith, *A Culture of Corruption: Everyday Deception and Popular Discontent in Nigeria* (Princeton, NJ: Princeton University Press, 2007).

a blessing could never have been viewed as a reward to compel a divine being to accomplish something immoral.

- *When appearing before a chief or king, or the elders of the community.* It was viewed as insensitive and unwise to turn up before those in authority with practically nothing. The gift was not a pay-off to the elders, who frequently went about as the judges and were relied upon to be just in the articulation and execution of their obligations.
- *When consulting diviners and priests.* Diviners and priests were regarded as intermediaries who could carry out the will of the gods. Bribing them to misconstrue what the gods were saying was unthinkable! Any attempt to do so would bring judgment. It is said that when somebody bribed a minister to help him acquire the ownership of some land, both the man and the cleric who took the reward passed on mysteriously.
- *When consulting medicine men and women.* A gift was often necessary to ensure the effectiveness of the medication prescribed. Given that some of these medicine men and women were prepared to use unorthodox and evil methods, the gift could well constitute a bribe to persuade them to use their powers to drive someone mad, kill someone, or make someone fall in love.

The above examples show that the motive for giving something is important when determining whether it is or is not a bribe. This researcher affirms that anything is bad if it is designed to make somebody act deceitfully or unfaithfully. However, if the thought process in giving a gift is not to gain some help or force a commitment now or later on, it is ethically acceptable.[6]

Given that it can sometimes be difficult to define motives clearly, gift-giving often blends with the desire to extract obligations and favors. Eric Otenyo, who has studied the ethics of the public services in Africa, observes that open administration endowments have ended up being rewards or actions to the degree that a "no blessing, no government" standard wins in numerous free workplaces in Kenya, Nigeria,[7] Ethiopia, the Congo, Tanzania, and other African nations.[8]

---

6. Otenyo, *Ethics and Public Service*, 42.

7. K. R. Hope, "Corruption and Development in Africa," in *Corruption and Development in Africa: Lessons from Country Case-Studies*, ed. K. R. Hope and B. C. Chikulo (New York: Palgrave, 2000), 17–39.

8. C. Bauer, "Public Sector Corruption and Its Control in South Africa," in Hope and Chikulo, *Corruption and Development in Africa*, 218–233.

Root Causes of Corruption

Ipsos Synovate, a research firm in Kenya, carried out a survey in August 2014 in which they did a random sampling of government officials on the issue of corruption. The results of their investigation showed that the police was the most corrupt institution, followed by the judiciary. The office of the presidency was found to be the least corrupt. The officials who were surveyed said that corruption was not an important problem facing the government compared to the security threats posed by Al-Shabaab. "Everyone does it" was the explanation they offered. However, the following are dangerous ethical perceptions that need to be addressed:

- One has the "right" to do something about one's interests if one's employer is not doing enough (e.g. small salary).
- The end justifies the means (corruption increases efficiency).
- There are worse "evils" in the world than corruption. It is a lesser evil compared to others.
- As long as other people are also involved in an action, it is justified.

Hope[9] and Bauer[10] have also commented on the subject of corruption, particularly in Africa. According to them, government leadership in a country can have a strong influence on corruption if there are no checks and balances for accountability and the rule of law. Auma-Osolo agrees that governments can easily control corruption. She affirms that bad leadership in Kenya has not only led to widespread deaths from both preventable and curable diseases (such as malaria, pneumonia, and tuberculosis), but has also made citizens victims of simple and easily managed problems, such as malnutrition, illiteracy, unemployment, hunger, unclean water, poor roads and shelter, child delinquency, drug addiction and trafficking, and short life expectancy, even though Kenya has an abundance of God-given natural resources which the government leaders can freely exploit and use in tackling these problems.[11]

---

9. Agola Auma-Osolo, *Why Leaders Fail and Plunge the Innocent into a Sea of Agonies: The Danger of Abnormal Politics* (Maseno: Maseno University Press, 2014), 357. See also Charles Hornsby, *Kenya: A History Since Independence* (London: I. B. Tauris & Co., 2012).

10. Susan Rose-Ackerman, *Corruption and Government: Causes, Consequences, and Reform* (Cambridge: Cambridge University Press, 1999), 297.

11. Rose-Ackerman, *Corruption and Government*, 457.

Consequences of Corruption

All governments control the delivery of important revenue and the burden of unreasonable expenses. The transfer of these positions and expenditures is for the most part under the control of public authorities who have discretionary power. Private individuals and firms that want ideal treatment might pay to get it. They are usually inclined to accept corruption, saying that this is just the way things are done in Africa. But corruption is an indicator that something has turned out badly in the administration of the country.[12] Organizations intended to represent the relationships between the citizens and the state are utilized for individual advancement and the procurement of advantages by the corrupt. The value component, so regularly a wellspring of financial productivity and a given for development, can, as pay-off, undermine the authenticity and viability of government. Corruption in Kenya – indeed, throughout Africa – has led to the following grave consequences that we should not ignore:[13]

- *Erosion of moral values.* Corruption perverts a nation's sense of right and wrong. In corrupt societies, the right becomes wrong, and the wrong becomes right.
- *Increased social evils.* Corruption provides fertile soil for tribalism, nepotism, fraud, dishonesty, and selfishness, and may even lead to murder.
- *Lack of transparency.* Corruption urges those in power to evade straightforwardness and responsibility. Calls for the public authorities to be straightforward and responsible provoke malevolent reactions.
- *Disregard of the rule of law.* Corruption encourages individuals, entities, and institutions to cut corners and ignore legal requirements. Obtaining justice can be difficult.
- *Oppression of the weak.* In corrupt societies, the poor and powerless suffer because only the wealthy and powerful have access to the courts.
- *Loss of public trust.* Corruption makes individuals hopeless because they don't believe that promises will be kept by those in public offices. They also have no confidence in the legislature and the framework of government.

---

12. This is very common in Kenya, especially with the county governments.

13. The health component that was devolved to county governments is not doing well. Nurses have gone on strike three times due to lack of salary, lack of medical facilities, and poor working conditions.

- *Adoption of a utilitarian ethic.* Corruption encourages people to believe that the end justifies the means. They then feel free to use immoral methods and to abuse other people's trust in the pursuit of their own interests. Some may even become so ruthless that they are prepared to indulge in ritual murder to ensure success.

- *Destruction of the moral fiber of society.* Corruption dulls people's consciences and results in a loss of respect for life and property.

- *Reduced productivity and increased incompetence.* In Kenya, officials do not take pride in the quality of the service that they provide, and consequently, poor service becomes the order of the day. The Commission for Higher Education decreed that standards of education are falling because teachers allow students to cheat in examinations, and unqualified students bribe their way into classes. People's security is traded off as building inspectors and the police acknowledge outside influences. The National Construction Authority (NCA) was formed because so many buildings in Nairobi were collapsing and killing people – a sign that building inspectors and police were being bribed to ignore strict building regulations. Manufacturing quality is sacrificed as inspectors agree to ignore deficiencies in products. This led to a lot of deaths in central Kenya through people drinking poor-quality alcohol. The government enforced a crackdown in 2015 and destroyed all illegal and poor-quality alcohol. Commercial contracts are given to whoever pays the largest bribe.[14] Poor-quality supplies or even the wrong supplies may be ordered, and bank officials enrich themselves with people's savings. Government officials launder money for criminal gangs.

- *Ineffective development and administration.* Kenya is lagging behind in development due to corruption. On 26 August 2015 the then president of the United States of America, Barack Obama, challenged Kenyans that regarding development, they had been on a par with South Korea at independence, yet "right now South Korea is way ahead of Kenya. The reason for this is corruption." He challenged the country to "pull together" in the fight against corruption. Kenya is not developed because corruption is on the rise, especially with the

---

14. The Public Private Partnership (PPP) mode of doing road infrastructure (design, build, and maintenance) has not started two years after it was instituted because banks that were supposed to finance road contractors have refused to do so out of fear of losing their funds. In the PPP modal, the government was only going to pay for a well-constructed road. The initiative is aimed at curbing corruption in the road-building sector.

establishment of the county governments through the enactment of the country's new constitution on 27 August 2010. Government officials allow the wealthy to evade taxes and pilfer funds intended for subsidies and pensions, while medical institutions[15] and the transport infrastructure deteriorate.[16] While accepting bribes to reduce the taxes or fees of some, they extort money from other individuals and organizations. Funds meant for development are diverted to their personal bank accounts.

- *Limited foreign and domestic investment.* Both internal and foreign investors are reluctant to invest in corrupt countries because of the political and economic instability that accompanies corruption. Adverse media reports regarding corruption signal that money spent in such a country will be wasted.

- *Undermining of democracy.* Although Kenya – and indeed many other African countries – has adopted a democratic system, corruption threatens the very existence of democracy. Polls are rigged, leaders are imposed on the people as in Kenya's 2002 general election, and some heads of state and presidents refuse to resign, while others change the constitution to continue running for president, as in Uganda, Rwanda, and Burundi. The corruption present in supposedly democratic systems has often been used to justify military takeovers.

The Christian Response to Corruption

A person responds to corruption depending on his or her understanding of it. The Word of God serves as a primary resource for a Christian willing to confront the menace of corruption. Examples in both the Old and New Testaments can teach Christians how to face corruption.

Corruption: Old Testament Perspective

The Old Testament regularly refers to "bribery" as corruption. Moses gives the following instruction in the book of Exodus: "Do not accept a bribe, for a bribe

---

15. Similar content is found in Deut 16:19.

16. Philip Graham Ryken, *Exodus: Saved for God's Glory* (Wheaton, IL: Crossway, 2005), 749.

blinds those who see and twists the words of the innocent" (Exod 23:8 NIV).[17] Ryken says that our eyes are closed to truth when bribery is involved because there can never be justice in such a case.[18] Bribery often leads to blind justice. The Israelite judges were cautioned against taking bribes so that they could provide equal justice to all and protect their legal system from abuse. From this we see that a bribe is any income that any government official receives to influence a decision in a certain way. This is an offense against the individual, the community to which he or she belongs, and ultimately God.[19] Giving gifts is customary as a sign of respect and love to a person; however, it is wrong if it is driven by the sole purpose of influencing an action.[20] Chianeque and Ngewa agree that professions like judges should never allow personal favoritism, friendships, or bribes to influence their judgment.[21]

King Solomon describes how justice is destroyed by the evil intent of bribes: "The wicked accept bribes in secret to pervert the course of justice" (Prov 17:23). There is no doubt that corruption imperils nobility and equity.[22] In Kenya, there is a saying that often overrides truth: "I'll scratch your back if you scratch my back." This ought not to be adequate, even if it is viable. At the point where sober-mindedness starts to decide whether an activity is satisfactory or not, judges get to be salespeople who offer "reality" to the outstanding bidder. As a consequence, vulnerable individuals become helpless, there is no social equity because professional people lose their sense of God, and life becomes savage.[23] Goldingay says that leaders turn into murderers when the legal system only benefits people in power.[24]

The book of Proverbs reveals various attitudinal aspects of bribery: "The greedy bring ruin to their households, but the one who hates bribes will live" (Prov 15:27). Murphy and Huwiler are of the opinion that the way the proverb

---

17. John Harold Walton and Victor Harold Matthews, *The IVP Bible Background Commentary: Genesis–Deuteronomy* (Downers Grove, IL: InterVarsity Press, 1997), 117–118, 241.

18. R. E. Clements, *The Book of Deuteronomy: A Preacher's Commentary* (Peterborough: Epworth, 2001), 75.

19. L. C. Chianeque and Samuel Ngewa, "Deuteronomy," in *Africa Bible Commentary*, ed. T. Adeyemo (Nairobi: WordAlive, 2010), 233.

20. E. K. Nsiku, "Isaiah," in Adeyemo, *Africa Bible Commentary*, 811.

21. Raymond C. Ortlund, *Isaiah: God Saves Sinners* (Wheaton, IL: Crossway, 2005), 44, 72.

22. John Goldingay, *New Testament Biblical Commentary* (Peabody, MA: Hendrickson, 2001), 38.

23. Roland E. Murphy and Elizabeth Huwiler, *Proverbs, Ecclesiastes, Song of Songs*, New International Biblical Commentary (Peabody, MA: Hendrickson, 1999), 77.

24. Richard J. Clifford, *Proverbs: A Commentary* (Louisville, KY: Westminster John Knox, 1999), 158, 189; T. Habtu, "Proverbs," in Adeyemo, *Africa Bible Commentary*, 776.

is constructed plainly shows that bribery and greediness go hand in hand.[25] When Solomon is writing about corruption, he mentions the short-term results, which are mostly positive to the giver of the bribe, but he also indicates the long-term adverse effects. In Proverbs 17:8, he writes that "A bribe is seen as a charm by the one who gives it; they think success will come at every turn." The bribe empowers the giver, making him or her feel important.[26] Jeremiah describes the same outcome of bribery:

> Like a partridge that hatches eggs it did not lay
>   are those who gain riches by unjust means.
> When their lives are half gone, their riches will desert them,
>   and in the end, they will prove to be fools. (Jer 17:11)

Allen refers to a popular belief that other birds have their eggs taken from their nests by partridges.[27] The young bird flies back to its kind after it has been hatched and reared by the partridge. Jeremiah sees a parallel between what happens to the bird and money obtained in wrong ways.

Those Who Resisted Corruption in the Old Testament

The Old Testament tells of officials who acted so faithfully and honestly with money given to them that no accounting was needed from them (2 Kgs 12:15; 22:7). The same is testified of Daniel: "At this, the administrators and the satraps tried to find grounds for charges against Daniel in his conduct of government affairs, but they were unable to do so. They could find no corruption in him, because he was trustworthy and neither corrupt nor negligent" (Dan 6:4). Daniel's faithfulness to God caused him to be faithful in all areas of his life. Christians should be encouraged by Daniel's example to be loyal citizens and conscientious and reliable workers.

Nehemiah likewise exhibited a lifestyle that merits mention (Neh 5:14–19). Having been designated governor in the land of Judah, neither he nor his allied laborers ate the food assigned to the governor. The past governors had laid heavy burdens on the general population to subsidize their extravagant way of life, and in the process ruined the already impoverished population. Out of worship for God, Nehemiah did not follow the same pattern. Despite what

---

25. Leslie C. Allen, *Jeremiah: A Commentary* (Louisville, KY: Westminster John Knox, 2008), 201.

26. Raymond Brown, *The Message of Nehemiah: God's Servant in a Time of Change* (Downers Grove, IL: InterVarsity Press, 1998), 96–98.

27. Exod 23:1; Walton and Matthews, *Genesis–Deuteronomy*, 117; Ryken, *Exodus*, 746.

might have been expected, he helped other people. For him, worship of God was not just about showing love; it impacted his daily life. He had compassion for others and showed liberality and astuteness by supporting others from his own salary. In this way, he prevented money from becoming his god.[28]

Standardized Rules for Christians Living in a Corrupt World

God puts a high premium on trustworthiness and honesty because they are the basis around which all human relationships revolve.[29] The people of God are instructed in Leviticus 19 not to steal, lie, or deceive one another. Throughout the chapter, there is a repetition of the phrase "I, YAHWEH," which indicates that while violating these laws may escape the eyes of human beings, it certainly won't escape the eyes of God, and it will not go unpunished.[30] The people of Israel were expected to live with integrity in their actions and words. In Kenya today – and throughout Africa – there is a need to establish a trustworthy society in which supervisors are not required to check on people. Tidball says that organizations that are set up in this manner will ultimately be cheap to run because the citizens themselves form a productive workforce.[31]

Above we mentioned that greed is at the heart of corruption. Solomon counters this attitude with the following proverb: "Better a little with righteousness than much gain with injustice" (Prov 16:8). Murphy and Huwiler state that the most valuable possession is a right relationship with God, not riches.[32] The problem with riches is that "Whoever loves money never has enough; whoever loves wealth is never satisfied with their income" (Eccl 5:10). The author of this book is making it clear that money and abundance never satisfy. The love of money brings disillusionment because riches and possessions are temporary in life.[33] First John 2:16–17 talks about the passing away of everything on the planet, including the longings of a corrupt person, the desires of his or her eyes, and the wishes of the world. Eternal life may be

---

28. Jacob Milgrom, *Leviticus: A Book of Ritual and Ethics*, A Continental Commentary (Minneapolis, MN: Fortress, 2004), 226.

29. Derek Tidball, *The Message of Leviticus* (Downers Grove, IL: InterVarsity Press, 2005), 238.

30. Murphy and Huwiler, *Proverbs, Ecclesiastes, Song of Songs*, 81.

31. Daniel C. Fredericks and Daniel J. Estes, *Ecclesiastes and the Song of Songs* (Downers Grove, IL: InterVarsity Press, 2010), 150.

32. Martinus C. De Boer, *Galatians: A Commentary* (Louisville, KY: Westminster John Knox, 2011), 351.

33. Robert Stutzman, *An Exegetical Summary of Galatians* (Dallas: SIL International, 2006), 239; De Boer, *Galatians*, 372.

experienced by those individuals who live according to the will of God. In his letter to the Galatians, the apostle Paul refers to this kind of life as living according to the Spirit and not according to the sinful nature (Gal 5:16–17). De Boer affirms that it is the Spirit of God in human beings that helps to overcome the power of the sinful nature.[34] Idolatry and selfish ambition are characteristics of the sinful nature (Gal 5:20). Paul exhorts the Colossian church to put to death whatever belongs to their earthly nature (Col 3:5), referring specifically to the greed that also equates to idolatry. In his mind, the sinful nature is crucified by those who belong to Jesus Christ and then decide to live by the Spirit in their everyday lives (Gal 5:24–25). Christians should make every effort to align their lives with the Spirit, as the Spirit is the regulative principle for the believer's conduct.[35]

The crowds that responded to John the Baptist's teaching asked how they should live (Luke 3:10–14). In his response, John specifically addressed a group of tax collectors and of soldiers, giving a specific answer to each group with the common theme of unselfishness. In his reply, he encouraged the demonstration of genuine love and justice, as well as contentment with their wages. The attitude of peace protects people from falling into the temptations associated with their particular professions.[36] Paul addresses the same matter in his words to Timothy (1 Tim 6:6–10). He argues that people who are not content with their possessions are never satisfied and hence never happy either. Discontent can lead to all kinds of sins because one is always craving more.[37] The author of the book of Hebrews advises readers to keep their lives from the love of money and instead be content with whatever they have, because God has promised not to leave nor forsake his people (Heb 13:5). Thus, according to Arthur, Christians ought to be the first to battle materialism and greed, since they have one who will battle for them, and God's support is more trustworthy than money in the bank.[38] Harvey[39] and Guthrie agree.[40]

---

34. A. E. Harvey, *A Companion to the New Testament* (Cambridge: Cambridge University Press, 2004), 36; Richard C. Blight, *An Exegetical Summary of Luke 1–11* (Dallas: SIL International, 2007), 127–130.

35. S. Andria, "1 Timothy," in Adeyemo, *Africa Bible Commentary*, 1476.

36. J. P. Arthur, *No Turning Back: An Exposition of the Epistle to the Hebrews* (London: Grace Publications, 2003), 223.

37. Harvey, *Companion to the New Testament*, 716.

38. G. H. Guthrie, "Hebrews," in *Commentary on the New Testament Use of the Old Testament*, ed. G. K. Beale and D. A. Carson (Grand Rapids, MI: Baker Academic, 2007), 991.

39. Quoted in Samuel Ngewa, "Galatians," in Adeyemo, *Africa Bible Commentary*, 1424.

40. This was said by former US President Barack Obama during his visit to Kenya (24–26 July 2015).

The book of James advises believers of Jesus Christ living in this corrupt world to rid themselves of filth and evil and instead humbly accept the Word of God which is planted in them and can save them (Jas 1:21). Christians should put on righteous living and strip themselves of their pre-Christian sinful lifestyles. Their lifestyles should now be in obedience to the Word of God, which is the new authority and guide in their lives. Peter tells Christians: "Be alert and of sober mind. Your enemy the devil prowls around like a roaring lion looking for someone to devour. Resist him, standing firm in the faith, because you know that the family of believers throughout the world is undergoing the same kind of sufferings" (1 Pet 5:8–9). Peter is alluding to the individual's perspective – that is, being spiritually sober, and having self-control and a clear mind. Christians can be ready and vigilant to stand against the devil's dangers and assaults if their minds are free from disarray and consuming interests. They will be able to stand firm against the evil if they hold fast to the gospel and the Christian community. The individual believer is strengthened by the fact that he or she is not alone but rather belongs to the community of God's heavenly kingdom.

Peter gives more consolation to believers in Jesus Christ in his second letter: "His divine power has given us everything we need for a godly life through our knowledge of him who called us by his own glory and goodness. Through these he has given us his very great and precious promises, so that through them you may participate in the divine nature, having escaped the corruption in the world caused by evil desires" (2 Pet 1:3–4). In this letter, the words "life" and "godliness" often stand for a single entity, the godly life. Peter argues that there is no reason why his readers should not live holy lives, because they have received everything needed to do so. Jude echoes the same message in verse 24: "To him who is able to keep you from stumbling and to present you before his glorious presence without fault and with great joy . . ." There is no doubt in Jude's mind that God will protect his children. This theme often recurs in the New Testament (John 17:11, 15; 2 Thess 3:3; 1 Pet 1:5; and Rev 3:10) and serves as a great encouragement to believers.

A Few Points for Christians to Consider When Confronting Corruption

In the introduction, we mentioned that corruption is everywhere in Kenyan society and indeed most societies in Africa. This research has shown that government programs have not been effective in fighting corruption. It is our opinion that this problem can be tackled from the grassroots level by involving everybody, including Christians, as whistle-blowers. We should no longer be satisfied with the "culture of silence" and "that's the way things are done in Kenya." As Christians, we ought to be reformers and engage in changing our Kenyan culture. This may mean tackling the corruption menace on two levels: *personal* and *public*. On the one hand, we should ourselves guard against the temptation to be corrupt and instead live exemplary lives, even when no one is watching us. On the other hand, when in public places, we ought to blow the whistle at whatever point we experience corruption. Action on both levels requires the right personal attitude in order to succeed.

Tackling Corruption: Personal Level

Believers are warned by the Word of God not to be arrogant and think that they cannot fall into temptation. Paul conveys this message unambiguously in several passages, including the following two:

> Brothers and sisters, if someone is caught in a sin, you who live by the Spirit should restore that person gently. But watch yourselves, or you also may be tempted. (Gal 6:1)

> So, if you think you are standing firm, be careful that you don't fall. (1 Cor 10:12)

The same message is conveyed in this proverb of the Akamba people of Kenya: "One in the woodpile does not laugh at one in the fire."[41] This means that Christians ought to be ready and make preparations for the threats and attacks of the devil. They should also be encouraged to live godly lives because Jesus has empowered them, and they have the promise that God can protect them.

Replacing one set of qualities with another does not automatically convert one to a godly life. The mind has an important role in inward change, and it is internal change that will bring about behavioral change. Paul refers to the "renewing of your mind" (Rom 12:2) and being "made new in the attitude of your minds" (Eph 4:23). Genuine change will bring about practical Christian living; the ability to break with the corrupt world is conceivable when the Holy Spirit transforms and reestablishes the mind.

Jesus Christ gave "the golden rule" in Matthew 7:12: "So in everything, do to others what you would have them do to you." This formed the climax of his Sermon on the Mount. The rule gives encouragement and instruction for life in this world. Living in conformity to the golden rule of Jesus Christ will uncover

---

41. Boniface Mwangi (@bonifacemwangi), Twitter, 15 February 2017, 2:52 a.m., https://twitter.com/bonifacemwangi/status/831818386216730624.

any hint of selfishness and narrow-mindedness in the life of the Christian and will advance personal uprightness and genuineness. Somebody who worked out how to apply the golden rule of Jesus Christ in his life is Nehemiah. He was also content with what he had, and this protected him from falling into temptation. Christians can follow his example, because God promises never to leave nor forsake us.

Tackling Corruption: Public Level

From a public standpoint, Christians ought to blow the whistle on corruption because it violates either personal, ethical, or moral beliefs. Jesus Christ used light and salt metaphors (Matt 5:13–16) to describe the influence of his followers in fighting corruption and moral decay in society. Where justice and righteousness are being jeopardized in society, Christians have no choice but to be whistle-blowers. They can improve the world by usefully being involved in all circles of life. We agree with former US President Barack Obama when he said that "all citizens must fight corruption."

The Kenyan government instituted the Ethics and Anti-Corruption Commission (EACC) to lead the "war" against corruption that is threatening Kenya's vision of being a strong middle-income economy by 2030. All Kenyans must support EACC for it to be effective. We should ensure there is democracy and a free press in the country to hold the government to account. We should lead in creating awareness of the negative consequences of corruption, such as a rise in public debt, a financial drain on the country, capital flight, higher taxation rates on nationals, lower levels of investment, hindrances to administrative expansion and efficiency, and misdirection of public assets. When all these adverse consequences of corruption are tackled, there will be more money to alleviate poverty in the country.

Attitude Needed to Fight Corruption and Succeed

No fight can be won with a wrong state of mind. In Galatians 5:22–23 Paul gives a list of attitudes to guide believers in their daily lives: "love, joy, peace, forbearance, kindness, goodness, faithfulness, gentleness, and self-control." They are obtained as a result of making a decision to accept Jesus Christ as one's Lord and Savior, not through strict obedience to the Old Testament law or through high moral aspirations. From the moment one accepts Jesus Christ as Lord and Savior, these new dynamics become visible in one's life because they are the work – or fruit – of the Holy Spirit.

Conclusion

Corruption is a vicious sin and a crime that destroys a nation and perverts its sense of right and wrong, good and bad. "The fact that corruption costs Kenya over 250,000 jobs every year"[42] shows that Kenya will continue to suffer if the evil of corruption is tolerated. The main solution is to reject all corrupt practices and embrace a position of straightforwardness and responsibility before God and our fellow citizens. We should follow the example of those in the Bible and in society who have fought corruption. This will require the involvement of all citizens, right from the grassroots level up through all levels of government administration. Most importantly, individuals should work out how to live according to "the golden rule" of Jesus Christ ("do to others what you would have them do to you"). This rule can ensure integrity and honesty by exposing greed and selfishness. Christians should also be willing to act with the proper attitude and think ethically by exposing corrupt individuals in society.

Bibliography

Adeyemo, T., ed. *Africa Bible Commentary*. Nairobi: WordAlive, 2010.

Allen, Leslie C. *Jeremiah: A Commentary*. Louisville, KY: Westminster John Knox, 2008.

Andria, S. "1 Timothy." In *Africa Bible Commentary*, edited by Tokunboh Adeyemo, 708–738. Grand Rapids: Zondervan, 2010.

Arthur, J. P. *No Turning Back: An Exposition of the Epistle to the Hebrews*. London: Grace Publications, 2003.

Auma-Osolo, Agola. Why Leaders Fail and Plunge the Innocent into a Sea of Agonies: The Danger of Abnormal Politics. Maseno: Maseno University Press, 2014.

Bauer, C. "Public Sector Corruption and Its Control in South Africa." In *Corruption and Development in Africa: Lessons from Country Case-Studies*, edited by K. R. Hope and B. C. Chikulo, 218–223. New York: Palgrave, 2003.

Blight, Richard C. *An Exegetical Summary of Luke 1–11*. Dallas: SIL International, 2007.

Blunt, Elizabeth. "Corruption 'Costs Africa Billions.'" BBC News online, Wednesday, 18 September 2002. Accessed 21 July 2015. http://news.bbc.co.uk/1/hi/world/africa/2265387.stm.

Brown, Raymond. *The Message of Nehemiah: God's Servant in a Time of Change*. Downers Grove, IL: InterVarsity Press, 1998.

---

42. John Karanja, "Evangelical Attitudes toward Democracy in Kenya," in *Evangelical Christianity and Democracy in Africa*, ed. Terence O. Ranger (New York: Oxford University Press, 2008), 67–94. See also Ariel Zirulnick, "Obama Highlights Kenya's Stubborn Corruption Problem," 26 July 2015, https://www.csmonitor.com/World/Africa/2015/0726/Obama-highlights-Kenya-s-stubborn-corruption-problem.

Chianeque, L. C., and Samuel Ngewa. "Deuteronomy." In *Africa Bible Commentary*, edited by Tokunboh Adeyemo, 311–397. Grand Rapids: Zondervan, 2010.

Clements, R. E. *The Book of Deuteronomy: A Preacher's Commentary*. Peterborough: Epworth, 2001.

Clifford, Richard J. *Proverbs: A Commentary*. Louisville, KY: Westminster John Knox, 1999.

De Boer, Martinus C. *Galatians: A Commentary*. Louisville, KY: Westminster John Knox, 2011.

Fredericks, Daniel C., and Daniel J. Estes. *Ecclesiastes and the Song of Songs*. Downers Grove, IL: InterVarsity Press, 2010.

Goldingay, John. *New Testament Biblical Commentary*. Peabody, MA: Hendrickson, 2001.

Grenz, Stanley J., and Jay T. Smith. *Pocket Dictionary of Ethics*. Downers Grove, IL: InterVarsity Press, 2003.

Guthrie, G. H. "Hebrews." In *Commentary on the New Testament Use of the Old Testament*, edited by G. K. Beale and D. A. Carson, 234–371. Grand Rapids, MI: Baker Academic, 2007.

Habtu, T. "Proverbs." In *Africa Bible Commentary*, edited by Tokunboh Adeyemo, 423–473. Grand Rapids: Zondervan, 2010.

Harvey, A. E. *A Companion to the New Testament*. Cambridge: Cambridge University Press, 2004.

Hope, K. R. "Corruption and Development in Africa." In *Corruption and Development in Africa: Lessons from Country Case-Studies*, edited by K. R. Hope and B. C. Chikulo, 17–39. New York: Palgrave, 2003.

Hope, K. R., and B. C. Chikulo, eds. *Corruption and Development in Africa: Lessons from Country Case-Studies*. New York: Palgrave, 2000.

Hornsby, Charles. *Kenya: A History since Independence*. London: I. B. Tauris & Co., 2012.

Milgrom, Jacob. *Leviticus: A Book of Ritual and Ethics*. A Continental Commentary. Minneapolis, MN: Fortress, 2004.

Murphy, Roland E., and Elizabeth Huwiler. *Proverbs, Ecclesiastes, Song of Songs*. New International Biblical Commentary. Peabody, MA: Hendrickson, 1999.

Ngewa, Samuel. "Galatians." In *Africa Bible Commentary*, edited by Tokunboh Adeyemo, 601–635. Grand Rapids: Zondervan, 2010.

Nsiku, E. K. "Isaiah." In *Africa Bible Commentary*, edited by Tokunboh Adeyemo, 511–554. Grand Rapids: Zondervan, 2010.

Ortlund, Raymond C. *Isaiah: God Saves Sinners*. Wheaton, IL: Crossway, 2005.

Otenyo, Eric E. *Ethics and Public Service in Africa*. Nairobi: Quest & Insight Publications, 1998.

Rose-Ackerman, Susan. *Corruption and Government: Causes, Consequences, and Reform*. Cambridge: Cambridge University Press, 1999.

Ryken, Philip Graham. *Exodus: Saved for God's Glory*. Wheaton, IL: Crossway, 2005.

Smith, Daniel Jordan. *A Culture of Corruption: Everyday Deception and Popular Discontent in Nigeria*. Princeton, NJ: Princeton University Press, 2007.

Stutzman, Robert. *An Exegetical Summary of Galatians*. Dallas: SIL International, 2006.

Tidball, Derek. *The Message of Leviticus*. Downers Grove, IL: InterVarsity Press, 2005.

Vorster, J. M. "Managing Corruption in South Africa: The Ethical Responsibility of the Church." Unpublished article, Faculty of Theology, North-West University, Potchefstroom, 2011.

Walton, John H., and Victor Harold Matthews. *The IVP Bible Background Commentary: Genesis–Deuteronomy*. Downers Grove, IL: InterVarsity Press, 1997.

Zirulnick, Ariel. "Obama Highlights Kenya's Stubborn Corruption Problem," 26 July 2015. https://www.csmonitor.com/World/Africa/2015/0726/Obama-highlights-Kenya-s-stubborn-corruption-problem.

3

Elements of Political Engagement in Emerging Urban Pentecostal Movements in Kenya

Kyama Mugambi

Associate Researcher, Centre for World Christianity, Africa International University

Abstract

The recent historical relationship between church and politics in Kenya has been varied, with some churches maintaining an activist position, others being loyalist, while still others have tried to maintain an apolitical stance. In the late 1990s, historian John Karanja predicted that younger charismatic churches would have an opportunity to make a contribution to this debate. What he did not anticipate were the specific ways in which this contribution would be made. Emerging urban Pentecostal movements have charted a unique path of engagement in politics and social transformation. This chapter outlines how these movements have participated in the discussion on national political events and issues using ways unavailable for their predecessors. The chapter notes the challenges of these avenues of engagement and looks into future possibilities for the church.

Key words: African Pentecostalism, Pentecostals and politics, urban Pentecostalism, Pentecostal charismatic churches, church and politics, Christian political activism, church and state in Africa

Introduction

"Let your vote count. Politicians who don't respect you don't deserve your vote. Your vote is your weapon against impunity, go register today."[1] These were the words of Boniface Mwangi broadcast to his 585,000 followers ahead of the 2017 elections in Kenya. A short succinct message of 140 characters, limited in length only by the format of the micro-blogging site Twitter. Mwangi, a well-known activist who has been arrested multiple times, has often been found in discourse that was at odds with the political establishment. A senior TED fellow, Mwangi often gave lectures addressing issues such as social justice, equity, and governance. Among his many distinctions is one he does not often shake off: he is an avowed Christian known to have long attended one of Nairobi's Pentecostal churches. In 2017 he declared his bid to join active politics by vying for a parliamentary seat for the Starehe Constituency in Nairobi. One of the first places he declared his intention was during an impromptu moment at his church, Mavuno Church Downtown. Many in the congregation met this renowned activist's announcement with excitement. He represents a shift in the way Christians in emerging urban Pentecostal churches will engage with national politics in the future.

This chapter explores different ways in which emerging movements engage with political discourse. It gives a chronological account of Christian political engagement in Kenya. We then interact with common perceptions and misconceptions that shape Christian engagement in Kenya, before launching into the key elements of this engagement. Our contention is that a section of emerging Christian communities have developed a holistic view of the gospel and regard discourse on political engagement as an aspect of the good news. These churches have devolved engagement to include both laity and clergy, broadening the platform for a more effective discourse.

In the late 1990s John Karanja described as varied the historical relationship between church and politics in Kenya. Some churches had an activist position, others were loyalists, while still others tried to maintain an apolitical stance.[2] He opined that self-interest and other narrow considerations shaped the political engagement of evangelicals in churches that were less established.[3]

---

1. Boniface Mwangi (@bonifacemwangi), Twitter, 15 February 2017, 2:52 a.m., https://twitter.com/bonifacemwangi/status/831818386216730624.

2. John Karanja, "Evangelical Attitudes toward Democracy in Kenya," in *Evangelical Christianity and Democracy in Africa*, ed. Terence O. Ranger (New York: Oxford University Press, 2008), 67–94.

3. Karanja, "Evangelical Attitudes," 67.

He postulated that the younger charismatic churches would make a significant contribution to this debate in the future. What he did not anticipate in his writing were the specific ways in which this contribution would happen. Our study in this chapter builds from where Karanja left off, examining the unique path of political engagement in emerging urban Pentecostal movements.

Kenyan Christian Political Engagement: 1950s–2000s

Terence O. Ranger noted that democracy is more than the removal of dictators and the introduction of multiparty elections. He defined it as the "achievement of participation in voting, in discussion, in self-assertion, and self-help, in the establishment of a democratic culture both within the church and state."[4] Ranger's definition is helpful in framing this discussion. Political engagement will be considered in this chapter as any effort to discuss, critique, reflect on, or otherwise mobilize action and opinion around the establishment of a democratic culture.

In broad terms Africa experienced three democratic revolutions. The first happened in the 1950s and 1960s, the result of which was the overthrow of colonial rule over Africans. The continent went on to experience the beginning of authoritarian and autocratic regimes.[5] Ranger suggests that the role played by the church then was unclear.[6] Though the church's official position on politics was not clearly articulated by missionaries, the message of the gospel as it was received by Africans was liberating for the disenfranchised. It was a motivating factor in the development of the anti-colonial movements.[7] One of the results of this empowering perspective of the gospel was a group of charismatic leaders who emerged from mission schools empowered with education and who took an active part in politics.

---

4. Terence O. Ranger, "Introduction," in Ranger, *Evangelical Christianity*, 9.

5. Ibid.

6. Before Kenyan independence, the Christian Council of Kenya, the forerunner of the National Council of Churches of Kenya (NCCK), was not entirely silent. It encouraged reflection on nationhood, albeit cautiously and without any emphasis on specific action. See, for example, Robert MacPherson, Sospeter Magua, and Paul D. Fueter, *Kenya Present and Future* (Nairobi: Christian Council of Kenya, 1960).

7. We agree here with Lamin Sanneh's view that the gospel empowered Africans through the translation process that began with the vernacularization of the Bible. Lamin O. Sanneh, *Translating the Message: The Missionary Impact on Culture* (Maryknoll, NY: Orbis, 1991), 105–123.

One such leader was Musa Amalemba, the first African in the legislative council in 1957 before the formation of the self-rule Kenyan government.[8] Amalemba first went to school at the Pentecostal school in Nyangori, then to the CMS school in Maseno. He was a skilled writer working as an influential journalist among Africans.[9] He even traveled to the UK for training before his entry into politics.[10] Amalemba became the minister for housing in the precolonial government.[11] His church in Nairobi, led at the time by Canadian missionaries, was not vocal against the colonial injustice. Church leaders such as John Kitts had strong negative sentiments towards the resistance movement.[12] For his part, Amalemba addressed sensitive issues by raising awareness of the complexity of the Mau Mau sentiments towards the Christians, pointing out the plight of the Kikuyu Christians, while making a case for the release of Kenyatta and his fellow freedom fighters.[13] *Pentecost* proudly wrote of him as "an African Pentecostal Member of the legislative council."[14] Outside Amalemba's political activities, the voice of the Pentecostal church was little short of mute in this difficult time. Amalemba was one of few Pentecostals whose understanding of the gospel seemed to free him from this non-participatory position.

Eventually, the African nations achieved independence, and many of them entered two tumultuous decades of upheaval under authoritarian regimes that were often punctuated with bloody coups. This led to a second democratic revolution challenging "one-partyism" and military rule.[15] The death of Kenyatta in 1978 initiated the autocratic, "one-party" Moi regime of the 1980s and 1990s. The mainline churches were not active in opposing the authoritarianism at the beginning. Their voice arose in the late 1980s into the 1990s through activist clergy who stepped into the limelight using their pulpits

---

8. Amalemba's achievements as a member of the church are recorded in the Pentecostal Assemblies of Canada Archival documents. *Pentecost,* a Pentecostal missionary periodical, provides a composite picture of this leader's life in the context of a church during Kenya's political turmoil in the 1950s. "New African Pentecostal Church in Nairobi: The Work Goes on in Kenya in Spite of Mau Mau," *Pentecost* 28 (June 1954): 10; John Kitts, "Threatened by Mau Mau," *Pentecost* 23 (March 1953); "Member of Kenya Legislative Council," *Pentecost* 45 (September 1958): 11.

9. Joanna Lewis, *Empire State-Building: War and Welfare in Kenya, 1925–52* (Athens, OH: Ohio State University Press, 2000), 261.

10. "New African Pentecostal Church in Nairobi," 10.

11. "Member of Kenya Legislative Council," 11.

12. John Kitts, "Pentecost in East Africa," *Pentecost* 32 (June 1955): 14; John Kitts, "Kikuyu Converts," *Pentecost* 30 (December 1954): 7.

13. A. C. Irvine, "Pentecost among the Tribesmen," *Pentecost* (June 1953): 6.

14. Donald Gee, "Kenya and Tanganyika," *Pentecost* (September 1960): 10.

15. Ranger, "Introduction," 9.

to challenge the state machinery. These efforts were often at personal great cost. In Kenya highly influential well-trained clergy, such as Manases Kuria, David Gitari, Henry Okullu, Alexander Muge, and Timothy Njoya, brought activism to the pulpit, contributing to the clamor for democracy in the country.[16] The National Council of Churches of Kenya (NCCK) gave institutional backing to many of these leaders whose churches were its members. It is notable that many newer Pentecostal charismatic churches (NPCCs) were not publicly militant against Moi's authoritarianism. Gifford theorized that these churches provided an empowering and enfranchising environment where participatory leadership, through volunteerism, modeled in microcosm what the public desired, but lacked, in the macrocosm of the national political dispensation. He observed the newness of recent African Pentecostal churches which provided free social space, solidarity, psychological security, and shelter.[17] According to Karanja and Gifford, these NPCCs did not, however, challenge the political status quo.[18] We will look at some of the motivations for that shortly.

The 2000s saw efforts to build a culture of effective electoral institutions, the clamor for transparency, and a strong resistance to "presidential third termism."[19] This political dispensation in Kenya was marked by the iconic search for a new constitution. The mainline denominations struggled to determine their relevance in this new era.[20] It was also during this time that newer Pentecostal charismatic movements increased in their significance among the masses. This era brought a mixed bag of blessings for Africa. The next couple of decades ushered in the reconstruction of a post-apartheid South Africa, the making of a new nation in South Sudan, and the strengthening of regional economic blocs, such as the East Africa Community (EAC) and the Southern African Development community (SADC). It also saw the rise to prominence of the African Union (AU), all against a volatile background of armed ethnic, religious, and political conflict in various hotspots. The mainline churches did not come across as forcefully as before in addressing the needs of this new season of change. In Kenya, the political elite along with the civil society put together the long-awaited constitution that was promulgated after a plebiscite in 2010. It needs to be said that churches under the umbrella of

---

16. Karanja, "Evangelical Attitudes."

17. Paul Gifford, *The Christian Churches and the Democratisation of Africa* (Leiden: Brill, 1995), 6.

18. Karanja, "Evangelical Attitudes"; Paul Gifford, *Christianity, Politics and Public Life in Kenya* (London: C. Hurst, 2009).

19. Ranger, "Introduction," 9.

20. Ranger, 16.

NCCK were a part of the process among many participants in a national effort for a new constitution.

As Kenya entered its second election cycle after the promulgation of the constitution, questions emerged as to the nature of Christian political engagement. Karanja postulated that evangelicals were likely to remain divided on the issues of governance so long as they held a theology that was uncritical of corrupt governance structures.[21] Having said that, he suggested that "One group of evangelicals will probably have an important future role in Kenyan political life. It consists of churches led by young charismatic leaders who enjoy an intense, if not fanatical following. These are the fastest growing ministries in Kenya."[22] He observed that "So far, the leaders of these ministries have shown no interest in political issues, preferring to concentrate instead on evangelistic crusades or missions and spiritually nurturing their followers. It is not clear whether they will take an interest in politics in the future and what form that will take."[23] It is this observation that we concern ourselves with.

Perceptions and Misconceptions of NPCC Engagement

According to Paul Gifford, the issue with African politics is the "neo-patrimonial nature" of the political elite. There doesn't seem to be a functional difference between the modes of exerting control during colonial times and in independent Africa.[24] He decried the weak engagement he perceived among leading evangelical church figures against these structures in the church in the 2000s. The danger in this scenario, he noted, was for evangelical Christianity to be used for political purposes.[25] This begs the question about what effective political engagement looks like. As noted above, there is a conspicuous absence of iconic activist leadership on the political front, especially among the evangelical churches, of which, in Kenya, the Pentecostal churches are a part.

Gifford's biggest indictment against the Pentecostal movement was what he called its "enchanted" worldview. This worldview, he says, renders African Christianity impotent because it jettisons a rationalism that is essential in

---

21. Karanja, "Evangelical Attitudes," 87–88.

22. Karanja, 88.

23. Karanja, 88.

24. Paul Gifford, "Evangelical Christianity and Democracy in Africa: A Response," in *Evangelical Christianity*, 225–230.

25. Gifford, "Evangelical Christianity."

addressing political and developmental issues.[26] Walls acknowledges that the African worldview has a holistic perspective which espouses a fluid interface between the physical and metaphysical.[27] What is in question are the ways in which this perspective is irrational, and whether it can only be detrimental to discourse on politics and social transformation.

Gifford is perceptive in his understanding of the conversionist nature of Pentecostal faith. There is often a heavy stress laid on the personal nature of the conversion experience. Such an individualistic faith experience focuses on personal experience at the expense of societal change. Maggay explained this defective idea. She stated that this perspective teaches that spiritual transformation through conversion is the only Christian response to social, political, or economic problems.[28]

Another misconception is an erroneous understanding of the need for and practice of political engagement. On one end of the scale is the practice of abstinence from all things political. As the old adage goes, "politics is a dirty game." Since politics is dirty, it is expected to corrupt even a Christian individual.[29] This is reinforced by the above-mentioned perspective of the personal nature of common expressions of evangelicalism. On the opposite end of the scale is subservience. Maggay explained that these perspectives come from Romans 13, where Christians are adjured to always obey the government.[30] This may also be further strengthened by a potential instinct for self-preservation. Karanja explained that in "the emerging charismatic ministries that are currently busy consolidating themselves, the fear of de-registration may keep them away from publicly expressing their views on issues of governance for the time being."[31]

Many of the inaccurate perceptions stem from an inadequate theological basis for political engagement as an aspect of Christian living. On this issue Maggay pointed out how Pentecostal leaders in places like Peru have a dualistic understanding of theology and politics. The two hardly come together in discourse. This observation highlights the need for a cohesive theological

---

26. Gifford expounds on this view extensively in Gifford, *Christianity, Development and Modernity in Africa* (London: C. Hurst, 2015).

27. Andrew F. Walls, *The Cross-Cultural Process in Christian History: Studies in the Transmission and Appropriation of Faith* (Maryknoll, NY: Orbis, 2002), 122–133.

28. Melba Maggay, "Confronting the Powers: The Church's Political Commitment," in *Holistic Mission: God's Plan for God's People*, ed. Brian Woolnough and Wonsuk Ma (Eugene, OR: Wipf & Stock, 2011), 192.

29. Maggay, "Confronting the Powers."

30. Maggay.

31. Karanja, "Evangelical Attitudes," 89.

approach to Christian engagement in politics. We now examine some ways in which newer Pentecostal charismatic churches have begun charting the way forward in terms of political engagement in spite of these misconceptions. This political engagement takes on forms different from the "iconic activist clergyman" model of the previous era of Christian political activism in Kenya. We begin with the pulpit.

Political Engagement from the Pulpit

The primary avenue for the communication of a church's theology is the pulpit. This is where the theology forged in the mind of preachers and informed by their contexts is shared. In the past, pulpit activism was proclamatory and prophetic in a manner to provoke, stir up, and otherwise challenge the status quo. It was not uncommon to find journalists in the late 1980s and early 1990s in Kenya following activist clergymen from historic mission churches to hear how their sermons would challenge the government of the day.[32] Today, a segment of influential NPCCs have chosen to use their sermons to articulate a cogent theology of personal responsibility for listeners to institute change in their political and social contexts. Far from being provocative or adversarial, these sermons are much more focused on urging the individual to bring about social transformation. While the sermons do challenge those in authority, the underlying assumption is the congregation's greater ability to influence societal change. We take Mavuno Church as an example of this.

Our data comprises selected sermons preached by different preachers at Mavuno Church between 2011 and 2013.[33] The Mavuno movement annually prepares a lectionary of sermons from different ministers from within, addressing different social issues.[34] Many of these sermons are posted in written form or video on the church blog and are available to many beyond the congregation. In this way, the audience reached is wider than the physical congregation in a specific location. The pastors at each Mavuno congregation preach most of the sermons "in parallel" across the campuses.

32. Stephen Muoki Joshua and Stephen Asol Kapinde, "'Pulpit Power' and the Unrelenting Voice of Archbishop David Gitari in the Democratisation of Kenya, 1986 to 1991," *Historia* 61, no. 2 (2016): 79–100, https://doi.org/10.17159/2309-8392/2016/v61n2a4.

33. Mavuno Church is an NPCC founded in Nairobi in August 2005 by Muriithi Wanjau. The church grew rapidly, attracting young urban professionals. As of 2016 the church had five campuses in Nairobi, five in other African countries, and church-planting work going on in an additional four countries. The church was seen as trendsetting in terms of its relevance of the messages to the demographic as well as in its use of modern technology and music.

34. *Blog.Mavuno*, accessed 21 November 2018, https://mavuno.wordpress.com/.

With reference to the data, one of the themes that emerged in relation to political participation is the notion that justice is instituted by individuals within a social system. In his sermon "Restore Justice," Muriithi Wanjau argued that his audience "must move away from seeing justice as the government's or civil society's responsibility. We need to understand that God holds his people accountable for the practice of justice in our nation, and in God's eyes, justice in our day-to-day dealings is even more important than our worship and prayers on Sunday."[35] One way to effect this justice is to eradicate poverty, not through handouts but by a commitment to economic empowerment. In the same sermon Muriithi stated that the answer to eradicating poverty in Kenyan society was "to break people out of poverty into a place where they own their means of production – which is what we call the 'middle-class.' That was the rationale behind the year of Jubilee."[36]

While the discerning middle class should exert their influence to address societal issues, the national leadership must also be kept accountable. In a sermon on leadership titled "The Leadership Brand," Linda Ocholla-Adolwa challenged her audience, saying that "When a leader becomes destructive it is my duty to select another leader in his place."[37] Teaching from 1 Kings 12:1–15 she cautioned against a compartmentalized understanding of Christian faith, saying, "We relegate certain things to the spiritual realm and certain other things to the secular realm. We compartmentalize life in such a way that to be Christian means certain kinds of actions and certain other kinds of actions are not part of what it means to be Christian."[38] Her rallying call was for people to pray for the nation at the church's evening of prayer, but also, very importantly, to go and register as a voter. On this she said, "The voter registration exercise has begun. Go and register to take charge of the future of this country."[39] She reinforced this view by saying that in order "for the next governor of Nairobi to be people-centered, I must be vigilant in demanding accountable leadership."[40] She went on to say, "Because of the power distance in our culture it is extremely difficult for us to challenge those in authority. Yet, to get the kind of leaders

---

35. Muriithi Wanjau, "Restore Justice," *Blog.Mavuno* (blog), 17 February 2013, https://mavuno.wordpress.com/2013/02/17/restore-justice/.

36. Wanjau, "Restore Justice."

37. Linda Ochola-Adolwa, "The Leadership Brand," *Blog.Mavuno* (blog), 25 November 2012, https://mavuno.wordpress.com/2012/11/25/3425/.

38. Ochola-Adolwa, "Leadership Brand."

39. Ochola-Adolwa.

40. Ochola-Adolwa, "The Widow & the Judge," *Blog.Mavuno* (blog), 20 November 2012, https://mavuno.wordpress.com/2012/11/20/3406/.

who are people-centered and who experience the world as others see it we will have to be vigilant."[41]

Simon Mbevi is a pastor and a former political aspirant who preaches often at Mavuno Church. Trained as a lawyer, he left the legal profession to focus on teaching about responsible masculinity, prayer, and national unity through his organization "Transform Nations."[42] In a sermon about elections at Mavuno, Mbevi taught that "The greatest challenge we have as a nation in transition is and will be leadership. Good and effective leaders are hard to find. At home, at the market place, in institutions, in the villages, and in the nation."[43] Mbevi observed that the Scriptures are not silent on leadership, and went on to draw out five leadership qualities in that sermon titled "Kiongozi Challenge." The qualities of such a leader, according to Mbevi, are conciliatoriness, care, character, competence, and compelling vision.[44]

These churches consider the pulpit an appropriate place for discourse on the Christian's responsibility for social transformation. The gospel is not an inert participant in the listener's context. It is the message that turns believers into salt and light, active ingredients vital for bringing about change. Thus, in addition to evangelism, the pulpit becomes one of the avenues for empowering Christians to become active participants in God's work on earth. These churches' view of discipleship extends beyond the narrow confines instituted by some churches. Such churches do not address the responsibility of believers to exercise their faith in matters of societal value. The preachers described above, and others like them, are well within their mandate when they use the pulpit to inspire hope and change in the holistic application of the good news.

Blogosphere: Where Clergy and Laity Influence Meets

A post on Facebook, the well-known micro-blogging site, says this of elected members of parliament: "We need to make them feel so small, not just to teach them that we are still their bosses, but to teach us not [to] worship them. We need to stop using 'Honorable' and *Mheshimiwa* when we talk to them. They can use those titles with each other, but we *wananchi* (Swahili for Citizen)

41. Ochola-Adolwa, "Widow."

42. "Transform Nations," Transform Nations, accessed 22 February 2017, http://transform-nations.net/.

43. Simon Mbevi, "Kiongozi Challenge," *Blog.Mavuno* (blog), 16 September 2012, https://mavuno.wordpress.com/2012/09/16/3355/.

44. Mbevi, "Kiongozi Challenge."

should stop using them. We need pastors to tell politicians who come to church to come forward to confess and repent to the people, not to donate money."[45]

Cyril Imo theorized that political engagement of evangelicals falls into three groups: evangelical politicians, evangelical ministers, and the evangelical low-status group.[46] The growth of social media, blogging, and other Internet-based spaces provides unique platforms where ministers and laity can engage in political discourse, each bringing their ideas to the table. The quote above represents a fourth category of engagement, that of the "social media-aware" laity who through social media exert significant influence on the listening and concerned public. Ministers and laity use the Internet platform in different ways. We will illustrate two approaches in this section. Let us take the examples of David Oginde, the presiding bishop of CITAM, and Muriithi Wanjau, the senior pastor of Mavuno Church.

Oginde maintains a blog known as the "Bishop's Blog." On the blog he engages in current affairs, giving his considered position on key issues. For example, in his 2015 article "By Their Inaction, Leaders Reducing President to a Manager," Oginde analyzed Kenya's leadership and concluded that there was a failure of leadership by those who worked with the president.[47] In the article, he quoted leadership examples from Europe, drawing parallels with the local situation. He also talked about some of his own experiences as a leader in the Kenyan context. He pointed to the value of responsible leadership among those whom the president has entrusted with the role of advising him. In another article, Oginde decried leaders for failing to seek counsel. He cited a personal example from within the church of the lack of advice given to leaders.

Oginde's articles offer a sober critique of Kenya's political leadership with none of the provocative and adversarial language common to previous activist clergy. The arguments are articulate, and forceful, and he does not shy away from touching on national scandals, the judiciary, or even the office of the president. He also addresses religious, social, and cultural challenges in society. In his writing we see an intentional drive to engage Christian values, biblical

---

45. Wandia Njoya, "The role of government, which is why we spend a lot of energy and time on elections, is to represent the people's interests," Facebook, 19 February 2017, accessed 20 February 2017, https://www.facebook.com/wandia.njoya/posts/1383427011709636; *Mheshimiwa* is Swahili for "the honorable one."

46. Cyril Imo, "Evangelicals, Muslims and Democracy: With Particular Reference to the Declaration of Sharia in Northern Nigeria," in Ranger, *Evangelical Christianity*, 37–66.

47. Bishop Dr David A. Oginde, "By Their Inaction, Leaders Reducing President to a Manager," *CITAMBlog* (blog), 20 July 2015, https://citamblog.wordpress.com/2015/07/20/by-their-inaction-leaders-reducing-president-to-a-manager/.

teaching, and sound reasoning. The blog provides a structured opportunity for the bishop of CITAM to respond to national issues.

Wanjau's blog articles carry out a similar function, providing a social and political commentary that is cogent and more conciliatory than confrontational. In one article, for example, referring to the British antislavery politician William Wilberforce, Wanjau wrote to his audience,

> I believe our own nation desperately needs Wilberforces today! We live in a time when greed has been enshrined as a virtue . . . It's not enough for us to express our disgust with the status quo on social media! We each need to begin to see our vocation as our space to bring about the reformation of manners. If you are a parent, you need to take your role of bringing up children with strong moral values seriously. If you are a media practitioner or entertainer, use your platform for the betterment of society. If you are an accountant or lawyer or farmer or marketer how is your practice or career or business not just adding to your bottom line but also helping create a better nation?[48]

In the blog Wanjau throws the responsibility for social and political change back to the audience. In doing this he inspires his audience to take up their responsibility for a better future. For example, in an article talking about Africa's potential, he began by stating, "Fifty years after independence however, I am no longer envious of my father's generation. For Kenyans of my generation who are fortunate enough to have an education, there has never been a better time to be alive!"[49] He went on: "As Africa's middle class, it is our responsibility to create the jobs and provide the solutions that will raise our continent out of poverty! . . . My prayer is that my generation will not either miss out on or misappropriate Africa's century!"[50] His tone and that of Oginde display measured language that is tailored to communicate forcefully without causing undue offense.

Some laity have taken the social media space as an arena for activism and political engagement. Some of them see it as their Christian calling to engage the powers that be. Their language is decidedly activist and often adversarial,

---

48. Muriithi Wanjau, "We Need a Reformation of Manners!," *Pastor M's Blog* (blog), 29 October 2013, https://greatnessnow.wordpress.com/2013/10/29/we-need-a-reformation-of-manners/.

49. Muriithi Wanjau, "Africa's Century," *Pastor M's Blog* (blog), 13 August 2013, https://greatnessnow.wordpress.com/2013/08/13/africas-century/.

50. Wanjau, "Africa's Century."

reminiscent of the clergy of yesteryear. One such activist is Njonjo Mue, a human rights lawyer with a graduate theology degree. Mue and other activists often use Facebook as their preferred blogging medium, though they can be found on other blogging sites. In one of his posts Mue urged Kenyans to take personal responsibility for the outcome of Kenyan political governance. He encouraged his readers to fight against mediocrity and strive for excellence until progress is achieved.[51] The militancy is evident, as is the urgency, in the tone of the speech. Mue often posts or reposts pithy quotes with an activist message that is relevant to the current context. Mue attends one of the influential Pentecostal churches and will often engage other Christians in animated discourse on politics and social justice issues.

Another activist blogger is Wandia Njoya. A lecturer with a PhD in literature, she also attends a Pentecostal church and does not see her activism as separate from the exercise of her faith. Her language is also provocative and activist in tone. Consider, for instance, her words in a post about a long-standing doctors' strike at the end of 2016:

> Much as our interests and those of the doctors intersect, we're really on our own, and without a voice in the formal discussion about something that affects us so fundamentally, economically, and physically. We're the ones who will pay the bills and who will use public hospitals, yet we have no voice. What is the use of voting, of paying taxes, if the people whom we elect don't represent us but represent their private interests? Why should we always have to seek audience with government? Government is not supposed to have an opinion. It's supposed to implement our opinion. We should be telling government we want universal healthcare, and we don't want to hear excuses about wage bill and [the] World Bank. And if they can't do it, we get another government that can.[52]

---

51. Njonjo Mue, "Conversations from the Edge: Essays, Speeches, Thoughts and Musings of Njonjo Mue," accessed 21 November 2018, http://njonjomue.blogspot.com/; Njonjo Mue, "Conversations from the Edge: The Glory of Kenya," 7 February 2012, https://njonjomue.blogspot.com/2012/02/glory-of-kenya.html.

52. Njoya, "The Role of Government."

Wandia and Mue represent a cadre of "social media-aware" laity who have taken activism to the Internet, reaching large audiences on a platform that also allows for feedback. Boniface Mwangi also uses both Facebook and Twitter.[53]

Engaging Kenyan Christian Professionals

Another major avenue for the engagement of an economically and intellectually empowered laity is professional forums. In this section we briefly look at two Kenyan forums. We begin with Christians for a Just Society (CFJS). It was founded in 1998 by a group of Christians who "believed that there was a role for Christians to play in the political, economic, and social affairs of our country and aimed at sensitising and mobilising Christians to get involved."[54] Their mission is to "mobilize and equip Christians for political engagement." They developed a church leaders program aimed at providing information and resources for leaders in churches to use when vetting and engaging with political leaders. They created another program to train practicing Christians who are aspiring to political office. They also have a women's program to develop women for political leadership.[55] CFJS holds member gatherings in the form of town hall meetings targeting the middle class to interrogate the visions and objectives of political aspirants. June is the CFJS National Justice month for teaching, mobilizing prayer, and acting against different types of injustice in the country.[56]

The Executive Leaders Network (ELNET), another professionals group, is linked to Life Ministry, an evangelism and discipleship organization working among students and professionals.[57] ELNET strives to build "leaders of integrity who can spearhead Kenya's holistic transformation."[58] The forum puts together gatherings of leaders to "[engage] and [empower] leaders to champion and

---

53. Boniface Mwangi, "Boniface Mwangi – Home," Facebook, accessed 20 February 2017, https://www.facebook.com/BonifaceMwangiBM; Boniface Mwangi (@bonifcaemwangi), "Since 2013 I have been charged five times, acquitted on one case, another case was thrown out and three are ongoing. Activism isn't a crime!" Twitter, 21 February 2017, 7:46 a.m., accessed 20 February 2017, https://twitter.com/bonifacemwangi/status/833930809648222208.

54. "Christians for a Just Society (CFJS)," accessed 21 February 2017, https://cfjs.wordpress.com/.

55. "Christians for a Just Society (CFJS)."

56. "Christians for a Just Society (CFJS)."

57. Life Ministry is a student discipleship ministry affiliated to CRU, Campus Crusade for Christ.

58. "ELNET Executive Leadership Network," accessed 22 February 2017, https://www.elnetkenya.org/.

influence the implementation of godly values in governance," and to encourage the church as a corporate body and individuals to participate proactively in governance issues.[59] The forum has a governance group which focuses on advocacy "on issues of concern to the church as the moral conscience of the nation," "policy formulation and law making – [participating] in the drafting of bills and implementation of the constitution," and "responsible citizenship," which includes "[holding] leaders accountable."[60] In the area of "responsible citizenship," the group aims to address issues of voter registration and empowerment, encouraging Christians to enter elective office as well as supporting candidates who uphold godly values. This group has a monthly governance forum in Nairobi as well as a parliamentarians support group. The Kenya Christian Professionals Forum also has a governance committee with objectives very similar to those of ELNET.[61]

The approach used in these forums is consultative, with monthly meetings constituted around various relevant matters. The tone of the forums is conciliatory and bipartisan. It is meant to encourage and affirm consensus approaches to political issues from a Christian perspective. The content is largely informative and inspirational. Its goal is to empower through information. These forums aim to exert quiet influence away from public and populist rhetoric. Policy material proposed at these forums has the potential to have a national impact at every level of society. For example, the moral framework for vision 2030 developed by ELNET, if implemented, can have a strategic impact on the national conversation on values. Importantly, these forums give the laity a voice in political engagement alongside their clergy.

Conclusion

When Karanja predicted that younger charismatic churches would likely make a significant contribution on the question of Christian political engagement, he was accurate.[62] He did not anticipate the specific ways in which this contribution would be made. Emerging urban Pentecostal movements have charted a unique path of engagement in politics and social transformation. I have argued that these churches see the gospel holistically. Political discourse

---

59. "ELNET Governance Group," accessed 22 February 2017, https://www.elnetkenya.org/elnet-governance-group/.

60. "ELNET Governance Group."

61. "Governance Committee," KCPF (Kenya Christian Professionals Forum), accessed 21 February 2017, https://www.kcpf.or.ke/governance-committee/.

62. Karanja, "Evangelical Attitudes," 88.

affects society, and these churches consider Christian engagement with this reality to be an aspect of the good news.

Building on past models, these churches cascade the role of activism to a wider group of clergy who are politically aware and who use their pulpits boldly to comment and teach on political issues. Their tone and manner are forceful, but much less adversarial than those of their predecessors. The emergence of blogging sites and social media platforms has expanded the audience to create a virtual constituency for this kind of engagement. While NPCC clergy cautiously engaged with the issues, the laity seized on them and were decidedly more adversarial. Using language reminiscent of the "activist clergy" of the 1990s, the laity forcefully advanced the agenda for change, carrying with them a sympathetic audience on the platforms.

Social media provides avenues for feedback, creating a format of debate that is closer to conversational dialogue. Multiple opinions can be heard on any social media platform. Christian professional forums provide a different approach which appeals to intellectual pursuits, using more tempered approaches aimed at exerting quiet influence. In sum, the dialogue today builds on the foundation laid in the past by broadening the discourse beyond a few activist clergy to a wider group of participants. This new season provides a scenario in which more voices meet with a wider audience through social media. This carries with it enormous opportunities as well as risks.

The role of evangelical church leadership must therefore evolve from being reactive to empowering the laity and younger clergy with sound theological foundations for meaningful engagement. This means that both pulpit and discipleship avenues will need to be fully engaged in discourse on how to engage politically, especially for the laity. Leadership within the church must also affirm those who choose to engage in public political discourse. Such affirmation should limit itself, in terms of the content and the practice of political engagement, to upholding biblical values. The church in general will also need to navigate the thin line between encouraging political debate in an increasingly open democratic space and avoiding being partisan. It should be possible for congregation members with different political inclinations to sit under the same teaching and draw out truth that will enrich the debate, steering it towards God's vision for citizens of earthly "kingdoms." The voice of Christian academia has been conspicuously absent in this dialogue. When it emerges, it will find its work cut out. The development of a cogent theological framework of political engagement will need to be its first task. We conclude by affirming what we see: that the Pentecostal church is not mute in its political engagement; it has just changed its language to speak more quietly to a wider audience that will understand the new language.

Bibliography

"Christians for a Just Society (CFJS)." Accessed 21 February 2017. https://cfjs. wordpress.com/.

"ELNET Executive Leadership Network." Accessed 22 February 2017. https://www. elnetkenya.org/.

"ELNET Governance Group." Accessed 22 February 2017. https://www.elnetkenya. org/elnet-governance-group/.

Gee, Donald. "Kenya and Tanganyika." *Pentecost* (September 1960): 10.

Gifford, Paul. *The Christian Churches and the Democratisation of Africa*. Leiden: Brill, 1995.

———. *Christianity, Development and Modernity in Africa*. London: C. Hurst, 2015.

———. *Christianity, Politics and Public Life in Kenya*. London: C. Hurst, 2009.

———. "Evangelical Christianity and Democracy in Africa: A Response." In *Evangelical Christianity and Democracy in Africa*, edited by Terence Ranger, 225–230. New York: Oxford University Press, 2008.

"Governance Committee." KCPF (Kenya Christian Professionals Forum). Accessed 21 February 2017. https://www.kcpf.or.ke/governance-committee/.

Imo, Cyril. "Evangelicals, Muslims and Democracy: With Particular Reference to the Declaration of Sharia in Northern Nigeria." In *Evangelical Christianity and Democracy in Africa*, edited by Terence Ranger, 37–66. New York: Oxford University Press, 2008.

Irvine, A. C. "Pentecost among the Tribesmen." *Pentecost* (June 1953): 6.

Joshua, Stephen Muoki, and Stephen Asol Kapinde. "'Pulpit Power' and the Unrelenting Voice of Archbishop David Gitari in the Democratisation of Kenya, 1986 to 1991." *Historia* 61, no. 2 (2016): 79–100. https://doi.org/10.17159/2309-8392/2016/ v61n2a4.

Karanja, John. "Evangelical Attitudes toward Democracy in Kenya." In *Evangelical Christianity and Democracy in Africa*, edited by Terence Ranger, 67–94. New York: Oxford University Press, 2008.

Kitts, John. "Kikuyu Converts." *Pentecost* 30 (December 1954): 7.

———. "Threatened by Mau Mau." *Pentecost* 23 (March 1953): 10.

———. "Pentecost in East Africa." *Pentecost* 32 (June 1955): 14.

Lewis, Joanna. *Empire State-Building: War and Welfare in Kenya, 1925–52*. Athens, OH: Ohio State University Press, 2000.

MacPherson, Robert, Sospeter Magua, and Paul D. Fueter. *Kenya Present and Future*. Nairobi: Christian Council of Kenya, 1960.

Maggay, Melba. "Confronting the Powers: The Church's Political Commitment." In *Holistic Mission: God's Plan for God's People*, edited by Brian Woolnough and Wonsuk Ma, 175–186. Eugene, OR: Wipf & Stock, 2011.

"Mavuno Church Blog." *Mavuno Church* (blog), 22 April 2014. https://mavuno.wordpress.com/.

Mbevi, Simon. "Kiongozi Challenge." *Blog.Mavuno* (blog), 16 September 2012. https://mavuno.wordpress.com/2012/09/16/3355/.

"Member of Kenya Legislative Council." *Pentecost* (September 1958): 11.

Mue, Njonjo. "Conversations from the Edge: Essays, Speeches, Thoughts and Musings of Njonjo Mue." Accessed 21 November 2018. http://njonjomue.blogspot.com/.

———. "The Glory of Kenya." 7 February 2012. https://njonjomue.blogspot.com/2012/02/glory-of-kenya.html.

Mwangi, Boniface. "Boniface Mwangi – Home." Facebook. Accessed 20 February 2017. https://www.facebook.com/BonifaceMwangiBM.

———. (@bonifacemwangi) "Let your vote count. Politicians who don't respect you don't deserve your vote. Your vote is your weapon against impunity, go register today." Twitter, 15 February 2017, 2.52 a.m. https://twitter.com/bonifacemwangi/status/831818386216730624.

———. (@bonifacemwangi) "Since 2013 I have been charged five times, acquitted on one case, another case was thrown out and three are ongoing. Activism isn't a crime." Twitter, 21 February 2017, 7.46 a.m. https://twitter.com/bonifacemwangi/status/833930809648222208.

"New African Pentecostal Church in Nairobi: The Work Goes on in Kenya in Spite of Mau Mau." *Pentecost* (June 1954).

"Nicholas Benghu for World Conference." *Pentecost* (March 1958): 2.

Njoya, Wandia. "The role of government, which is why we spend a lot of energy and time on elections, is to represent the people's interests." Facebook, 19 February 2017. Accessed 20 February 2017. https://www.facebook.com/wandia.njoya/posts/1383427011709636.

Ochola-Adolwa, Linda. "The Leadership Brand." *Blog.Mavuno* (blog), 25 November 2012. https://mavuno.wordpress.com/2012/11/25/3425/.

———. "The Widow and the Judge." *Blog.Mavuno* (blog), 20 November 2012. https://mavuno.wordpress.com/2012/11/20/3406/.

Oginde, Bishop Dr David A. "By Their Inaction, Leaders Reducing President to a Manager." *CITAMBlog* (blog), 20 July 2015. https://citamblog.wordpress.com/2015/07/20/by-their-inaction-leaders-reducing-president-to-a-manager/.

Ranger, Terence O. "Introduction." In *Evangelical Christianity and Democracy in Africa*, edited by Terence Ranger, 3–36. New York: Oxford University Press, 2008.

———, ed. *Evangelical Christianity and Democracy in Africa*. New York: Oxford University Press, 2008.

Sanneh, Lamin O. *Translating the Message: The Missionary Impact on Culture*. Maryknoll, NY: Orbis, 1991.

"Transform Nations." Transform Nations. Accessed 22 February 2017. http://transform-nations.net/.

Walls, Andrew F. *The Cross-Cultural Process in Christian History: Studies in the Transmission and Appropriation of Faith*. Maryknoll, NY: Orbis, 2002.

Wanjau, Muriithi. "Africa's Century." *Pastor M's Blog* (blog), 13 August 2013. https://greatnessnow.wordpress.com/2013/08/13/africas-century/.

———. "Restore Justice." *Blog.Mavuno* (blog), 17 February 2013. https://mavuno.wordpress.com/2013/02/17/restore-justice/.

———. "We Need a Reformation of Manners!" *Pastor M's Blog* (blog), 29 October 2013. https://greatnessnow.wordpress.com/2013/10/29/we-need-a-reformation-of-manners/.

4

Promoting Biblical Principles of Good Governance in Africa

Paul M. Mbandi

Executive Director of Missions Afield Leadership Development Africa (MALDA)

Abstract

Those who read and listen to African news related to leadership of governments and of private and civil society organizations will agree that most of the problems in Africa are associated with bad governance. In this chapter, the author first highlights some governance-related problems that are mainly experienced in Africa. Second, the author defines the key terms that are used in the chapter. Third, as a Christian theologian, the writer develops the biblical principles of good governance: godly character, delegation, right knowledge and skills, inclusiveness, concern for the poor, accountability and transparency, respecting the rule of law, equity and responsiveness, sacrificial servanthood, and transformational leadership. Fourth, the writer discusses how church leaders could promote the implementation of these biblical principles of good governance among government officers, public servants, and politicians. Church leaders have a key role to play in modeling the above biblical principles of good governance and in teaching them to others in order to reduce governance crises and the corruption in many Africa nations.

Key words: Africa, governance, character, servanthood, inclusiveness, poor, transparency, and equity

Introduction

Those who read and listen to African news related to government leadership will agree that many crises in Africa are associated with poor governance. For example, the Libyan crises began in 2011, leading to the ousting and death of Muammar Gaddafi. Since that time Libya has experienced civil war and violence due to a power struggle among the many competing militias that participated in the ousting of Gaddafi. Up to the time of writing, the "Government of National Accord" formed by the Tobruk Government and the General National Congress (GNC) is still struggling to take control of Libya's major oil terminals.

In January 2017 we witnessed civil unrest in Gambia when the president Yahya Jammeh refused to hand over power after losing the presidential election to Adama Barrow.[1] It took a threat of imminent invasion by Senegal's army for Jammeh to step down from power. Several African countries have experienced civil unrest and violence because sitting presidents have manipulated elections or handled them unfairly, in order for them to remain in power.

The headline of the *Kenya Daily Nation* on 27 October 2016 read: "Inside Story of Sh5bn Jubilee Health Scandal." The story alleged that the above billions went missing due to manipulation of payment systems to allow double payments. In 2016 almost 2 billion Kenyan shillings were lost through untrustworthy companies that allegedly provided services or supplies to National Youth Service (NYS). This was captured in the *Kenya Daily Nation* headline on 17 November 2016: "Scandals: See No Evil, Hear No Evil." The story was summarized in the following words: "After discovering that a lot more than Sh1.8 billion may have been stolen at National Youth Service, an exasperated Parliament is venting its anger on officials who go round in circles looking busy and waxing virtuous but appear careful to achieve nothing in getting to the bottom of the growing pile of financial scams in the government department."[2]

At the time of writing this chapter, on 3 March 2017, the medical doctors working in government hospitals in Kenya had been on strike for more than eighty days. They were asking for better pay and improved working conditions. The attempts by Health Cabinet Secretary Cleopa Mailu, his Principal Secretary

---

1. According to Sky News on 18 January 2017, many businesses were closed down and as many as 26,000 people had fled Gambia for Senegal due to the fear of civil war, https://news.sky.com/story/senegal-troops-invade-the-gambia-as-adama-barrow-sworn-in-as-president-10734802.

2. *Kenya Daily Nation* (Nairobi), 17 November 2016.

Nicholas Muraguri, and county governors had not resolved the stalemate. The judicial attempt to imprison the officials of Kenya Medical Practitioners, Pharmacists and Dentists Union (KMPDU) made the situation worse, for the doctors in private hospitals and universities joined their counterparts in striking in protest on the streets. The alleged loss of 5 billion from the ministry of health made many people sympathetic to the doctors' demands. Also during the writing of this chapter, the lecturers in government universities were on strike demanding better pay. The above corruption scandals and civil servants' strikes are confirmation that governance in public sectors is a major problem in many countries in Africa.

We have experienced many attempts to impeach County Governors in Kenya, as well as physical fights in the National and County Assemblies. These stories of corruption are duplicated in many countries in Africa. Many of them continue to experience violence and instability due to problems associated with governance.

On the one hand, according to Iva Bozovic, lack of transparency and accountability, as well as corruption, are to blame for the misuse of public resources in many governments and lack of information regarding citizens' rights.[3] On the other hand, transparency, accountability, and anti-corruption play a major role in building effective institutions, improving governance and service delivery.[4]

Although the focus of this paper is on governance in the public sector, governance problems are not limited to that sector. They are also experienced in businesses and corporate organizations. Governance problems are even experienced in parachurch organizations and churches. I am a minister with the Africa Inland Church (AIC) Kenya. Currently, we have two AICs: the AIC Kenya, which is led by Rev Dr Silas Yego, as the Presiding Bishop; and the "original" AIC, which is led by Rev David Mbuvi as Bishop. Attempts to reconcile these church leaders and their respective followers have been futile. Local churches continue to defect from AIC Kenya to the "original" AIC due to leadership issues, especially those related to resource management. For example, in 2017 Muisuni AIC in Kangundo Region defected from AIC Kenya to the "original" AIC due to leadership disagreements related to the management of Kangundo children's home.

---

3. Iva Bozovic, "Building Transparency, Accountability, and Anti-Corruption into the 2015 Development Framework," discussion paper, ed. Anga Timilsina and Diana Torres (New York: United Nations Development Programme, September 2014), 5.

4. Bozovic, "Building Transparency," 7.

On 5 June 2015, a headline of an article in *Standard Digital* read: "Preachers Wilfred Lai and Arthur Kitonga Lock Horns in Court over Church." According to the report, Bishop Kitonga of Redeemed Gospel Church, Kenya, and Lai of Jesus Celebration Center (JCC) in Mombasa were "locked in a legal battle over the ownership of a church in Makindu, Makueni County."[5] These problems associated with governance are evidence that most government and non-government leaders in Africa do not understand and embrace biblical principles of good governance. Thus, the purpose of this chapter is to set out the biblical principles of good governance and to explore how church leaders could promote their implementation, especially among government ministers and politicians. The biblical principles of governance developed in this chapter are also applicable to businesses, corporate organizations, and different institutions.

In this chapter I have attempted to develop biblical principles of good governance based on theological reflections on key biblical passages that have implications for governance. Although I do not engage in detailed exegesis of the passages, work has been done to ensure that the implications drawn from the passages are supported by the context of the passages. I have also consulted other relevant literature on governance. In an effort to find out how church leaders could practically encourage the biblical principles of good governance among governing officers and public servants, I interviewed several church leaders on this matter.

I believe that the Bible provides fundamental principles of good governance and that church leaders, including professional theologians, should consciously strive to practice and promote the implementation of these principles among government ministers and public servants at all levels of governance. If governing bodies understood and embraced biblical principles of governance, the bad governance that negatively affects citizens, public servants, and all other stakeholders would be minimized.

First, it is important to explain how I will use certain key terms in this chapter.

---

5. For more information, see the article by Willis Oketch at *Standard Digital*, https://www.standardmedia.co.ke/article/2000164642/preachers-wilfred-lai-and-arthur-kitonga-lock-horns-in-court-over-church. It is known that pastors of Redeemed Gospel Churches in Kenya are divided over who is their bishop. Some churches and pastors claim allegiance to Rev Wilfred Lai as the bishop, while others uphold Rev Arthur Kitonga as the bishop.

Explanation of the Key Terms

Governance: According to Webster's New Twentieth Century Dictionary, the word "governance" comes from a Latin word *gubernare*, which means the "exercise of authority, control, management, and power of government."

In its attempt to reflect on the definition of governance, the Institute on Governance in Canada, states "Governance determines who has power, who makes decisions, how other players make their voice heard and how account is rendered."[6] Thus, "governance is how society or groups within it, organize to make decisions."[7] In simple language governance has also been understood as the processes for making and implementing decisions. Based on these explanations, the main aspects of governance can be summarized as authority, the decision-making process, stakeholders' participation, and accountability. Given these dimensions of governance, we need to have a broad understanding of decision-making that involves the development of policies or procedures and their implementation in order to have control in governance. The International Federation of Accountants Consultation (IFAC) captured the above nuances in its explanation of governance: "governance comprises the arrangements put in place to ensure that the intended outcomes for stakeholders are defined and achieved."[8] According to these explanations, it is clear that good governance should focus on delivering services to the stakeholders.

Governing minister: In this chapter I use "governing minister" in a broad way that includes a cabinet minister, permanent secretaries, governors, people working under governors, and other government officers who have been entrusted with authority and responsibility in managing resources. Thus, governing ministers are to be understood as persons or a group entrusted with the responsibility to develop strategic directions, policies, and accountability of public resources for the purpose of serving the public interest. The practice of having ministers and governors is not foreign to the Bible. According to 1 Kings 4:1–7, King Solomon had chief officials (ministers) who served in the administration of the affairs of the state. The king also had twelve governors who served in the administration of the twelve districts of Israel (1 Kgs 4:7–19).

Church leader: In this chapter, "church leader" is used in a broad sense to refer to church elders and especially church ministers who serve as teaching

---

6. "Defining Governance," accessed 31 August 2016, https://iog.ca/what-is-governance/.

7. "Defining Governance."

8. "Good Governance in the Public Sector," International Federation of Accountants Consultation (IFAC), June 2013, http://www.ifac.org/system/files/publications/files/Good-Governance-in-the-Public-Sector.pdf 8.

elders (pastors). This includes bishops and archbishops who are overseers of several churches or a denomination. "Church leader" also includes professional Christian theologians who are involved in teaching theology and training church leaders.

This leads us to the development of the biblical principles of good governance.

Biblical Principles of Good Governance

According to the Old Testament, principles of good governance are revealed mainly through a good relationship between the ruler and the people, as well as through the relationship between God and the rulers. According to the New Testament, principles of good governance are expressed mainly through the relationships of Jesus and his followers to the authorities of the time.[9] We begin by developing biblical principles of good governance based on Jethro's advice to Moses in Exodus 18:13–27.

According to the story, Jethro (the father-in-law of Moses) witnessed Moses judging the people of Israel and teaching them God's statutes from morning to evening (Exod 18:13–16). Jethro advised Moses to look for able men and delegate the work to them.[10] It is generally agreed by those who have studied the history of Israel that during this period there was no difference between the sacred and the secular in Israel's legal system. It is understood that Jethro's advice to Moses was directly related to judicial administration. Therefore, there are many principles of governance that can be developed from this passage and applied to different levels of governance in public sector and other organizations.

The Principle of Delegation for Effectiveness in Governance

Based on Jethro's advice to Moses, governors should delegate work in order to be effective and efficient. According to the story, Jethro intervened because he witnessed a lack of effectiveness and efficiency: many people were standing

---

9. "Bible Study 1: On Good Governance," http://clients.squareeye.net/uploads/anglican/documents/governance.pdf accessed 20 March 2017.

10. Moses's father-in-law said to him, "What you are doing is not good. You and the people with you will certainly wear yourselves out . . . Look for able men from all the people, men who fear God, who are trustworthy and hate a bribe, and place such men over the people as chiefs of thousands, of hundreds, of fifties, and of tens. And let them judge the people at all times. Every great matter they shall bring to you . . . and they will bear the burden with you" (Exod 18:17–18, 21–22).

"around [Moses] from morning till evening" waiting for his services (Exod 18:13–14). The work was too heavy for Moses to bear, and he was wearing out both himself and his people (v. 18). We can infer from this that governors of state or of any other organization should use downward delegation to avoid doing everything themselves. The fact that different officials were put in charge of thousands, hundreds, fifties, and tens shows that they served at various levels of civil courts depending on their abilities and the complexity of the cases. Thus, there is a need to have government ministers who can serve at different levels in order to make delivery of services in a particular state effective and efficient. Effectiveness is an essential principle of good governance for it ensures that the governing bodies provide quality services to stakeholders; efficient services demonstrate good value for money.[11] The idea of downward delegation in order to enhance effectiveness is also in agreement with the devolution of governance.

The Principle of Right Qualification

Jethro advised Moses to "look for able [capable] men from all the people" (v. 21). It is important to underscore the word "able" – that is, persons with the ability to get the work done, not just anyone. It is important for governors to select ministers who are qualified for their jobs. Therefore, those entrusted with the responsibility of recruitment, appointing, or selecting government ministers should give jobs to those who have the relevant knowledge and skills for a particular office or task. Unfortunately, most leaders fail in this principle. Instead of following institutions' policies and recruitment procedures to search for qualified persons, many leaders give positions of governance to friends, relatives, people of their ethnic group, or their political loyalists. Those who have witnessed such unethical practices in different states and organizations agree that the consequences have been detrimental to both the leaders and the recipients of the services.

The Principle of Inclusiveness

Moses was advised to have co-governors from "all the people." No doubt Moses was required to have co-governors from different tribes of Israel and not from one tribe only. It is essential for governance to be inclusive. From

---

11. British and Irish Ombudsman Association, *Guide for Principles of Good Governance* (British and Irish Ombudsman Association [BIOA], October 2009), 8.

this directive, we can infer that it is important for presidents and governors to have ministers and other civil officers from different ethnic groups, religions, and regions in order to have a wide representation and fair distribution of government and leadership positions. Unfortunately, most government appointments and recruitments are politically influenced and are not inclusive. Thus, appointments or the selection of government ministers needs to be based on relevant knowledge and skills, as well as a fair distribution of governance positions based on regions, qualifications, ethnic groups, and other essential factors. Inclusiveness in governance also ensures the representation and participation of all stakeholders.

The Principle of Godly Character

Moses was advised by Jethro to select persons "who fear God" (v. 21). From a biblical perspective, Jethro was referring to a holy fear. According to J. D. Douglas, "holy fear" comes from the believer's apprehension of God. Following Martin Luther, Douglas pointed out that the natural person cannot have a genuine fear of God, for it is God-given.[12] It is this holy fear that enables believers to revere God and obey his commands, shunning evil (Jer 32:40; Gen 22:12; Heb 5:7). Thus, it is vital for governors and ministers to have godly character.

It is the holy fear of God that results in good character. This is confirmed by what the Bible teaches about the fear of God. "The fear of the LORD is the beginning of wisdom" (Prov 9:10a). King Solomon asked God to give him wisdom in order that he might "govern" the nation of Israel "and discern between good and evil" (see 1 Kgs 3:9). The fear of God is considered to be the secret of uprightness (see Prov 8:13) and the whole duty of a human being (see Eccl 12:13). Many would agree that public officers who are committed to uprightness should not participate in or support corruption.

Nehemiah, who was appointed governor of Judah by the Persian emperor (King Artaxerxes), demonstrated a godly character that should be emulated by governors of all times and in all places. According to Nehemiah's testimony, he did not place a heavy burden on his people as the previous governors did, due to his reverence for God. He states,

> Moreover, from the twentieth year of King Artaxerxes, when I was appointed to be their governor in the land of Judah, until his

---

12. J. D. Douglas, "Fear," in *New Bible Dictionary*, ed. I. Howard Marshall, A. R. Millard, J. I. Packer, and D. J. Wiseman, 3rd ed. (Downers Grove, IL: InterVarsity Press, 2008), 365.

thirty-second year – twelve years – neither I nor my brothers ate the food allotted to the governor. But the earlier governors – those preceding me – placed a heavy burden on the people and took forty shekels of silver from them in addition to food and wine. Their assistants also lorded it over the people. But out of reverence for God, I did not act like that. Instead I devoted myself to the work of this wall. All my men were assembled there for the work; we did not acquire any land. (Neh 5:14–16)

According to this passage, even Nehemiah forfeited some governor's privileges – for example, the food allocated to him as the governor. His behavior was in contrast to that of many government leaders of today, who illegally acquire public resources, especially land, through corruption. And this behavior of Nehemiah's is explicitly attributed to his godly character or "reverence for God" (see v. 15).

If today's government ministers and politicians had this reverence for God, we would not be experiencing the magnitude of corruption, especially the "stealing" of public resources that we continue to witness. I concur with Peter Zephaniah,[13] who strongly associates most of the governance problems that we have in Kenya with government officers who do have the relevant knowledge and skills, but lack good character.

The Principle of Concern for the Poor

According to Nehemiah 5:1–13, when the poor cried out to Nehemiah, he listened and acted promptly by ordering the "nobles and officials" of the day to stop oppressing their fellow citizens. He gathered them together and gave them an order saying, "Let us stop charging interest! Give back to them [the poor] immediately their fields, vineyards, olive groves and houses, and also the interest you are charging them – one percent of the money, grain, new wine and olive oil" (Neh 5:10b–11 NIV).

The success of Nehemiah in leading the nation of Israel in rebuilding the wall of Jerusalem regardless of the opposition from their enemies is attributed to the way he treated his people with compassion and justice. This is revealed in Nehemiah's prayer when he was facing opposition from Israel's enemies. He prayed, "Remember me with favor, O my God, for all I have done for these

---

13. Peter Zephaniah of Nairobi, interviewed by the author, 26 February 2017. Zephaniah (not his real name) is vice chancellor of one of the Christian universities in Nairobi and speaks at leadership seminars and conferences at different levels.

people" (Neh 5:19 NIV). It should be noted that in the preceding verses (vv. 17–18) he explains how he forfeited the food allocated to him due to the needs of the poor. Nehemiah's concern for the poor and for justice for the oppressed is still relevant to our contemporary governments. Like Nehemiah, today's government leaders should have a genuine and action-oriented concern for the poor and the oppressed, especially poor widows and orphans. Governors should be ready to listen and to act in response to the outcry of the oppressed, regardless of their ethnic group or geographical location. For example, in Kenya, we have many helpless orphans who are unable to access basic resources, particularly food, clothing, shelter, education, and medical care.

The Principle of Accountability and Transparency

According to Exodus 18:21, Moses was advised to select "trustworthy [persons] who hate dishonest gain." Here the Bible provides us with a biblical principle of good governance from both positive and negative points of view. Positively, the Hebrew word *'emeh*, translated as "trustworthy," has the idea of dependability, truthfulness, faithfulness, and uprightness of character. Thus, faithfulness and anti-corruption are fundamental biblical principles of good governance, which in turn are demonstrated through accountability and transparency. Thus, government officers have an obligation to report, explain, and be answerable to their followers, stakeholders, or community that entrusted them with the responsibility of leading and managing their resources.

Negatively, governors are to be people who "hate dishonest gain." In the passage, "dishonest" is the opposite of "trustworthy." When we talk about dishonest gain, we tend to think of large-scale corruption. However, we need to have a broad understanding of corruption that includes the common temptations of bribery and economic manipulation that are indulged in by leaders in different organizations and at different levels of governance. If government ministers were trustworthy and hated dishonest gain, we would not be wrestling with the financial scandals that we have continued to experience in Kenya, such as those involving 5 billion in the ministry of health and 1.8 billion in the National Youth Service.

In governance studies, these biblical principles of trustworthiness and honesty are equivalent to the principle of integrity. According to the British and Irish Ombudsman Association (BIOA), integrity is a key principle of good governance. The Association defines integrity as "Ensuring straightforward dealing and completeness, based on honesty, selflessness and objectivity, and ensuring high standards of probity and propriety in the conduct of the [governing body's] affairs and complaint decision-making."[14] Integrity ensures impartiality and objectivity in executing all state services, as well as the faithful application of policies that deal with conflict of interest.

The Bible is full of examples of leaders who demonstrated the principle of integrity. For example, in 2 Corinthians 8, Paul and his colleagues demonstrated trustworthiness and honesty in administering the gifts that were gathered for the needy church in Jerusalem. According to the background of the chapter, Paul had been encouraging different churches, including the churches in Corinth, to give generously for the purpose of helping the poor in Jerusalem. The Macedonian churches did so.[15] However, the churches in Corinth had relaxed, due to an unfounded suspicion that Paul and his colleagues were using the donations for their own benefit. Therefore, in 2 Corinthians 8, Paul encouraged the Corinthian churches to contribute by appealing to his integrity in managing the gifts. He wrote,

> And we are sending along with [Titus] the brother who is praised by all the churches for his service to the gospel. What is more, he was chosen by the churches to accompany us as we carry the offering, which we administer in order to honor the Lord himself and to show our eagerness to help. *We want to avoid any criticism of the way we administer this liberal gift. For we are taking pains to do what is right, not only in the eyes of the Lord but also in the eyes of man.* (2 Cor 8:18–21 NIV, emphasis added)

The churches' act of choosing a person to be involved in the administration of their gifts, and Paul's commitment to avoid criticism by doing what was right before God and others, demonstrate the importance of inclusiveness, accountability, and transparency in governance.

The churches' act of choosing a person of good reputation to be involved in the administration of their gifts not only enhances trustworthiness, but it also demonstrates the participatory principle of good governance. In other words, Paul gave the stakeholders an opportunity to participate in the administration of the resources by choosing someone to be involved in it. Therefore, from Paul's example we can infer that through inclusive, accountable, and transparent governance, the public should be able to participate in, follow, and evaluate the dealings of government officers, including the decision-making and execution

---

14. British and Irish Ombudsman Association, *Guide for Principles of Good Governance*, 7.

15. Paul told the Corinthian churches that "they [the Macedonian churches] gave as much as they were able, and even beyond their ability" (2 Cor 8:3 NIV).

procedures. It is important to keep in mind that corruption does not exist where governance is characterized by accountability and transparency.

The Principle of the Rule of Law and Justice

Psalm 72:1–7 is a prayer for righteous judgment that is attributed to King Solomon. In this prayer, he asks God to give the king the ability to judge people in righteousness and justice.[16] This clearly indicates that the rule of law and justice is a biblical principle of governance that is essential for government ministers or servants. Thus, those involved in governance should strive to follow the rule of law and regulations when dealing with all matters of governance. Decision-making processes should always be based on the relevant rules and regulations that have been agreed upon by the authorities and stakeholders.

For example, in awarding a tender to an organization, the officers concerned should ensure that the relevant government acts and legislation are duly followed in order to be fair and to provide equal opportunities to the people involved. Failure to follow the rule of law and justice in matters of governance has many bad consequences. According to Bernard Wanyama,[17] when people know that they are not going to be held accountable for their evil actions (like corruption), they are most likely to continue those actions, and others tend to be attracted to such practices.

Justice and objectivity in the application of rules and policies are very important, for they provide checks and balances. Many would agree that the separation of the powers of the executive and judiciary, as well as the independence of the latter, is key to the effective application of the rule of law. For example, in 2017 President Trump's executive immigration order banning people from seven Muslim-majority countries from entering the USA was put on hold by state judges who followed the rule of law and justice. Effective checks and balances in a state or any organization can take place where there is a clear separation of powers in all arms of government. The officers involved in each arm of governance need to exercise their duties with justice, objectivity, and independence. This allows them to perform those duties with freedom, or without unwarranted pressure from the other arms of government.

---

16. The psalmist says, "Endow the king with your justice, O God, the royal son with your righteousness. May he judge your people in righteousness, your afflicted ones with justice" (Ps 72:1–2 NIV).

17. Bernard Wanyama of Nairobi, interviewed by the author, 21 February 2017. Wanyama (not his real name) is a senior pastor in an evangelical church who has been involved in training pastors in Christian universities.

Proper implementation of the rule of law and justice requires that the government will punish those who commit evils such as corruption. The Bible clearly teaches that God establishes governing authorities and that they are his ministers, or servants, for punishing evil (see Rom 13:1–7; 1 Tim 2:2; Titus 3:1). Therefore, it is a biblical principle that government should punish evildoers. Many Kenyans are aware that the officials of the printing company in England that printed the election papers for the Independent Electoral and Boundaries Committee (IEBC) in 2013 were convicted of corruption and punished. The punishment included serving time in jail. However, it is well known that their Kenyan counterparts (the people who were dealing with the procurement of the above service) were not convicted or punished for the "Chicken gate IEBC scandal." This leaves Kenyans with many questions to be answered in relation to the government or judiciary commitment to the implementation of the rule of law and punishment therein. By embracing justice and impartiality, the Bible clearly promotes a legal framework that impartially enforces the law. Thus, good governance demands an effective judicial system that implements the rule of law and justice independently and without compromise. Many would agree that corruption and injustice roam free in many countries in Africa, and that the rule of law does not exist for those in positions of power or who can pay their way out. This makes it hard to bring positive governance reforms, especially in the public sector.

The Principle of Equity and Responsiveness

Responsiveness has to do with sensitivity to the needs of the community that one is serving. According to Psalm 72:4, the king "[defends] the afflicted among the people" and "[saves] the children of the needy."[18] Biblically, a godly king is expected to have compassion for the vulnerable and those who are oppressed. The psalmist describes such a king: "He will take pity on the weak and the needy and save the needy from death. He will rescue them from oppression and violence, for precious is their blood in his sight" (Ps 72:13–14 NIV). Thus, a biblical principle for those involved in governance is that they should be equitable and responsive to the needs of all people, including the weak, the vulnerable, and minorities. Good governors in any context should value all those under their authority and consider their interests when making decisions at all levels of governance. In other words, their voices should be heard.

---

18. Ps 72:12 repeats this task of the king: "For he will deliver the needy who cry out, the afflicted who have no one to help."

Unfortunately, in most cases, government ministers and politicians do not give help to the needy or to those who deserve it. Many times government financial assistance – for example, a bursary for school fees – is "sold" to people who do not need it, while leaving needy children unable to access the education that should be provided for them.

In their article "Governance Egalitarianism in Jesus' Teaching," Clive Beed and Cara Beed point out that Jesus's model of governance was characterized by egalitarianism.[19] Synonyms of egalitarianism include social equality, classlessness, consensus, fairness, impartiality, and equal opportunity. Therefore, leaders in government offices and corporate organizations who would like to embrace Christ's model of governance should strive to prioritize the above values. The opposite of egalitarianism is inequality.

In order for governance to be equitable and responsive to the real needs of the people, it should be participatory. Participation in governance entails that anyone affected by or with an interest in a decision should have the opportunity to directly or indirectly participate in the process of making that decision. Thus, the old idea of "the government by the people for the people" should not end with the election or appointment of leaders or governors for a state. Participation in governance should enable people to have a voice in and give legitimacy to what takes place in an organization. All stakeholders should participate in decision-making, whether directly or indirectly through institutions or committees that represent their interests. Community Development Society proposes four ways of promoting community participation and engagement, which include the following: (1) Promoting "active and representative participation" on decision-making; (2) engaging the community in "learning and understanding" all community issues well; (3) enhancing "the leadership capacity of the community members; (4) engaging strategies for "the long term sustainability and well-being of the community. [20] It should be noted that such participation in governance is best implemented where the freedoms of association and speech are valued and encouraged.

In most state governments in Africa, the leaders tend to suppress the freedoms of association and speech, for they are afraid of their bad governance practices being unmasked. Suppressing the freedoms of association and speech prevents not only criticism of the government, but also the constructive

---

19. Clive Beed and Cara Beed, "Governance Egalitarianism in Jesus' Teaching," *Anglican Theological Review* 97, no. 4 (2015): 587.

20. "4 Ways to Promote Community Participation and Engagement," accessed 25 November 2018, https://www.comm-dev.org/blog/entry/4-ways-to-promote-community-participation-and-engagement.

participation of the stakeholders. A leader who embraces biblical principles of governance should not sacrifice constructive participation through fear of criticism. A competent governor must be able to mediate the different interests of stakeholders with the aim of reaching a broad consensus on what is best for all stakeholders, based on the rules and policies of the organization.

The Principle of Sacrificial Servanthood

Proper theological reflection on biblical principles of governance, especially based on the New Testament, supports what could be termed "the sacrificial servant" principle of governance. Paul's command to the Corinthian Christians to "follow my example, as I follow the example of Christ" (1 Cor 11:1) needs to be understood as a universal command to all Christians. Given the Reformers' emphasis on the priesthood of all believers, we cannot escape the fact that Christians need to view themselves as serving God in whatever work they are involved in, including governance.

Many theologians agree that central to Christ's work was his sacrificial death for the forgiveness of sin and salvation for people. It was Christ's sacrificial attitude and interest in others that led him to take the "nature of a servant" and to humble himself to the point of death on the cross (Phil 2:6–8). All Christians, including those in governance, are commanded by the Scriptures to imitate this attitude of Christ (Phil 2:4–5).[21] Thus, the sacrificial servant principle is essential for good governance. Government ministers who are characterized by a sacrificial servant attitude will not be driven by "selfish ambition" at the expense of the interest of others. Unfortunately, many leaders in government and of corporate organizations are driven by selfish ambition rather than by serving people. When Nehemiah was governor of Judah, he demonstrated this principle of sacrificial servanthood by declining some of his privileges in order to more effectively meet the needs of the people he was governing (Neh 5:18–19).[22] No wonder he was a successful leader who accomplished much for God and the nation of Israel.

---

21. "Each of you should look not to your own interests, but all to the interest of others. Your attitude should be the same as that of Christ" (Phil 2:4–5 NIV 1985).

22. "Each day one ox, six choice sheep and some poultry were prepared for me, and every ten days an abundant supply of wine of all kinds. In spite of all this, I never demanded the food allotted to the governor, because the demands were heavy on these people. Remember me with favor, my God, for all I have done for these people" (Neh 5:18–19 NIV).

Christ's sacrificial servant attitude was tied to his "servant leadership" style.[23] Thus, governance should be guided by a selfless servant spirit in which the goal is to always serve those whom one leads. Serving them should include developing their personal lives and meeting their holistic needs.

The Principle of Transformational Leadership

Transformational leadership is a leadership approach that causes a change in individuals and social systems. In this approach, leaders act as role models and motivators. They offer vision, encouragement, morale, and satisfaction to those they lead. Transformational leaders strive to create valuable and positive change in those they lead, with the end goal of developing followers into leaders.[24] A careful study of the Bible reveals several models of transformation leadership; however, due to space, we will highlight only three here. First, the book of Numbers illustrates how Moses was characterized by charisma, inspiration, and concern for his followers, rather than by selfishness.[25] Second, Jesus Christ coached and inspired the disciples to continue actualizing his vision and mission after his departure. Jesus focused on the needs of his followers and on empowering them, even to the point of suffering on the cross. Third, the apostle Paul worked selflessly for the purpose of bringing transformation to many, and empowering persons like Timothy and Titus to continue making disciples (see 2 Tim 2:1–2; Titus 2:1–10).

In the above three biblical examples, we see models of transformational leadership that incorporate individualized consideration, others-centeredness, empowerment of others, inspirational influence, and visionary leadership. Transformational leadership provides a broader view of leadership that augments other leadership models. It emphasizes the needs, values, and morale of others. Thus, in accordance with transformational leadership characteristics, the goal should be to motivate those in governance positions to transcend self-interest for the good of the society and the communities that they represent.

---

23. The phrase "servant leadership" owes much to Robert K. Greenleaf's essays on servant leadership, which have rightly been called "A Journey into the Nature of Legitimate Power and Greatness." Robert Greenleaf, *Servant Leadership: A Journey into the Nature of Legitimate Power and Greatness* (Mumbai: Magna, 2003).

24. In Num 13, Moses sent twelve spies to Canaan. Among them was Joshua, whom he prepared and motivated to take over the leadership after Moses's death (see Deut 31).

25. In Num 11–12, 14, Moses pleaded with God on behalf of the Israelites who had complained before God. God listened to Moses, withheld punishment, and provided food for the Israelites.

Implementing the Principles of Good Governance

Having established the above biblical principles of good governance, how can church leaders (both pastors and theologians) promote their implementation among government ministers and other officers? In addition to surveying the literature, I interviewed four knowledgeable and experienced church leaders in order to find practical ways to implement the principles of good governance.

After discussing the biblical principles of good governance with Wanyama,[26] I asked him how we could promote the implementation of these principles among public governors and officers. In response, he said that, first, many church leaders need to correct their own bad governance practices in order to have the moral authority to correct government ministers and promote good governance. Otherwise, government officers could ask church leaders to set their own houses in order before teaching or correcting them. He pointed out that good governance begins with good processes of recruitment, appointment, or election of governing officers. He claimed that many church leaders have lost the moral authority to correct government in this matter of appointment and election. He himself has witnessed church elections in different denominations and local churches that were not free, fair, or transparent. He gave as an example one denomination in Kenya that had not conducted elections for bishops for more than ten years.

Another interviewee, Harold Kimanthi,[27] made a similar observation. He too emphasized that church leaders need to model the biblical principles of good governance in their churches and denominations in order to promote their implementation in the public sector. He lamented that, in his view, most contemporary church leaders are mainly serving for selfish gain rather than advancing the gospel. They have forgotten that the church belongs to God and they are just stewards. He referred to 1 Peter 5:1–4, where church leaders are instructed not to be "greedy for money" (NIV 1985), but to be "examples to the flock." He said that church leaders should strive to model and to teach what the Bible says: "Let each of you look not only to his own interests, but also to the interests of others" (Phil 2:4).

Second, Wanyama proposed that church leaders should avoid being "pocketed" by government ministers and politicians. Otherwise, it negatively

---

26. The real names of all the church leaders mentioned here have been changed for anonymity.

27. Harold Kimanthi of Nairobi, interviewed by the author, 23 February 2017. Kimanthi is a retired pastor and university lecturer who has been involved in various church leadership positions, including serving as bishop in an evangelical denomination in Kenya.

affects their authority and freedom to correct and to challenge governing ministers to practice biblical principles of good governance. While church leaders cannot prevent government ministers and politicians giving to church projects and other needs, church leaders need to be wise and diligent to avoid being compromised to the point of losing their prophetic voice as God's ministers.

Third, according to Wanyama, church leaders need to re-examine and change their approach to correcting government ministers and politicians, as well as their methods of promoting good governance. He suggested that it is better for church leaders to correct and advise government leaders privately before confronting or attacking them publicly.[28] To simply attack them publicly fails to demonstrate the distinction between the approach of politicians and that of church leaders. Church leaders should not downplay or ignore the power of persuasion and of correcting in love that is demonstrated and taught in the Bible. For example, in 2 Samuel 12 the prophet Nathan rebuked King David privately for having arranged the death of Uriah and taken his wife Bathsheba. David responded by confessing his sin. Although David and his house experienced serious consequences because of his sinful act, God spared his life because he confessed his sin. In our discussion, Wanyama acknowledged that private and persuasive approaches might not always work, but it is worth attempting them before using public confrontation or attack.

Fourth, Wanyama insisted that leaders from different churches and denominations should speak objectively and with one voice when correcting government and promoting good governance. Denominational leaders and church leaders need to avoid being compromised by particular political parties or powerful politicians to the point of becoming partisan and promoting divisive politics. In order for this to take place, denominational leaders need to meet together and discuss their response to particular government issues. This could be done under umbrellas, such as the National Council of Churches in Kenya (NCCK). It is more likely that government leaders will consider the proposals of church leaders when they speak with one voice about an issue.

Fifth, church leaders need to be prepared to rebuke and to publicly challenge government leaders for their bad governance when the above diplomatic and private approaches fail. This point came after much theological reflection on the implications of the story of John the Baptist when he rebuked King Herod, as recorded by Luke and Matthew: "But when John rebuked Herod

---

28. This is the method that was advocated by Jesus Christ in Matt 18:15–20. The process of correcting a brother or sister begins by first approaching him or her privately. If this does not work, one should then involve two to three witnesses, and then finally the church.

the tetrarch because of his marriage to Herodias, his brother's wife, and all the other evil things he had done, Herod added this to them all: He locked John up in prison" (Luke 3:19–20 NIV). According to Matthew 14:1–12, John was eventually beheaded at the order of King Herod to fulfill the request of Herod's wife through her daughter.

Our discussion of the story of John the Baptist led to the conclusion that sometimes church leaders should be prepared to suffer for speaking the truth or rebuking government leaders. The renowned pastor-theologian Martin Luther King Jr. relentlessly fought racism and discrimination against African Americans in the USA. Like Martin Luther King, today's church leaders need to be prepared to challenge evil practices regardless of the cost. We know that Martin Luther King was eventually killed for his stand against racism and discrimination, but his legacy and message forever changed the relationship between African Americas and Anglo-Americans.[29]

The writer also interviewed Zephaniah[30] on this subject. He started by dividing governance into two main levels: first, the level of developing rules, policies, and procedures; and second, the level of implementation that includes monitoring and evaluation. He suggested that the main challenge of governance lies at the second level of governance due to lack of good character and the appropriate skills needed to implement services according to the rules and policies of the state.

Zephaniah emphasized the need for both good character and appropriate skills in order to implement the principles of good governance. For him, it is no use having a government minister with the appropriate knowledge and skills but without good character, and vice versa. When asked what he meant by good character, Zephaniah talked about integrity. He explained this as equivalent to the faithfulness, trustworthiness, and transparency that is mainly demonstrated by those who have a genuine fear of God or godly character.[31] Thus, in order to promote good governance, pastor-theologians have an obligation to model and to instill godly character in all the people in their churches and public places where God has placed them. In addition, the

---

29. For example, in King's famous speech in Washington, known as "I Have a Dream," he said, "I have a dream that my four little children will one day live in a nation where they will not be judged by the color of their skin but by the content of their character." Although he was killed for his stand against racism, many would agree that he continues to live, for his message continues to have an impact across the generations. Americans have a Martin Luther King Jr. Day each year, when they remember and celebrate his achievements.

30. Zephaniah is vice chancellor of a Christian university in Kenya and has written on the area of leadership. He has also been involved in leadership seminars and conferences worldwide.

31. See the discussion of godly character under the fear of God earlier in this chapter.

Word of God plays an important role in bringing about "real heart change."[32] We also acknowledged that instilling good character in a person is a lifelong and complex cultural process that requires more than church ministers. All Christians need to participate in promoting a culture of hard work and integrity in order to minimize corruption.

In order to deal with the problem of incompetent government ministers, Zephaniah talked about the need to emphasize diligence, fairness, and objectivity in selecting and electing government leaders in order to ensure that they have the appropriate knowledge and skills for a particular task. This should be backed up by continuous training for government officers, in place of the so-called "benchmarking experience trips" outside the country that consume millions in taxpayers' money but add minimal value to governance, if any.

The International Federation of Accountants Consultation (IFAC) of June 2013 developed guidelines for implementing good governance principles that clearly complement Zephaniah's suggestions. According to the consultation draft, implementing principles of good governance in the public interest requires several things.

First, it requires "strong commitment to integrity, ethical values, and the rule of law."[33] Expanding on this statement the consultants explained the importance of integrity and ethical values when dealing with public resources:

> The public sector is normally responsible for using a significant proportion of national resources raised through taxation to provide services to citizens. Public sector entities are accountable not only for how much they spend but also for the ways they use the resources with which they have been entrusted. In addition, they have an overarching mission to serve the public interest in adhering to the requirements of legislation and government policies. This makes it essential that the entire entity can demonstrate the integrity of all its actions and has mechanisms in place that encourage and enforce a strong commitment to ethical values and legal compliance at all levels.[34]

Thus,

---

32. Zephaniah referred to the book by Timothy S. Lane and Paul David Tripp, *How People Change* (Greensboro, NC: New Growth Press, 2006), 195.

33. "Good Governance in the Public Sector," International Federation of Accountants Consultation (IFAC), June 2013, http://www.ifac.org/system/files/publications/files/Good-Governance-in-the-Public-Sector.pdf, 13.

34. "Good Governance," 13.

Ethical values and standards . . . should form the basis for all [government] policies, procedures, and actions, as well as the personal behavior of its governing body members and other staff.[35]

Such codes of conduct should guard against conflict of interests and other malpractices that interfere with objectivity and openness in the provision of services. Clear and open codes of conduct assist in reassuring the public that the governing body is committed to ethical values and integrity in all its dealings.[36]

Second, implementing good governance principles requires acting in the public interest through "openness and comprehensive stakeholders' engagement."[37] That means there is a need to encourage governing bodies and public servants to develop a transparent mechanism of communication and consultation in order to effectively engage with citizens, service users, and interested institutional stakeholders in a particular region. The IFAC underscores the importance of comprehensive engagement of stakeholders in implementing good governance: "Few public sector entities can achieve their intended outcomes solely through their own efforts. Public sector entities also need to work with institutional stakeholders to improve services and outcomes, or for accountability reasons. Developing formal and informal partnerships with other entities, both in the public sector and other parts of the economy, allows entities to use their resources more efficiently and achieve their outcomes more effectively."[38]

Third, promoting principles of good governance requires "implementing good practices in transparency and reporting to deliver effective accountability."[39] Thus, in transparent governance, the management of public resources should be open and accessible to all stakeholders, including citizens, service users, and public servants. According to IFAC, "accountability reports should be written and communicated in an open and understandable style appropriate to the intended audience."[40] Governing ministers and senior management officers need to demonstrate that they have implemented public projects and services and have used government resources effectively. There is need to provide public reports regularly so that the stakeholders can evaluate whether the governing

---

35. "Good Governance," 14.
36. "Good Governance," 14.
37. "Good Governance," 17.
38. "Good Governance," 18.
39. "Good Governance," 39.
40. "Good Governance," 39.

body is delivering value for money and managing the available resources in the public interest.

Good practice in reporting needs to include both internal and external audit reports. The external audit report needs to be conducted by qualified professionals who cannot be compromised in order to cover mismanagement of resources or corruption among the members of the governing body or senior management officers.

Finally, in order to find out how church leaders could promote biblical principles of governance in the public sector, I also interviewed Stephen Matata.[41] According to Matata, church leaders could promote the implementation of good governance by teaching and encouraging all those involved at different levels of governance to be committed to the biblical principle of resisting "selfish ambition." He said that those involved in governance should be guided by the biblical principle of minding the "interests of others."[42] According to Matata, if governing officers took into account the interests of their people, they would engage all stakeholders in determining projects or services that were vital and a priority to people. Unfortunately, in his view, most governing ministers decide and implement public projects in line with selfish economic and political ambitions, rather than serving the real and pressing needs of their communities. Thus, according to Matata, church leaders need to model and promote a culture where acting in the public interest, rather than for selfish gain, is the standard of good governance.

Matata emphasized that church leaders need to minister to people holistically. This includes teaching them socio-political and economic responsibilities. Thus, church leaders need to teach people how to identify and elect leaders with integrity and ethical values. In most cases, people emphasize secular knowledge, skills, and a person's ability to buy votes, rather than integrity. He said that when people "buy their positions," their first priority is usually to get their money back and to reward those who assisted them in buying the position, rather than to serve the public. Matata agreed with Zephaniah's observation that the main challenges of governance are associated with the characters of the governing officers. Therefore, according to both Matata and Zephaniah, church leaders have a responsibility to promote good

---

41. Stephen Matata of Machakos, interviewed by the author, 27 February 2017. Matata is a church leader who at one time served as a chairman of a county council. Therefore, he understands the challenges of leadership in the government and in the church.

42. "Do nothing out of selfish ambition or vain conceit. Rather, in humility value others above yourselves, not looking to your own interests, but each of you to the interests of the others" (Phil 2:3–4 NIV).

governance by transforming people's characters so that they embrace the biblical principles of good governance.

Conclusion

In this chapter I have exposed the crises associated with bad governance and developed the biblical principles of good governance: godly character, delegation, right knowledge and skills, inclusiveness, concern for the poor, accountability and transparency, respecting the rule of law, equity and responsiveness, sacrificial servanthood, and transformational leadership. I have further proposed that church leaders could promote the implementation of these principles by modeling and teaching them. Thus, this chapter serves as an encouragement to church leaders to understand and model these biblical principles of good governance and to promote their implementation among governing ministers and public servants at all levels of governance. Doing so would enhance good governance and thereby reduce the governance crises and corruption scandals that we continue to witness in Kenya and in many other nations.

Bibliography

"4 Ways to Promote Community Participation and Engagement." Accessed 25 November 2018. https://www.comm-dev.org/blog/entry/4-ways-to-promote-community-participation-and-engagement.

Beed, Clive, and Cara Beed. "Governance Egalitarianism in Jesus' Teaching." *Anglican Theological Review* 97, no. 4 (2015): 587.

Bellon, Emmanuel O. *Transformational Leadership through Value Based Training*. Orlando: International Leadership Foundation, 2011.

"Bible Study 1: On Good Governance." Accessed 20 March 2017. http://clients.squareeye.net/uploads/anglican/documents/governance.pdf.

Bozovic, Iva. "Building Transparency, Accountability and Anti-Corruption into the 2015 Development Framework." Discussion paper, edited by Anga Timilsina and Diana Torres. New York: United Nation Development Programme, September 2014.

Douglas, J. D. "Fear." In *New Bible Dictionary*, edited by I. Howard Marshall, A. R. Millard, J. I. Packer and D. J. Wiseman. 3rd ed. Downers Grove, IL: InterVarsity Press, 2008.

Greenleaf, Robert. *Servant Leadership: A Journey into the Nature of Legitimate Power and Greatness*. Mumbai: Magna, 2003.

"Good Governance in the Public Sector." International Federation of Accountants Consultation (IFAC), June 2013. Accessed 1 September 2016. http://www.ifac.org/system/files/publications/files/Good-Governance-in-the-Public-Sector.pdf.

Guide for Principles of Good Governance. British and Irish Ombudsman Association (BIOA). October 2009.

Institute of Governance (IOG). "Defining Governance." Accessed 31 August 2016. https://iog.ca/what-is-governance.

Lane, Timothy S., and Paul David Tripp. *How People Change.* Greensboro, NC: New Growth Press, 2006.

Oketch, Willis. "Preachers Wilfred Lai and Arthur Kitonga Lock Horns in Court over Church." *Standard Digital*, 5 June 2015. https://www.standardmedia.co.ke/article/2000164642/preachers-wilfred-lai-and-arthur-kitonga-lock-horns-in-court-over-church.

Part II

Christian Higher Education

5

Effect of Numerical Church Growth on Pastoral Care and Administration

Elkanah Kiprop Cheboi
PhD Candidate, Africa International University

Abstract

Undoubtedly, church-planting initiatives and missionary work carried out in Africa during the twentieth century led to the numerical growth of the church. However, the maximum impact is yet to be realized. The numerical growth of the church has presented new challenges in the areas of pastoral care and administration. The provision of effective pastoral care and equipping of pastors to lead the growing number of churches is still an area of great concern. This research investigated the effect of numerical church growth on pastoral care and administration in churches in Africa Inland Church in Marakwet Region, Kenya, a context where many pastors serve more than one congregation. Pastoral care functions that are affected, and the effect of numerical growth on pastors serving more than one congregation, are highlighted. In addition, the study looked at possible interventions that can help a church grow numerically (quantitatively) as well as in depth (qualitatively) through effective pastoral care and administration. The qualitative study used a hermeneutical phenomenological research strategy to get an in-depth understanding of the research questions. Semi-structured interviews were used to understand the experiences of pastors who oversee more than one congregation. Additional perspectives were sought from lay leaders and elected church officials. The study showed that pastoral care functions were negatively affected in cases where there was numerical growth of the church but with no pastors to lead each congregation. Also, the demanding pastoral responsibilities have negatively affected the few pastors who serve in such contexts. Although the numeric growth of the church in Africa is commendable, there is still much to be done to promote pastoral care and administration in each congregation. The church must invest in the training of pastors and lay leaders for ministry to match the pace of the multiplication of congregations. In addition, the church must come up with strategies and policies that govern both aspects of numerical church growth/church planting, and pastoral care and administration.

Key words: church growth, administration, church health, pastoral care, pastors, local church/congregation

Introduction

The church-planting initiatives and mission work carried out in Kenya during the twentieth century resulted in steady numerical growth of the church. However, the geographical spread of the church and the numerical gains have brought about new challenges. At the turn of the twenty-first century, some church leaders not only acknowledged the numeric success the church in Africa has achieved, but also recognized the need for leadership training to sustain new congregations, and for the equipping of more pastors to cope with the overall growth and the retention of those already in service.[1] This call seems to have received little attention, because the challenge has persisted. Many new local churches that were planted, especially in rural areas, are being led by lay leaders who are not equipped with the right knowledge and skills to execute pastoral care responsibilities and administration. As a result, the few trained pastors find themselves overseeing several congregations or local churches, and therefore becoming less productive in their discharge of pastoral care and administrative duties. This is a concern that should cause church leaders and churches to look again at their church-planting policies, administration, and pastoral care.

Further, the fact that the numeric growth or multiplication of churches has outpaced the increase in number of pastors should stimulate a great concern and a conversation among church planters, theological educators, pastors, lay leaders, and church administrators in the Global South. This is a critical

---

1. Jose B. Chipenda and All Africa Conference of Churches, eds., *The Church of Africa: Towards a Theology of Reconstruction*, African Challenge Book Series 2 (Nairobi: AACC, 1991), 2.

issue that needs to be deeply studied because, historically, most of the studies concerning church growth have largely been about qualitative and quantitative aspects. Many discussions on church growth presume that a local congregation has at least one pastor. But this is far from the reality in many of the churches, especially in rural parts of Africa. Also, very few authors have explored how the multiplication of congregations without a corresponding increase in the number of pastors affects pastoral care and administration.

Purpose of the Study

This study sought to discover the effects of numerical church growth on pastoral care and administration. It focused on the effects of the numeric growth on the pastor, and on pastoral care duties and administrative functions when a local church has no pastor of its own.

Significance of the Study

This study on the effects of numerical growth on pastoral care and administration in selected local churches of Africa Inland Church (AIC) Kenya in Marakwet Region, the northwestern part of Rift Valley, is of importance in several ways. First, the research will be a source of valuable information for church leaders and pastors of Africa Inland Church, especially in planting churches and planning, and in execution of pastoral care and administrative duties. It is hoped that this research will encourage the church, pastors, and church leaders to embrace research as a tool for enhancing the growth of the church. Second, it will be a source of information for church councils to consider when crafting church policy or laws that deal with church planting and pastoral care and administration. Third, the research will be a source of information for church leaders and pastors from other denominations facing similar challenges, or for other researchers who may want to compare findings with research carried out in other contexts. Fourth, the research can provide valuable information for consideration by curriculum developers when coming up with pastoral programs to address the felt and dynamic needs of the church.

Research Questions

1. What pastoral care and administrative functions has numerical growth of AIC in Marakwet Region affected?

2. What are the implications of numerical growth for AIC pastors serving in Marakwet Region?

3. How has the leadership of AIC Marakwet Region prepared to handle these effects of numerical growth on pastoral care and administration in the past and in the present?

Sub-Questions

1. What are the ecclesiological functions that have been affected by having few pastors among many local churches?

2. How can both the numerical growth of the church in Marakwet Region and pastoral care be sustained?

3. How has the church-to-pastor ratio affected the pastors serving in Marakwet Region?

Assumptions

1. The numerical growth of the church in AIC Marakwet Region has negatively affected the quality of pastoral care and administration.

2. There is inadequate preparation of both pastors and lay leadership to cope with the numerical increase in church growth in AIC Marakwet Region.

3. The numerical growth in AIC Marakwet Region has caused strain on pastors serving in the region.

Limitations

This study is not generalized to all AIC churches in Kenya or to other denominations because it only seeks to study the effects of numerical growth on pastoral care and administration in AIC Marakwet Region. Other AIC regions and other denominations were not studied. This limitation does not, however, diminish the significance of the study because the results can be compared with what other researchers have found in other contexts. Also, the sample size used for this study is relatively small; however, while conducting the research, the researcher reached a level of satisfaction based on the pattern of responses received.

Delimitation

This research was confined to discovering the effects of numerical church growth on pastoral care and administration and the laid-down strategies to improve pastoral care in local churches with no pastors. Therefore, other AIC church regions were not studied. Data collection was confined to the available church records and interviews of selected regional church officials, pastors, and church leaders.

Research Objectives

This study will:

1. Determine the pastoral care and administrative functions that have been affected by having few pastors among many local churches in AIC Marakwet Region.

2. Determine the implications of numerical growth of churches for AIC pastors serving in Marakwet Region.

3. Discover the levels of preparedness and the interventions of the leadership of AIC Marakwet Region (in the past and present) in handling the effects of numerical growth on pastoral care.

Literature Review

McGavran, who is widely regarded by many as the twentieth-century father of the Church Growth Movement, has written extensively on church growth with an emphasis on quantitative church growth.[2] Wagner and McGavran have also jointly explored the quantitative aspects of church growth in several works. In this present study, Elliot's highlighting of six functions of ministry that are necessary for effective and sustainable church growth is helpful. The key functions of ministry highlighted are shepherding, fellowship, worshiping ministry, missional ministry, education ministry, and stewardship.[3] Another important work by Rainer highlights various aspects of church growth,

---

2. Donald A. McGavran and C. Peter Wagner, *Understanding Church Growth*, 3rd ed. (Grand Rapids, MI: Eerdmans, 1990).

3. Ralph H. Elliott, *Church Growth That Counts* (Valley Forge, PA: Judson, 1982).

including leadership, laity, evangelism, worship, small groups, church planting, and planning.[4] In his book, church growth is also related to pastoral care.

Olson, in chapter 9 of his book, highlights the principle of "Each Congregation: One Pastor."[5] He advocates that each local church or congregation should have one ordained pastor. He argues that for congregations to serve their purpose of bearing witness to the kingdom of God, "congregations must have a strong, compassionate, courageous, and clearly identified leader. When this essential leadership role is divided and shared, the evangelical mission of the church suffers greatly."[6] But, as mentioned above, achieving this ideal is far from possible in many churches in Africa, especially in rural areas.

On the other hand, church growth has also been presented in qualitative terms. Schwarz, the scholar behind Natural Church Development, is well known for his eight qualitative characteristics/indicators of growth.[7] He argues for "a leadership that concentrates on *empowering* others, a ministry that is *gift-oriented*, spirituality that is *passionate*, church structures that are *functional*, a worship service that is felt to be *inspiring*, small groups that are *holistic*, evangelism that is *need-oriented*, and relationships that are *loving*."[8] Schwarz looks at church growth in qualitative terms, in contrast to the earlier-mentioned extensive publications and propagation of a quantitative approach. This study, however, looks at the effects of church growth (both numeric and geographical), not in relation to the eight indices of Schwartz, but in relation to the pastor and aspects of pastoral care and administration.

McKee, in his dissertation, explored the relationship between church health and growth by focusing on eight characteristics of church health: intentional evangelism, mobilized laity, transforming discipleship, engaging worship, passionate spirituality, empowering leadership, authentic community, and effective structures.[9] In his work, church health was compared with indices of

---

4. Thom S. Rainer, *The Book of Church Growth: History, Theology, and Principles* (Nashville: Broadman & Holman, 1993).

5. Mark A. Olson, *Moving beyond Church Growth: An Alternative Vision for Congregations*, Prisms (Minneapolis: Fortress, 2002), 86.

6. Olson, *Moving beyond Church Growth*, 86.

7. Christian A. Schwarz, *Paradigm Shift in the Church: How Natural Church Development Can Transform Theological Thinking* (Carol Stream, IL: ChurchSmart Resources, 1999).

8. Schwarz, *Paradigm Shift*, 242.

9. Scott B. McKee, "The Relationship between Church Health and Church Growth in the Evangelical Presbyterian Church" (PhD diss., Asbury Theological Seminary, 2003). Accessed 22 February 2016. https://place.asburyseminary.edu/cgi/viewcontent.cgi?referer=https://www.google.com/&httpsredir=1&article=1185&context=ecommonsatsdissertations.

growth, and a positive relationship between health and growth was discovered. The evaluative study employed stratified convenience sampling.

A limited amount of research has been done in the area and context that this research explores. But in his book, Philip Morrison acknowledges, based on his teaching and pastoral experience, the great challenge that the numerical growth of the church in Africa has caused.[10] He notes that many theological institutions train pastors with the assumption that they will eventually work in a church department or a single congregation. Yet the reality in the field for most of these pastors is quite different. Many of them end up becoming overseers of more than one congregation; certainly, this comes with enormous responsibility and significant effects on the pastor and the discharging of pastoral functions and administration. Morrison only advances leadership training as the solution to this problem.

It is worth noting that in the same context within which this study was carried out, Zablon Jacob had in the past investigated missiological issues that affected church growth in AIC Marakwet Region and suggested proposals for further expansion of the church.[11] This research involved the use of interview questionnaires, and church documents, minutes, and publications. The study, carried out in the same church context, ascertained the numerical growth of the church as a reality (something that forms the basis for this chapter) and looked at the challenges facing church growth from a missiological perspective.

Church Administration and Management

On church administration and management, two major books by Carnahan[12] and Welch[13] were consulted. The books highlight key areas in pastoral leadership and administration, such as planning, organizing, leading, and controlling/evaluation. The discharge of these administrative functions of the pastoral office in a local church requires a pastor who will coordinate office functions with the lay leadership.

---

10. Philip E. Morrison, *The Multi-Church Pastor: A Manual for Training Leadership in a Multi-Church Setting* (Allentown, PA: Gratia Veritas, 2004).

11. Jacob Kibor Zablon, "The Growth and Development of the Africa Inland Church in Marakwet Kenya" (master's thesis, Nairobi Evangelical Graduate School of Theology [NEGST], 1992).

12. Roy E. Carnahan, *Creative Pastoral Management* (Kansas City, MO: Beacon Hill Press of Kansas City, 1976).

13. Robert H. Welch, *Church Administration: Creating Efficiency for Effective Ministry*, 2nd ed. (Nashville: Broadman & Holman, 2011).

A book written by Adams[14] was found to be helpful in relating leadership, administration, and management to pastoral care. Good leadership, planning, and management is biblical and encouraged by the Holy Spirit. Adams argues that leadership and management is part of the work of pastoral care that an overseer should not omit. Further, according to Ford, Jesus embodies transformational leadership that should be applied to church leadership.[15] Separate studies by Ngasura[16] and Lang'at[17] highlight strategies for effective pastoral leadership and church-planting strategies in the Kenyan context with biblical foundations for leadership and healthy church growth.

Pastoral Care

Pastoral counseling as a key aspect of pastoral care was highlighted by Patton.[18] Other components of pastoral care as presented by White include worship, spiritual leadership, pastoral visitation, personal counseling, and pastoral evangelism.[19] The book details pastoral ministries in the local church which become affected when a congregation does not have a pastor of its own.

From a Western context, Fletcher explores the issue of ministry demands on the pastor. His work highlights the functional need for an executive pastor to facilitate policy-and-vision implementation in elder-led churches.[20] The research examined causative factors relative to the senior pastor and church growth, as well as the roles of the executive pastor. The research employed case-study interviews consisting of unstructured questions. Fletcher argues that the

14. Jay E. Adams, *Shepherding God's Flock: A Handbook on Pastoral Ministry, Counseling, and Leadership* (Grand Rapids, MI: Zondervan, 2016).

15. Leighton Ford, *Transforming Leadership: Jesus' Way of Creating Vision, Shaping Values and Empowering Change* (Downers Grove, IL: InterVarsity Press, 1991).

16. Philip K. Barar Ngasura, "Key Strategies in Effective Pastoral Leadership in the Africa Gospel Churches, Kenya: Biblical Foundations for Leadership and Healthy Churches" (PhD diss., Liberty Baptist Theological Seminary, December 2012), accessed 22 February 2016, http://digitalcommons.liberty.edu/cgi/viewcontent.cgi?article=1732&context=doctoral.

17. Lang'at Joshua Kibet, "An Investigation into the Factors That Influenced Numerical Growth of Deliverance Church Eastleigh in Nairobi, Kenya from 1981 to 2006" (Master's thesis, Missions, Nairobi Evangelical Graduate School of Theology [NEGST], 2006).

18. John Patton, *Pastoral Care in Context: An Introduction to Pastoral Care* (Louisville, KY: Westminster John Knox, 1993).

19. R. E. O. White, *A Guide to Pastoral Care: A Practical Primer of Pastoral Theology* (Basingstoke: Pickering & Inglis, 1983).

20. David Fletcher, "Case-Studies of Policy and Vision Implementation by the Executive Pastor" (PhD diss., Dallas Theological Seminary, May 2004), accessed 22 February 2016, www.dts.edu/download/degrees/dmin/DTS%20-%20David%20Fletcher%20(D.Min.)%20-%20Dissertation.pdf.

management crisis of the overburdened senior pastor has led to the rise of the executive pastor. Because the senior pastor is overburdened, Fletcher argues for the role of executive pastor.[21] Since the phenomenon in Fletcher's study is far removed from the reality in most African churches, the challenges of the senior pastor in this research were looked at in tandem with the challenges of a pastor overseeing several churches. Also, the pressures on the pastor, church growth, and the pastor's job description were areas highlighted in Fletcher's research that were helpful to my own research work.

Methodology

The qualitative research employed a phenomenological research approach to understand the effects of numerical church growth on the pastoral care and administration of a local church. The phenomenological approach identifies "the 'essence' of human experiences concerning a phenomenon" and seeks to understand "the lived experiences."[22] In this study, the lived experiences of church officials, selected lay leaders or elders from selected local churches, and pastors who oversee more than one congregation were considered.

Data was collected from available church documents at the AIC regional church office to determine the laid-down policies and procedures guiding church planting, pastoral care, and administration. In addition, data was collected using open-ended interview questions to get in-depth views and opinions from the participants. A total of eighteen interviews were carried out with six lay leaders from selected churches, six pastors, and six regional elected church officials.

The researcher used purposeful sampling in selecting the participants. This is a type of sampling that strategically selects participants who will "best help the researcher understand the problem and the research question."[23] From the group, the six AIC Marakwet regional church officials provided information concerning the regional scope of the issue and the strategies they used both in the past and in the present to address the subject. The six pastors were those who had oversight of more than one local church. The six sampled lay leaders (two per local church) were communicants in churches with a pastor who served in multiple churches within AIC Marakwet Region. The lay leaders

---

21. Fletcher, "Case-Studies," 246.

22. John W. Creswell, *Research Design: Qualitative, Quantitative, and Mixed Methods Approaches*, 2nd ed. (Thousand Oaks, CA: Sage, 2003), 15.

23. Creswell, *Research Design*, 185.

were also chosen on the condition that they had been members of the local church for a period of not less than five years; because of this, they are able to give rich information concerning areas in local church ministry that were affected by the lack or absence of a pastor.

Data Analysis and Findings

The interviews of the eighteen representative participants in three categories (regional officials, lay leaders, and pastors) enriched the study with reliable and in-depth information concerning the phenomenon. The following research questions guided the data analysis:

1. What pastoral care and administrative functions has numerical growth of AIC Marakwet Region affected?

2. What are the implications of numerical growth for AIC pastors serving in Marakwet Region?

3. How has the leadership of AIC Marakwet Region prepared to handle the effects of numerical growth on pastoral care and administration in the past and in the future?

Data Analysis of Question 1: What Pastoral Care and Administrative Functions Has Numerical Growth of AIC Marakwet Region Affected?

In order to analyze the data collected from the field, the data was categorized, and similar responses placed under common categories that yielded different headings. The categories or headings used are *church administrative functions*, *special pastoral functions*, *shepherding functions*, and *pastoral leadership*. These headings signify the aspects of pastoral care that are affected in cases where there is a multiplication of churches set against low numbers of pastors. Statistical Package for the Social Sciences (SPSS) software was used in data analysis.

The findings indicated that *shepherding functions*, as an aspect of pastoral care, were affected by numerical church growth. The specific aspects of shepherding functions were counseling, visitation, and preaching/teaching. Table 5.1 shows that all the respondents interviewed thought that each of the shepherding functions was affected at the same measure (at 33.3%). This finding makes each of the three aspects equally important. The frequency table (table 5.1) gives a summary of the responses of the church officials, lay leaders, and pastors, and indicates the distribution of the aspects of shepherding functions.

Table 5.1: Summary of responses from participants concerning shepherding functions that are affected by the numerical growth of the church

Shepherding Functions

		Frequency	Percent	Valid Percent	Cumulative Percent
Valid	Counseling	6	33.3	33.3	33.3
	Visitation	6	33.3	33.3	66.7
	Preaching and Teaching	6	33.3	33.3	100.0
	Total	18	100.0	100.0	

Table 5.2 shows how specific aspects of *church administration functions* (planning, organizing, leading, and controlling) are affected when there is a numerical increase in congregations set against few pastors. The two key functions that received priority in relation to pastoral care were organizing and leading, each scoring 33.3 percent. They were followed by planning and controlling, at 16.7 percent each. Table 5.2 shows the distribution of the aspects of church administration.

Table 5.2: Summary of responses from participants concerning church administration functions that are affected by the numerical growth of the church

Church Administration Functions

		Frequency	Percent	Valid Percent	Cumulative Percent
Valid	Planning	3	16.7	16.7	16.7
	Organizing	6	33.3	33.3	50.0
	Leading	6	33.3	33.3	83.3
	Controlling	3	16.7	16.7	100.0
	Total	18	100.0	100.0	

The frequency table 5.3 shows the findings in areas of *pastoral leadership.* These areas were fellowship, worship, discipleship, evangelism and missions, and departments (youth, children, men, and women). The findings revealed that in the pastoral leadership category, discipleship was the outstanding aspect of pastoral care that was affected, scoring 33.3 percent. The other aspects all scored 16.7 percent each.

Table 5.3: Summary of responses from participants concerning pastoral leadership functions that are affected by the numerical growth of the church

Pastoral Leadership

		Frequency	Percent	Valid Percent	Cumulative Percent
Valid	Fellowship	3	16.7	16.7	16.7
	Worship	3	16.7	16.7	33.3
	Discipleship	6	33.3	33.3	66.7
	Evangelism and Missions	3	16.7	16.7	83.3
	Departmental (Youth, Children, Men, and Women) Involvement	3	16.7	16.7	100.0
	Total	18	100.0	100.0	

Finally, the frequency table 5.4 shows the *special pastoral functions* that are affected when churches lack a full-time pastor. These functions included the Lord's Table, baptisms, dedications, weddings/marriages, and funerals. The findings indicated that the Lord's Table (scoring 33.3%) was the key aspect of special pastoral care that was affected, above the other aspects listed. The rest of the aspects scored 16.7 percent each.

Table 5.4: Summary of responses from participants concerning special pastoral functions that are affected by the numerical growth of the church

Special Pastoral Functions

		Frequency	Percent	Valid Percent	Cumulative Percent
Valid	Lord's Table	6	33.3	33.3	33.3
	Baptisms	3	16.7	16.7	50.0
	Child Dedications	3	16.7	16.7	66.7
	Weddings and Marriages	3	16.7	16.7	83.3
	Funerals	3	16.7	16.7	100.0
	Total	18	100.0	100.0	

Summary of the Findings of Research Question 1

The findings indicate that the three aspects under the *shepherding functions* category (counseling, visitation, and preaching and teaching) are equally affected when a local church has no pastor. Interestingly, the functions that affect pastoral care the least were the *special pastoral functions*; each aspect scored 16.7 percent, except for the Lord's Table, which is served once per month. The reason given for this phenomenon was that these functions only happen occasionally and can be carried out by any visiting pastor and not necessarily a local church pastor. The Lord's Table scored higher than the rest because those interviewed saw it as important and needing to be served regularly – preferably on a monthly basis.

The prominent aspects of pastoral care that scored the highest (33.3%) in each category were counseling, visitation, preaching and teaching (in shepherding functions), organizing and leading (in church administration functions), discipleship (in pastoral leadership), and the Lord's Table (in special pastoral functions). They are the specific aspects of pastoral care and administration that are most affected when a local church does not have its own pastor.

Generally, items under the shepherding functions category scored more highly than items in any other category. They were followed by those in the church administration category, and then by the pastoral leadership and special pastoral functions categories. This highlights the critical role of shepherding functions (counseling, visitation, and preaching and teaching) and church administration in a local church/congregation.

For each of the aspects that scored 16.7 percent, an explanation was offered. For example, planning and controlling (church administrative functions) were deemed to be functions that could be done by a local church council or board. Other respondents thought planning and controlling could be done occasionally, either by the local church itself or by the next level of the church hierarchy. Some aspects of pastoral leadership functions that scored 16.7 percent (fellowship, worship, evangelism and missions, departmental leadership) were interpreted as aspects that affect pastoral care but do not need close or constant supervision. These were areas where lay leaders could be empowered to serve. All the aspects that scored 16.7 percent can be interpreted as important functions of pastoral care and administration, but as secondarily affected compared to those aspects that scored 33.3 percent.

Data Analysis of Question 2: What Are the Implications of Numerical Church Growth for AIC Pastors Serving in Marakwet Region?

The data collected for this research question was organized into three categories: effects on the pastor's personal life, pressures on family life, and pressures of pastoral ministry. This research question targeted pastors and regional church officials for reliable information. The frequency table 5.5 indicates the findings on the effect of overseeing many churches on the pastor's personal life. The findings indicate that pastors face three risks/challenges: burnout (33.3%), little time for devotional life (33.3%), and facing high expectations (33.3%).

Table 5.5: Summary of responses from participants concerning implications of the numerical growth of the church on pastor's personal life

Effect on the Pastor's Personal Life

		Frequency	Percent	Valid Percent	Cumulative Percent
Valid	Burnout	6	33.3	33.3	33.3
	Little Time for Devotional Life	6	33.3	33.3	66.7
	High Expectations	6	33.3	33.3	100.0
	Total	18	100.0	100.0	

Table 5.6 indicates that the families of pastors are also affected when pastors have many pastoral roles and churches to oversee. The findings indicate that pastors must deal with three issues: inadequate family time (33.3%), low pay (50%), and parental challenges (16.7%).

Table 5.6: Summary of responses from participants on pressures on pastor's family life

Pressures on Family Life

		Frequency	Percent	Valid Percent	Cumulative Percent
Valid	Inadequate Family Time	6	33.3	33.3	33.3
	Low Pay	9	50.0	50.0	83.3
	Parental Challenges	3	16.7	16.7	100.0
	Total	18	100.0	100.0	

The research found out that pastors were also affected by pressures from pastoral ministry. The responses were categorized and are presented in frequency table 5.7. Some factors creating pressure in pastoral ministry are varied congregational needs (33.3%), decreased productivity (33.3%), distance and means of transport (16.7%), and leadership challenges (16.7%).

Table 5.7: Summary of responses from participants on pressures of pastoral ministry

Pressures of Pastoral ministry

		Frequency	Percent	Valid Percent	Cumulative Percent
Valid	Varied Congregational Needs	6	33.3	33.3	33.3
	Decreased Productivity	6	33.3	33.3	66.7
	Distance and Means of Transport	3	16.7	16.7	83.3
	Leadership Challenges	3	16.7	16.7	100.0
	Total	18	100.0	100.0	

Summary of the Findings of Research Question 2

These findings indicate that the responsibility placed upon a small number of pastors each overseeing several congregations negatively affects the personal life, the family life, and the ministry life of the pastor. The responsibility of taking care of several churches overwhelms and strains the ability of the few pastors involved. Pastors must cope with high ministry expectations, sustain their devotional time, and avoid burnout. In addition, low pay was one of the greatest aspects that affected a pastor's witness as a provider for his family. Other identified areas that a pastor must wrestle with in such contexts were varied congregational needs, decreased productivity because of increased workload, and distance and the means of transport to get from one church to another.

Data Analysis of Question 3: How Has the Leadership of AIC Marakwet Region Prepared to Handle the Effects of Numerical Growth on Pastoral Care and Administration in the Past and in the Future?

The research findings for this question revealed that the AIC regional leaders in the past foresaw the problem of having too few pastors to cope with the increasing number of congregations. The responses are divided into past and present interventions.

Past Interventions

The church leadership in the past sent and supported pastors who went to Bible colleges. However, the number of pastors being equipped for church ministry never matched the pace at which churches were planted. The church also moved about ten pastors from local churches to serve in church-sponsored high schools to serve as chaplains. Those chaplains are still attached to neighboring churches to carry out pastoral care and administration. The AIC regional church also established a Bible college in Kapsowar in 2012 to train pastors locally while they continue in ministry. Additionally, a training center giving short courses was established at Kapsigoria. This training center runs periodic week-long courses for lay leadership and refresher courses for pastors who have been in ministry for a long time. The interventions to promote pastoral care and administration were only implemented five years ago.

Present Interventions

Findings revealed that the regional church is establishing a Savings and Credit Cooperative (SACCO) for pastors. This is part of an effort to help pastors and their spouses access loans with friendly interest to educate their children and run their personal projects as they carry on the work of ministry. Reportedly, the church is in the process of developing its land assets to provide a steady income to support the work of ministry and hire more pastors. The church plans to invest resources in the church library at the regional offices for pastors to access books and materials for ministry. In addition, the church leadership is considering licensing and ordaining ministers who have been in ministry for a long time so that they can be officially allowed to administer church ordinances. As reported, this is expected to ease the discharge of pastoral functions and avoid straining the few ordained pastors. From the findings, the church's preparedness in the past to handle pastoral care and administration was inadequate. Much attention and focus was given to church planting in areas where there was no church. And since there were few pastors, elders took over the running of the local church through local church councils, with inadequate preparation. Of course, lay leadership and support is vital to the existence and sustenance of any local church; but still the office of the pastor remains relevant and important in relation to pastoral care and administration.

Conclusion and Recommendations

It can be concluded that all the research assumptions were confirmed to be true. Pastoral care functions are negatively affected when a local church has no pastor. This happens when numeric church growth is pursued at the expense of provision of quality pastoral care and administration. According to the findings, the pastoral care and administrative functions that are disabled are (in order): shepherding functions (counseling, visitation, and preaching and teaching), administrative functions (planning, organizing, leading, and controlling), pastoral leadership (fellowship, worship, discipleship, evangelism and missions, departments), and special pastoral functions (the Lord's Table, baptisms, dedications, officiating at weddings/marriages, and funerals).

The welfare of the pastors who take care of the growing numbers of churches should be taken into consideration. The findings indicated that demanding pastoral responsibilities affect the pastor's personal life, family life, and ministry productivity. The church should have a strategy in place that seeks to reduce the ratio of churches to pastors. The church should work to ensure that each local church has at least one pastor and equipped laity. This will not only help the pastors who are already under strain, but will also improve the level of pastoral care and administration in the churches. This should also be coupled with a strategy to improve the remuneration of pastors.

The findings also indicated that the church leadership anticipated a scarcity of pastors as compared to the number of churches that were planted. There were some initiatives launched to mitigate the problem. However, the challenge remains since most of the past interventions were implemented less than five years ago. Therefore, the level of preparedness to cope with the increasing numbers of congregations was inadequate. Church-planting strategies and policies should take into consideration the provision of quality pastoral care and administration for each congregation that is planted. Present interventions need to be enhanced to promote the welfare of the pastors and to ensure that the church maintains its steady numeric growth with consideration for and emphasis on the pastoral care and administration of the local church.

If the church is to experience steady growth and effective pastoral care and administration, the church leadership needs to come up with strategies and policies that govern both aspects of numerical church growth and pastoral care and administration. The Great Commission, Matthew 28:19–20, shows that the church needs to reach out to the world but at the same time maintain its teaching function. The two undeniable mandates in the Great Commission are "Go . . ." and ". . . teach." The church should not only seek growth quantitatively by "going out," but also provide quality pastoral care and administration by executing its teaching functions. Additionally, to cope with the problem of too few pastors among many churches, the church needs to consider investing in equipping lay leaders to effectively assist in the pastoral care and administrative responsibilities.

Bibliography

Adams, Jay E. *Shepherding God's Flock: A Handbook on Pastoral Ministry, Counseling, and Leadership*. Grand Rapids, MI: Zondervan, 2016.

Carnahan, Roy E. *Creative Pastoral Management*. Kansas City, MO: Beacon Hill Press of Kansas City, 1976.

Chipenda, Jose B., and All Africa Conference of Churches, eds. *The Church of Africa: Towards a Theology of Reconstruction*. African Challenge Book Series 2. Nairobi: AACC, 1991.

Creswell, John W. *Research Design: Qualitative, Quantitative, and Mixed Method Approaches*. 2nd ed. Thousand Oaks, CA: Sage, 2003.

Elliott, Ralph H. *Church Growth That Counts*. Valley Forge, PA: Judson, 1982.

Fletcher, David R. "Case-Studies of Policy and Vision Implementation by the Executive Pastor." PhD diss., Dallas Theological Seminary. May 2004. Accessed 22 February 2016. www.dts.edu/download/degrees/dmin/DTS%20-%20David%20Fletcher%20 (D.Min.)%20-%20Dissertation.pdf.

Ford, Leighton. *Transforming Leadership: Jesus' Way of Creating Vision, Shaping Values and Empowering Change*. Downers Grove, IL: InterVarsity Press, 1991.

Kibet, Lang'at Joshua. "An Investigation into the Factors That Influenced Numerical Growth of Deliverance Church Eastleigh in Nairobi, Kenya from 1981 to 2006." Master's thesis, Missions, Nairobi Evangelical Graduate School of Theology (NEGST), 2006.

McGavran, Donald A., and C. Peter Wagner. *Understanding Church Growth*. 3rd ed. Grand Rapids, MI: Eerdmans, 1990.

McKee, Scott B. "The Relationship between Church Health and Church Growth in the Evangelical Presbyterian Church." PhD diss., Asbury Theological Seminary, 2003. Accessed 22 February 2016. https://place.asburyseminary.edu/cgi/viewcontent. cgi?referer=https://www.google.com/&httpsredir=1&article=1185&context=ec ommonsatsdissertations.

Morrison, Philip E. *The Multi-Church Pastor: A Manual for Training Leadership in a Multi-Church Setting*. Allentown, PA: Gratia Veritas, 2004.

Ngasura, Philip K. Barar. "Key Strategies in Effective Pastoral Leadership in the Africa Gospel Churches, Kenya: Biblical Foundations for Leadership and Healthy Churches." PhD diss., Liberty Baptist Theological Seminary, December 2012. Accessed 22 February 2016. http://digitalcommons.liberty.edu/cgi/viewcontent. cgi?article=1732&context=doctoral.

Olson, Mark A. *Moving beyond Church Growth: An Alternative Vision for Congregations*. Prisms. Minneapolis: Fortress, 2002.

Patton, John. *Pastoral Care in Context: An Introduction to Pastoral Care*. Louisville, KY: Westminster John Knox, 1993.

Rainer, Thom S. *The Book of Church Growth: History, Theology, and Principles*. Nashville: Broadman & Holman, 1993.

Schwarz, Christian A. *Paradigm Shift in the Church: How Natural Church Development Can Transform Theological Thinking*. Carol Stream, IL: ChurchSmart Resources, 1999.

Welch, Robert H. *Church Administration: Creating Efficiency for Effective Ministry*. 2nd ed. Nashville: Broadman & Holman, 2011.

White, R. E. O. *A Guide to Pastoral Care: A Practical Primer of Pastoral Theology*. Basingstoke: Pickering & Inglis, 1983.

Zablon, Jacob Kibor. "The Growth and Development of the Africa Inland Church in Marakwet Kenya." Master's thesis, Nairobi Evangelical Graduate School of Theology (NEGST), 1992.

6

Integration of Faith, Life, and Academia to Achieve Transformational Education

Elizabeth Mburu

Langham Literature Regional Coordinator (Africa), Langham Publishers

Abstract

"Integration" is a word that is heard quite often in Christian universities. As part of our educational processes, we ought to endeavor to shape the worldview of every student towards a biblical worldview. However, many find that it is a challenge not only to fit our Christian calling in the educational arena, but even more so to define ways in which we, as educators, can adequately prepare students to exert a Christian influence in society. This paper will propose that the relationship between faith, life, and academia naturally flows out of an understanding of worldview. One's worldview will dramatically affect one intellectually, physically, socially, economically, and morally. Consequently, a major goal of education in Christian universities ought to be to shape the worldview of the learners so that how they "are" in society reflects Christlikeness. This paper will define a philosophy of integration that uses worldview as its basis. The model proposed emphasizes "being" rather than "doing."

A specific case study of the academic discipline of business will be used to demonstrate how integration can be successfully achieved at the three levels of:

- Curriculum development
- Course syllabus development

- Delivery of selected topics within a course

Key words: assumptions, business, culture, curriculum, integration, transformation, worldview

Introduction

"Integration" is a word that is heard quite often in Christian universities.[1] However, many find that it is a challenge not only to fit our Christian calling in the educational arena, but even more so to define ways in which we, as educators, can adequately prepare students to exert a Christian influence in society. It is not always clear whether the students who leave our universities are able to integrate their faith, academia/academic discipline, and practice. Do they become agents of transformation and the influencers of the ideologies, philosophies, beliefs, and practices of the world, or do the products of our Christian universities find themselves influenced instead?

Magesa observes that many Christians often display a compartmentalization of life that he identifies as two thought systems.[2] His observation is accurate. Indeed, Christian educators often observe this "silo" effect in students. However, I would add that the thought systems are not two, but rather three where education is concerned. While faith and life are the two compartments, one's academia (or academic discipline) must be taken into consideration. This is because the knowledge and skills acquired as a result of higher education must themselves shape and be shaped by the individual.

Different institutions have different philosophies of integration. However, integration entails more than merely including a few courses from the discipline of theology, praying before a class, or peppering classes with Scripture. Indeed, the anecdotal evidence bears witness to the fact that this approach is not effective. The solution to the dichotomous thinking we see in our students is for educators in Christian universities to deal with the root cause of this compartmentalization. Our task then is to develop a system whereby the three components, namely faith, life, and academia, are decompartmentalized and integrated into a cohesive whole. The result of this cohesive whole is a truly

---

1. For instance, the integration of faith and psychology has been an ongoing discussion in many Western universities for more than four decades. Fernando L. Garzon and M. Elizabeth Lewis Hall, "Teaching Christian Integration in Psychology and Counselling: Current Status and Future Directions," *Journal of Psychology & Theology* 40, no. 2 (2012): 155.

2. As documented by Richard J. Gehman, *African Traditional Religion in Biblical Perspective*, rev. ed. (Nairobi: East African Educational Publishers, 2005), 6.

biblical worldview that influences the student's faith, engagement with the world, and application of his/her academic skills and knowledge within his/her area of influence. This is transformational education.

This chapter will propose that the relationship between faith, life, and academia naturally flows out of an understanding of worldview. This is because one's worldview dramatically affects one intellectually, emotionally, physically, socially, economically, and morally. As part of our educational processes in Christian universities, we ought to endeavor to shape the worldview of every student towards a biblical worldview. This chapter will, therefore, define a philosophy of integration that uses a biblical worldview as its basis, and then use a specific case study of the academic discipline of business to demonstrate how integration can be successfully achieved at the levels of curriculum development, course syllabus development, and delivery of selected topics within a course. The focus is on the curriculum for two reasons: it is the vehicle through which "educational values and commitments actually become embedded in practice" and "educational vision takes root."[3]

The definition of biblical worldview adopted in this chapter borrows from Sire's in recognizing that worldview is holistic and is not external to but an integral part of the self.[4] A biblical worldview can, therefore, be defined as *the orientation of the self to all of life that is the foundation of the expression of our identities as redeemed human beings in relationship with God, others, and the world, and that is consistent with the biblical metanarrative in all its aspects.* To come to a view of the world that is integrated, there is the need to recognize the value of allowing all areas of one's life to flow from biblical assumptions. As Pazmino explains with regards to biblical and theological foundations of Christian education, "The Scriptures function as the final authority and serve as the filter through which all other truths are examined for their consistency with a Christian world and life view."[5] Since worldview is a broad subject, this chapter has isolated several essential elements of worldview, particularly relating to the African context, to inform the discussion. These include ultimate

---

3. Robert W. Pazmino, *Foundational Issues in Christian Education*, 3rd ed. (Grand Rapids, MI: Baker Academic, 2008), 234.

4. James W. Sire, *Naming the Elephant: Worldview as a Concept* (Downers Grove, IL: InterVarsity Press, 2004), 122.

5. Pazmino, *Foundational Issues*, 58.

reality, external reality, anthropology, epistemology, ethics, theodicy, history/ time, and art.[6]

This chapter does not intend to propose a new biblical/theological or even philosophical foundation of Christian education.[7] It is hoped that the ideas proposed can be incorporated into existing curricular foundations to enhance the curriculum development and delivery aspects of the education process.

Rationale for Integration

One might ask whether integration is necessary, possible, or even to be rejected. The paradigm proposed by H. Richard Niebuhr has been used by Christian educators to address the question of the relationship between education and the context in which one finds oneself. He proposed that there are at least five ways in which one could view the relationship between Christ and culture (or between the Christian and his/her context). These five ways are Christ against culture, Christ of culture, Christ above culture, Christ and culture in paradox, and Christ the transformer of culture.[8] These perspectives are particularly significant for education in a Christian context since one's stance determines one's educational philosophy with regards to integration. A philosophy that rejects integration is based on the belief that Christ is the sole authority and that any claims of culture are to be rejected. Adherents to a rejection of integration may also argue that Christ and culture are in opposition to each other.

This chapter would argue that Christ is the transformer of culture. From the onset of creation, we were called to stewardship. This is the command to exercise responsible dominion over the earth, subdue it, and develop its latent potential (Gen 1:26–28; cf. Gen 2:15). Because the scope of dominion is all creation, there is no secular/sacred distinction. It, therefore, applies to the spiritual, the social, and the natural world, and necessarily implies the exercise of proper stewardship through our work and through our broader mission as servants of Christ. Plantinga argues that one's vocation is to be a

---

6. Most of these reflect those identified by a number of worldview specialists such as Sire, Holmes, and Nash, but a few, such as time/history and aesthetics, have been included because of their relevance to African worldview formation.

7. For a brief overview of historical and philosophical foundations of education and major proponents, see Michael J. Anthony and Warren S. Benson, *Exploring the History and Philosophy of Christian Education* (Grand Rapids, MI: Kregel, 2003), 381–409; and Gerald L. Gutek, *Historical and Philosophical Foundations of Education* (Upper Saddle, NJ: Pearson Education, 2005).

8. See views from David J. Hesselgrave, *Communicating Christ Cross-Culturally* (Grand Rapids, MI: Zondervan, 1978, 1991).

prime citizen of the kingdom of God, no matter where one finds oneself in the fabric of society.[9] Fulfilling the call to stewardship is one way a Christian can attain to this prime citizenship.

Stewardship includes the development and the improvement of the creation that is about us, all to the glory and honor of God (cf. Gen 3:23; 9:1; Ps 8; Rom 8:20–21). When we read these verses, we recognize that we must develop a paradigm of integration that feeds into a range of disciplines with the aim of transforming the world around us into what God himself intended.

The Practical Necessity for Integration: A Case Study of Lake Victoria Fishermen

An article published by *The Star* newspaper on 14 January 2014 reported the devastating consequences of a small car wash business situated on the shores of Lake Victoria.[10] The business is located in Gabba, a fish-landing site in Kampala, Uganda. Fishermen have fished these waters for generations and depended on the fish of these waters for subsistence and for commercial purposes. This lake, the second largest freshwater lake in the world, boasts the world's largest freshwater fishery. Moreover, it is the source-feed of the river Nile, which itself supports an estimated 30 million riparian populations. According to a 2007 Lake Victoria Fisheries Organisation report, its total output is estimated at one million tonnes, worth $650 million. It provides employment for thousands of people.

However, this thriving business began to experience a decline from 2005. The reason? Pollution of the water after the establishment of numerous car wash stations along the shores of the lake. Most of the soaps used in these illegal car washes are the culprit. They contain phosphates and other chemicals that harm fish and water quality. While the car wash business is thriving, unfortunately the fishing business is in decline.

While the washing of cars is not negative, since it demonstrates that the individuals involved are hardworking and desire to earn a living, it does beg the question as to whether this example contradicts what a biblical worldview tells us should be the right approach to business. Is God concerned about the destruction of water life? What should our attitude to the environment be?

---

9. Cornelius Plantinga Jr., *Engaging God's World: A Christian Vision of Faith, Learning, and Living* (Grand Rapids, MI: Eerdmans, 2001), 108.

10. Carl Odera, "Kenya: The Lake Victoria Basin in Distress," *The Star*, 14 January 2014, AllAfrica, http://allafrica.com/stories/201401140576.html.

What is our responsibility with regards to the welfare of other human beings? Does the end justify the means?

Worldview and Integration

A snare that many people fall into is believing that just because they know the contents of their Bible and can quote Scripture and discuss theology, their approach to life is biblical, when in fact it is secular or rooted in spiritual beliefs that are a part of their culture. To make the transition from this wrong perspective, believers must ground their entire orientation to life in a cohesive biblical base. A major goal of education in Christian universities ought to be to shape the worldview of the learners so that how they will "be" in society reflects Christlikeness. It is natural, then, to have a philosophy of integration that is hinged on worldview.

According to Sire, worldview has pretheoretical, presuppositional, and theoretical aspects.[11] The pretheoretical encompasses those things which we know intuitively and without which we cannot think at all. So, for example, every culture has the concept of an ultimate reality. The next aspect is the presuppositional. While many presuppositions have a pretheoretical base, this is not always the case. Presuppositions, or assumptions, refer to those beliefs which, although we may be able to give reasons for them, we cannot prove. To continue the example above, this means that the form of one's belief in an ultimate reality will vary from culture to culture. The final aspect is the theoretical. It is influenced by both the pretheoretical and the presuppositional aspects and consists of that which arises from the mind's conscious activity.[12] These assumptions are what form the foundation for worldview.

A philosophy of integration must consider how worldview is formed in an individual. There are at least three levels of worldview formation or acquisition. The most basic level is the unconscious level. The second level involves changing one's worldview by preference. The third level – the one that is most relevant to the discussion in this chapter – is the conscious level. At this level, there is deliberative choice and one is aware of the process. Educators must empower students to interrogate their assumptions as this is the level at which conscious change can begin to take place. Fortunately, assumptions (and by extension, worldviews) are dynamic. This dynamic nature implies constant change at every level in response to the data received from interacting with the

---

11. Sire, *Naming the Elephant*, 77.

12. Sire, 77.

environment and from internal influences. At all these levels, one must avoid fostering a fragmented understanding and development of a worldview. A holistic approach recognizes that worldview incorporates all areas of life, with changes in one area impacting the others. This means that one must consider these aspects in the development and delivery of curriculum.

What about culture? Every individual is situated within a certain cultural context and lives in general conformity to that context. Culture includes the values and social mores of a society, as well as all the learned patterns of behavior that make that society unique. It has been recognized as the key influence on worldview. Regardless of the form a culture takes, the individual within that culture is influenced and shaped by it, both consciously and unconsciously. In formulating and developing a biblical worldview, therefore, one must recognize one's own cultural assumptions and separate these from the unchanging, universal biblical assumptions that are the basis of a biblical worldview.

Worldview also has an individual and a communal character. Individuals have beliefs and values that are uniquely theirs. At the same time, communities hold things in common, hence the communal character of worldview. This is significant for the educational endeavor, as it informs not just the content that educators pass on, but the teaching methodology as well, particularly for more communal cultures such as those in Africa. A point to note is that while there are numerous African worldviews, there are commonalities that make it possible to examine African worldview as a single entity.

Integration Model

The integration model proposed is an interactive system. The student, who is at the center of this model, comes into a Christian university with a particular worldview. We, the educators, have the responsibility to shape the faith, life, and academia of the student holistically. Curricula generally emphasize behavioral objectives (i.e. what the student ought to do) through the cognitive, affective, and behavioral domains. While the integrated approach proposed here does not minimize the validity of these objectives, the greater goal has to do with "being" rather than "doing," a model based on Pazmino's curricular foundations which he draws from Titus 2:1–15. He points out the following:

> In general terms, Titus is encouraged to teach various groups *to be* something or other. No doubt knowing, feeling, and doing are implied in the call to be, but a concern for being implies a larger purpose, a larger vision. Titus is to be concerned with character formation, the values persons are embracing and living out. Good

works and conduct flow from sound doctrine and from a person's being in a right relationship with God and others. Christian educators must be concerned for Christian values and virtues, which persons are called upon to embody in their very lives.[13]

The end result of the educational process is a transformed individual with an internalized biblical worldview that enables him/her to transform his/her world. This is the distinction between "being" and "doing."

The starting point is, therefore, the student's worldview (whatever that might be), and the three mid-points are faith, life, and academia. These are in constant interaction with each other, with influence flowing from one to the other until they come to a cohesive point. Each contributes to the totality of the resultant product in that faith affects life and academia, life affects academia and faith, and academia affects life and faith. As the student goes through the educational process, his/her worldview begins to experience shifts – some subtle and others not so subtle. The apex of this process is a biblical worldview, rightly understood, and informing the faith, life, and academic discipline of the student (see diagram).

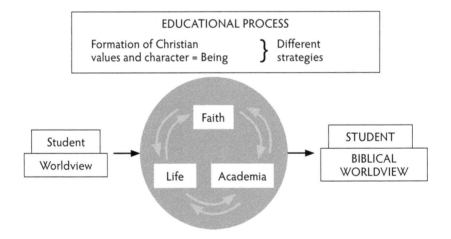

Actualizing Integration

Having understood the integration model, how can it be actualized? As the curriculum and the courses are developed and implemented, the educator must consciously keep in mind the following: the elements of worldview that are

---

13. Pazmino, *Foundational Issues*, 249.

essential in guiding valid integration questions, and the need to use strategies that will encourage holistic learning.

During the preparation of each curriculum, course, and topic, the educator must ask and answer at least three questions. This must be done intentionally.

1. How does worldview influence a student's understanding of how this curriculum/course/topic relates to his/her faith, life, and academic discipline?

2. What objectives should the educator incorporate in the curriculum (including the course outlines) that challenge students to begin to integrate?

3. Does the course content uncover issues that require reflective integration?

During the delivery of each course, the following questions can guide one in their integration:

1. What elements of worldview are relevant to the topic at hand?

2. What are the assumptions that undergird the relevant elements of worldview, as they relate to the topic? As educators, we are concerned not just with the "what" but also with the "why."

3. How do these assumptions inform the values and the character of the student in terms of his/her "being"?

4. Which educational strategy is most effective in delivering the desired content to achieve the goal of integration?

5. Have concrete examples and a proper biblical response to these issues been incorporated as part of the course material, in the form of illustrations, analogies, case studies, and so forth?

The sections following will provide a discussion of the elements of worldview as well as the educational strategies necessary for integration using the case study of a business curriculum.

Elements of Worldview with Emphasis on a Business Program

As we have noted above, to come to a view of the world that is integrated, there is the need to recognize the value of basing all areas of one's life on biblical assumptions. At the same time, when approaching business from a biblical perspective, we must keep in mind that "A Christian approach to business is not a cookbook of simplistic recipes for resolving complex business problems. . . .

the responsibility for determining what is fair and achieves business objectives in light of biblical principles requires hard thinking, creative problem solving, and careful implementation."[14] The elements of worldview discussed below provide a biblical base by identifying key assumptions that are essential to the formation of every worldview. These assumptions will then be used as the foundation for the formulation of the business curriculum's philosophy, goals, and expected learning outcomes. Implications of how the categories of worldview identified in this chapter intersect with a business curriculum will be given at the conclusion of each category.

Ultimate Reality

What functions as "god" in the lives of individuals and communities? In more technical terminology, what is the ultimate reality? That which is self-existent? Different answers can be given to this question: God, the gods, the material cosmos, and so forth.[15] In an African worldview, this is understood as the Supreme Being. As Turaki points out, Africans have a "concept, perception, notion or awareness of a universal God and Creator."[16] In the hierarchy of spiritual beings and powers, the Supreme Being occupies the highest and greatest position.[17] However, we must be cautious not to assume that the Supreme Being worshiped in various African religions is the God who has revealed himself in Scripture.[18] The common starting point is the self-existence of God.

One's understanding of ultimate reality, therefore, forms the foundation for everything else and defines the path that one's worldview takes. In the biblical worldview, as Sire convincingly argues, "everything is first and foremost determined by the nature and character of God."[19]

---

14. Richard C. Chewning, John W. Eby, et al., *Business through the Eyes of Faith* (New York: HarperCollins, 1990), 5.

15. See the approach by James W. Sire, *The Universe Next Door*, 5th ed. (Downers Grove, IL: IVP Academic, 2009), 22–23, who handles the question of worldview using philosophical categories. This is the perspective adopted in this chapter.

16. Yusufu Turaki, *Foundations of African Traditional Religion and Worldview* (Nairobi: WordAlive, 2006), 28.

17. Turaki, *Foundations*, 29.

18. See Samuel Waje Kunhiyop, *African Christian Theology* (Nairobi: HippoBooks, 2012), 44.

19. Sire, *Naming the Elephant*, 55.

Implications for Faith, Life, and Academia?

The underlying assumption regarding ultimate reality is that God is the creator and life-giver and therefore deserves glory. A basic question that the program would have to address with relation to this category would be: What is the underlying philosophy of the program? How are the students to orient themselves so that they gain an accurate understanding of this ultimate reality in relation to the material they are learning? The following is an example of a philosophy statement that achieves this.

> The philosophy of the program is to empower students to attain and develop godly qualities through:
>
> - *Holistic transformational development:* The program provides an avenue for development of specific character traits such as integrity and morality.
> - *Professional development:* The program equips students with skills, attitudes, and knowledge for effective service, and empowers students to develop and promote biblical values in the business fraternity.
> - *Academic development:* The program provides opportunities for students to develop and demonstrate excellence in research and scholarship and an attitude of lifelong learning.

Chewning et al. suggest that business for the Christian is "an institutionalization of God's intentions for us to work and to serve each other. . . . Business is a legal structuring of work where we express our dominion over creation. It affords us opportunities to plan, organize, lead, follow, and develop skills in a number of areas – all mirroring godly qualities."[20] Consequently, the curriculum must guide its students toward this theocentric orientation where they are taught to recognize that God comes first and that the goal as Christian business people is to glorify him.

External Reality

What is the nature of the world around us? Is this reality comprised only of the physical, or is there a spiritual realm with which humankind interacts actively, whether knowingly or unknowingly? Did it come into being by chance, or was there a first cause? A fundamental philosophical belief that defines both the traditional and the modern African worldview is the belief that the world is

---

20. Chewning et al., *Business*, 7.

spiritual rather than material.[21] The spiritual realm is in constant interaction with the seen, physical world. Indeed, the "world is permeated with divinities and spirits who can have positive and negative effects on every aspect of life."[22]

One's conception of the world in which one lives, whether accurate or inaccurate, determines how one chooses to interact with that world.

Implications for Faith, Life, and Academia?

An underlying assumption of external reality is that human beings have been given responsible dominion over this world. With this assumption in mind, a basic question that the curriculum would have to address would be: What should the students understand their responsibility to nature and the community to be? Perhaps even more specifically: What is the extent of corporate social responsibility?

- Let organizations control all exploitation of nature and regulate society completely?
- Within reason balance economic and ecological policies?
- Promote the individual's right to the good life, and therefore supply the means for unhampered employment without regard for nature and society?

Naturally, an accurate biblical understanding of external reality will affect how the student will relate to the world around him/her since s/he properly understands it to be the intentional creation of a God who is concerned with every aspect of his world and is intimately involved in it. Students should be encouraged to build businesses and social ventures that will transform their lives and their communities.

Anthropology

This area deals with the question of the nature of human beings and their interrelationships within a social framework. Several questions arise when one considers this category. How should humankind regard itself? What is the essential nature of humankind? How should we treat one another? Many African myths attest to the fact that God created not just the universe, but humankind as well. Many myths go on to explain how an offence committed by humankind led to the separation between human beings and God. However,

---

21. Turaki, *Foundations*, 34.

22. Kunhiyop, *African Christian Theology*, 53.

unlike the biblical story, none suggest that there was an effort to heal this rift in the relationship.[23] Numerous stories, proverbs, and songs also highlight the importance of relationships in community.

How human beings regard themselves is essential in directing their thoughts and behavior regarding God (or the ultimate reality they choose), themselves, and others around them.

Implications for Faith, Life, and Academia?

Regarding anthropology, an underlying assumption is that human beings are made in the image of God, but they need his salvation. This assumption is crucial when one considers the human resource element in organizations. As educators train students, they must sensitize them to basic human resource issues in the workplace. A basic question that the curriculum would have to help students address in relation to this category would be: How are people selected for employment? There are at least three options:

- Hire a close relative.
- Hire a relative or friend of someone in the organization.
- Hire the best person for the job.

Our educational process must bring our students to the point where they are able to affirm that human beings have worth and are created for a purpose. That purpose includes involvement with, and nurture of, other human beings. Fairness and justice in the workplace must be promoted.

Epistemology

The question of whether or not we can "know" has troubled philosophers through the ages. Beyond that, can what we know be verified? And how do we know? Knowledge cannot be divorced from human life; it is an integral part of daily living and hence must be taken into account in formulating any worldview.

Implications for Faith, Life, and Academia?

An underlying assumption of epistemology is that all truth is God's truth, hence truth is objective regardless of the source. A basic question that the curriculum would have to address in relation to this category would be: What is the purpose of knowledge acquisition?

---

23. Kunhiyop, 69.

- To gain knowledge that will enable one only to pass exams?
- To benefit oneself at the expense of the society?
- Or to gain practical wisdom that is applicable to everyday life and that benefits the society?

Our educational process must bring our students to the point where they understand that faith and reason should be understood as being complementary and hence must be used together to come to a cohesive biblical worldview. The educational process should, therefore, endeavor to help students grow in knowledge, both intellectually and spiritually, in a manner that reflects godly wisdom and that promotes the growth of the society.

Ethics

In this age in which we live, the question of what is morally right and wrong is no longer so easy to answer. Is morality a relative concept or are there some basic standards that are part of every culture? Clearly, a sense of right and wrong is inherent in every human being, but different cultures may be more flexible in defining this concept. For instance, African ethics focuses on the society as opposed to the individual. It is communal morality that regulates and controls conduct.[24]

Implications for Faith, Life, and Academia?

An underlying assumption is that all ethics is based on the character of God. A basic question that the curriculum would guide students in addressing would be: How does an organization arrive at making proper moral judgments with regards to its products?

- Focus only on the needs and social conditions of the culture in which the organization is located, regardless of whether or not there is a moral conflict with another culture that would be affected?
- Exercise fluidity in making moral judgments depending on how the organization feels about situations at any given time?
- Maximize benefits as long as it benefits the organization?
- Maximize benefits as long as it benefits the majority?

---

24. Samuel Waje Kunhiyop, *African Christian Ethics* (Nairobi: HippoBooks, 2008), 5.

Ethicists have identified at least four ethical categories that guide societies: cultural relativism, emotivist ethics, ethical egoism, and utilitarianism.[25] Our educational process must bring our students to the point where they can affirm that the major "secular" ethical theories today cannot be our standard. The moral rules we adopt must be based on the unchanging standards found in Scripture.

Theodicy

This is an area that has received many explanations but no ultimate answers. The question is, why is evil and suffering allowed to prevail? This is especially significant for Africa, where suffering appears to be a part of everyday life. One's basic presuppositions about this issue guarantee a particular kind of response during times of suffering and hardship, and that goes back to one's conception of the ultimate reality. For instance, the general African understanding is that suffering is a punishment that results from offending the Supreme Being or any of the entities in the spiritual hierarchy.[26] This is known as retribution theology.

Implications for Faith, Life, and Academia?

An underlying assumption of theodicy is that God is sovereign, even over evil and suffering. A basic question that the curriculum would have to address in relation to this category would be: What is an organization's involvement in situations where suffering is apparent?

- Try to alleviate suffering at all costs?
- Ignore suffering since it is a basic reality of life?
- Balance one's involvement, recognizing that it is not feasible to eradicate all the suffering in the world?

Our educational process must bring our students to the point where they acknowledge that God is in control of his world at all times and any suffering experienced is all part of his greater purpose. Although we as human beings may not understand what he is doing, he remains sovereign and just.

---

25. Arthur F. Holmes, *Ethics: Approaching Moral Decisions*, 2nd ed. (Downers Grove, IL: InterVarsity Press, 2007), 18–50.

26. See discussion in Elizabeth Mburu, "Is God a God of Retribution?" in *Christianity and Suffering: African Perspectives*, ASET, ed. Rodney L. Reed (Carlisle: Langham Global Library, 2017), 201–225.

History/Time

The question of how God is involved in the world is one that has troubled humankind since the beginning of time. Does God have his hand on human history, or are we simply going through meaningless motions as we move forward in time? The Western concept of time as linear, with an indefinite past, present, and indefinite future, did not exist in traditional African thinking. In Africa, time generally emphasizes the event as opposed to the passage of time. There are also at least two ways to understand the relationships of past, present, and future in Africa. One is two-dimensional with a long past, a present, and virtually no future.[27] Alternatively, there is a future, but it is merely a continuation of the present.[28] This understanding influences how one orders one's life with regards to the immediate and the distant futures.

Implications for Faith, Life, and Academia?

The underlying biblical assumption is that the past, the present, and the future are all important and contribute to God's eternal purpose in some way. A basic question that the curriculum would have to address in relation to this category would be: What is the temporal focus of life? Or more specifically: What goals should an organization have?

- Focus on the past, since the goals of the past are sufficient, and no change is necessary?
- Focus on the present, so that the goals of the organization reflect the present demands?
- Focus on the future, so that the goals of the organization are directed towards trends and the situation of the future?

Our educational process must bring our students to the point where they acknowledge that God has his hand on human history. Moreover, while the world is orderly, it is not, like the African understanding, determined or programmed. Our decisions are therefore significant.[29] Consequently, time should be used wisely.

---

27. John S. Mbiti, *African Religions and Philosophy* (1969; repr., Nairobi: East African Educational Publishers, 1992), 78.

28. J. N. K. Mugambi, *African Heritage and Contemporary Christianity* (Nairobi: Longman Kenya, 1989), 83.

29. Sire, *Universe*, 32.

Art

Finally, one's relationship to art or aesthetics forms an integral part of our worldview. Whether through song, poetry, stories, drama, or the graphic arts, this category is an essential component of life in Africa. While this category has largely been ignored in worldview discussions, it is obvious that we miss out on an important element since aesthetics demonstrate that worldview consists of more than abstract ideas or theoretical concepts.[30] The arts embody and express human values and are consequently an integral part of life.

Implications for Faith, Life, and Academia?

The underlying assumption in aesthetics is that "Artistic inventiveness is a reflection of God's unbounded capacity to create."[31] A basic question that the curriculum would therefore have to address would be: How can an organization maintain and contribute to the aesthetic beauty around us?

- Should we consider architectural principles of design and symmetry in constructing physical structures that house our organizations?
- Should an organization consider only the utilitarian aspects, regardless of how ugly the structure may be?
- Or should organizations seek a balance?

Our educational process must bring our students to the point where they seek to preserve and develop the beauty around them. God has placed beauty in his world, and the only appropriate response to this gift is to enjoy it and to add to it where possible.

Having identified the categories that are essential for guiding the process of integration, we will now look at the strategies necessary for effective integration.

Teaching/Learning Strategies Necessary for Integration

Different approaches must be implemented if the process of worldview acquisition is to be effective. Hence, there is the need to emphasize different forms of teaching/learning to promote holistic growth in individual areas. Apart from the more traditional methods of lecture and discussion in a

---

30. Leland Ryken, "The Creative Arts," in *The Making of a Christian Mind: A Christian World View and the Academic Enterprise*, ed. Arthur Holmes (Downers Grove, IL: InterVarsity Press, 1985), 105.

31. Sire, *Universe*, 35.

classroom setting, the following are a few suggestions intended to encourage holistic learning with the goal of the formation of a biblical worldview.

Self-Confrontation: Exercises in which students are led in a process of self-discovery through an examination of their individual and common cultures is the first step in recognizing the influence of culture on one's worldview. Once individuals begin to realize that they have been influenced tremendously by culture, they will be in a better position to begin to confront those areas of their lives that are not in conformity with a biblical worldview. This is an exercise that is best done in a group setting, but individuals should be challenged to engage in reflective self-analysis in order to be able to contribute to the group. Books on cultural anthropology, as well as individuals who specialize in this area, should be utilized for this process.

Mentoring: One-on-one mentoring is another strategy that is of invaluable help in integration. Ideally, a mentor should strive to help his/her protégé achieve steady growth and progress in all areas of life. Having a more mature believer "guide" you through life and provide an accountability structure is not that difficult to accept in a communal environment such as ours in Africa, where community is still a key value.

Intentional Exposure: Intentional exposure to a variety of situations is one key way to help students in the integration process. This exposure may take a variety of forms. Case studies provide a unique opportunity to reflect on situations before we encounter them. A good approach would be to create scenarios that cause dissonance among the students in the group and then guide them toward the appropriate way to respond to that dissonance. Role plays and simulations also provide unique opportunities to act out our responses in different situations. Moreover, they give one the confidence to respond rightly if, and when, a similar situation arises, because the scenario has already been processed.

Life Experiences: A strategy that works well when handled correctly is much like the support groups common to counseling. Individuals are encouraged to share their real-life experiences in a group setting. The group has the responsibility to help the one sharing sort through the issue and evaluate his/her response to the experience. In addition, people in the group who have not had a similar experience have the advantage of sharing in the discussion and filing what they learn for future reference. This works best for students who are already practicing within their field. Practicums are also an effective way of exposing students to real-life situations. As Pazmino points out, blending content and experience is one key to an effective, life-transforming curriculum.[32]

What about content? A business program has a clearly defined content. The challenge is to include content that will promote the development of a biblical worldview without compromising the core content that is needed for the acquisition of a valid business degree. Biblical instruction is crucial because it provides the content on which worldview is built. The authority of God's Word as the basis for right living must be constantly emphasized. Acquisition of correct doctrine is necessary if one's worldview is to be consistent with the biblical metanarrative. In this regard, including a Bible survey and theology course, coupled with hermeneutics, is essential. One of the essential aspects to include in every class session is a discussion of a biblical approach to organizational issues. Such discussions would be of significant help in making the Christian faith more relevant in a rapidly changing world.

Conclusion

In conclusion, we must ask ourselves a crucial question: Given the framework proposed, what do we hope to achieve by integrating faith, life, and academia in our approach to education? I would say that, first, we must understand that worldview develops within a cultural context and that it both informs and is informed by our culture. Second, worldview is dynamic and is constantly being changed at every level in response to the data received from interacting with one's environment and from internal influences. So, as we continue to challenge our students in the classroom to think critically about issues in our world and to respond biblically to them, we are in effect transforming the culture of our organizations, and ultimately of the society, because these students are the very ones who will go out and disseminate this "new" way of thinking about our world. In the preface to their book, Chewning et al. affirm that this is indeed possible. They write, "God calls us as Christians to look at all of life, including business, 'through the eyes of faith.' This means that we are called to see the world as God does. We look to biblical principles to guide our decisions and to form our values."[33]

---

32. Pazmino, *Foundational Issues*, 233.

33. Chewning et al., *Business*, 5.

Bibliography

Anthony, Michael J., and Warren S. Benson. *Exploring the History and Philosophy of Christian Education*. Grand Rapids, MI: Kregel, 2003.

Chewning, Richard C., John W. Eby, et al. *Business through the Eyes of Faith*. New York: HarperCollins, 1990.

Garzon, Fernando L., and M. Elizabeth Lewis Hall. "Teaching Christian Integration in Psychology and Counselling: Current Status and Future Directions." *Journal of Psychology & Theology* 40, no. 2 (2012): 155–159.

Gehman, Richard J. *African Traditional Religion in Biblical Perspective*. Rev. ed. Nairobi: East African Educational Publishers, 2005.

Gutek, Gerald L. *Historical and Philosophical Foundations of Education*. Upper Saddle, NJ: Pearson Education, 2005.

Hesselgrave, David J. *Communicating Christ Cross-Culturally*. Grand Rapids, MI: Zondervan, 1978, 1991.

Holmes, Arthur F. *Ethics: Approaching Moral Decisions*. 2nd ed. Downers Grove, IL: InterVarsity Press, 2007.

Kunhiyop, Samuel Waje. *African Christian Ethics*. Nairobi: HippoBooks, 2008.

———. *African Christian Theology*. Nairobi: HippoBooks, 2012.

Mbiti, John S. *African Religions and Philosophy*. Reprint 1969. Nairobi: East African Educational Publishers, 1992.

Mburu, Elizabeth. "Is God a God of Retribution?" In *Christianity and Suffering: African Perspectives*, ASET series, edited by Rodney L. Reed, 201–225. Carlisle: Langham Global Library, 2017.

Mugambi, J. N. K. *African Heritage and Contemporary Christianity*. Nairobi: Longman Kenya, 1989.

Odera, Carl. "Kenya: The Lake Victoria Basin in Distress." *The Star*, 14 January 2014. AllAfrica. http://allafrica.com/stories/201401140576.html.

Pazmino, Robert W. *Foundational Issues in Christian Education*. 3rd ed. Grand Rapids, MI: Baker Academic, 2008.

Plantinga, Cornelius Jr. *Engaging God's World: A Christian Vision of Faith, Learning, and Living*. Grand Rapids, MI: Eerdmans, 2001.

Ryken, Leland. "The Creative Arts." In *The Making of a Christian Mind: A Christian World View and the Academic Enterprise*, edited by Arthur Holmes, 105–131. Downers Grove, IL: InterVarsity Press, 1985.

Sire, James W. *Naming the Elephant: Worldview as a Concept*. Downers Grove, IL: InterVarsity Press, 2004.

———. *The Universe Next Door*. 5th ed. Downers Grove, IL: IVP Academic, 2009.

Turaki, Yusufu. *Foundations of African Traditional Religion and Worldview*. Nairobi: WordAlive, 2006.

7

Integrating a Biblical Worldview and STEM: Implications for the Kenyan Public University and Theological Education

Kevin Muriithi
Youth Pastor, Presbyterian Church of East Africa and Co-founder of Apologetics Kenya

Abstract

An increasing focus on infrastructure development as the backbone for Kenya's vision 2030 presupposes an emphasis on STEM (Science, Technology, Engineering, and Mathematics) education in order to guide the nation's developmental and educational agenda. In medical practice for instance, although frequent strikes are mitigated through policy frameworks, much more is needed. A similar case can be made for building collapses that have been popular in the recent decade. The author proposes an integration of a biblical worldview with STEM disciplines so as to anchor students in their lives and practice. Several challenges to this proposal include (1) a syncretism that downplays the role of biblical authority for the STEM evangelical student and professional; (2) a dichotomy between STEM and a biblical worldview that sees them at odds; and (3) collapsing such a proposal to merely an abstract level. This paper seeks this integration in a bid to show how it can be practical and life-transforming for STEM practitioners and can impact theological institutions. This can be done through (1) developing a holistic worldview that sees STEM in the providential plan of God; (2) encouraging the investigation of technology and science within theological education; and (3) STEM evangelicals speaking about how their faith has a bearing on their life and practice. The effect of doing this for students would be a faith that is engaged with the technological context of the twenty-first century, with its underlying dependence on a scientific worldview; and, considering the long-term effect of proclaiming the gospel to STEM students, enriching theological education, as well as transforming the cultural contexts of our societies with a biblically informed worldview. The chapter begins by framing the topic within an African context; it then discuss issues surrounding integration of faith and STEM; and finally, it draws out implications for the Kenyan public university and theological education.

Key words: biblical worldview, evangelical, faith, integration, naturalism, scientism, STEM, theological education, worldviews

Introduction: Framing the Conversation for a Biblical Worldview for Africa

The "Africa rising" narrative of the first decade of the twenty-first century has multifaceted implications. Economists have observed the increasing significance of the Global South, claiming that Africa houses six of the fastest-growing economies with average rates of growth above 6.5 percent in nations as diverse as Tanzania, DRC, Kenya, Ethiopia, and Rwanda.[1] Not limited to an economic perspective, the global shift southwards has also been observed by missiologists. Some have lamented that the increasing demographic of African Christians may indicate the malaise of a Christianity that is only "an inch deep." Yet this upsurge indicates an opportunity that Africa can carve out in shaping global Christianity as well as through cultural engagement within the wider public sphere.

It is commendable that the Africa Society of Evangelical Theology is, at the time of writing in 2017, seeking constructive ways of framing a theological discourse that is outward-looking in the fields of governance and education, and not merely inward-looking. In the early 1990s, Mark Noll, the notable

---

1. John Mbu, "Despite Headwinds, Africa's Economy Is Still Strong," World Economic Forum, 29 July 2016, accessed 25 October 2016, https://www.weforum.org/agenda/2016/07/african-economic-situation-the-fundamentals-still-remain-strong/.

evangelical historian, sounded the alarm in his magnum opus by beginning with the claim that "the scandal of the evangelical mind is that there is not much of an evangelical mind."[2] Noll lamented that as the modern-day inheritors of the Reformers, evangelicals had abandoned a vibrant intellectual tradition which had borne fruit in the cultivation of the minds and hearts of the Christians in the cultures in which they sojourned. By the phrase "life of the mind" Noll reorients us to the necessity of viewing everything from a Christian worldview, including the arts, politics and governance, engineering and science, as well as culture, in general.[3] Closer to home, the theologian Samuel Waje Kunhiyop voiced similar concerns for the African context. In his summons in the same decade, the principal challenge for African Christianity was to address contemporary existential concerns such as witchcraft, childlessness, and poverty.[4] Twenty years after these calls, while the African theological enterprise has sought to address these cultural issues mostly within the academy, the effect on lay Christians is still in question. A notable danger in such contextualization is syncretism, yet a relevant Christianity is one that "scratches where the modern African is itching."[5]

---

2. Mark Noll, *The Scandal of the Evangelical Mind* (Grand Rapids, MI: Eerdmans, 1994), 1.

3. Worldview thinking has long been proposed more cogently in the writings and works of Abraham Kuyper (*Lectures on Calvinism*) and Herman Bavinck (*Reformed Dogmatics*), which are seeing a contemporary revival. See, for instance, John Bolt, *Bavinck on the Christian Life* (Wheaton, IL: Crossway, 2015). For a more historical treatment of worldviews, see David K. Naugle, *Worldview: The History of a Concept* (Grand Rapids, MI: Eerdmans, 2002). A more popular and introductory work on worldview is James W. Sire, *The Universe Next Door: A Basic Worldview Catalog* (Downers Grove, IL: InterVarsity Press, 1997). For worldview thinking within the context of African traditional religions and way of life, see Yusuf Turaki, *African Traditional Religion and Worldview* (Nairobi: WordAlive, 2006). Although this chapter leans towards a more cognitive approach to worldview, James K. A. Smith observes that the affections are just as necessary. His thesis, which can provide grounds for further research, is that a more embodied perspective of worldview would be largely informed by looking at our rituals, practices, and liturgies; in his own words, "before we articulate a worldview, we worship." See James K. A. Smith, *Desiring the Kingdom: Worship, Worldview and Cultural Formation* (Grand Rapids, MI: Baker Academic, 2009), 33. With particular reference to the public university, he sees educational pedagogies as means of "moral formation," thereby noting that students are formed less by the information given in formal classes and more by relationships, practices, and rituals within their wider educational communities (Smith, *Desiring the Kingdom*, 112). In sum, worldviews are not only a matter of foundational orientations of the mind but are also a matter of the heart. In order to communicate the gospel authentically, we have to bridge scriptural exegesis and cultural exegesis. "We need to learn how to live in a multicontext world, to build bridges of understanding and relationship between different contexts, and to judge between them." See Paul G. Hiebert, *The Gospel in Human Contexts: Anthropological Explorations for Contemporary Missions* (Grand Rapids, MI: Baker, 2009).

4. Samuel Waje Kunhiyop, "Christian Relevance in Modern Africa," *Africa Journal of Evangelical Theology* 16, no. 1 (1997): 3–16.

5. Kunhiyop, "Christian Relevance," 9.

An example from the Western context may be illustrative of what such contextualizing may mean. Alvin Plantinga, a respectable Christian (reformed) philosopher from Notre Dame, acknowledged that "Augustine was right; that the contemporary western intellectual world, like the world of his times, is a battleground or arena in which rages a battle for our souls."[6] He noted the intellectual strongholds of relativism, anti-realism, and scientism that Christian scholarship has to address in a world that is not neutral. Awarded the Templeton Prize in 2017, Plantinga has managed to bring back the discourse on Christian theism to a discipline that has largely been atheistic or at the very least agnostic within the Western historical tradition. To what end, then, can we borrow from Noll's, Kunhiyop's, and Plantinga's concerns to frame this discourse within the context of engineering students in Kenyan public universities?

We propose a reframing of the views long held by some evangelicals on the relationship of science and theology in order to follow Paul's injunction, which bears resemblance to Plantinga's war analogy, to "take every thought captive to obey Christ" (2 Cor 10:3–6). Paul here defends his ministry, acknowledging the opposition, the "strongholds" within his vocational context. While Kunhiyop rightly claims that a relevant Christianity is one that addresses cultural concerns, we would like to bring to attention the crucible within which this unbiblical and secular enculturation occurs – that is, the public universities. From research conducted among youth who have left the church in Nairobi, it was discovered that one of the underlying reasons for their walking away from the church is an increasing view that only scientifically verifiable truths can be relied upon, a perspective that J. P. Moreland terms "scientism."[7] He agrees with Plantinga that scientists do not hold unbiased views, but may sometimes be strongly opposed to a biblical worldview. Moreland critiques this view on science by claiming that science has its limits.[8] A healthy proposal is a multidisciplinary approach that makes use of philosophy, theology, and science in order to reclaim a thoroughly biblical worldview. Within the public university, this multidisciplinary approach would seek to incorporate theology into engineering curricula or make use of theological resources in order to commend the gospel to students who may be intellectually curious.

---

6. Alvin Plantinga, "On Christian Scholarship," in *Christian Scholarship in the Twenty First Century: Prospects and Perils*, eds. Thomas M. Crisp, Steve L. Porter and Gregg A. Ten Elshof (Grand Rapids, MI: Eerdmans, 2014), 18–33.

7. Kevin Muriithi Ndereba, "Youth Worldviews among the De-churched in Nairobi and Implications for Ministry" (Master's thesis, International Leadership University, 2015).

8. J. P. Moreland, *Christianity and the Nature of Science* (Grand Rapids, MI: Baker, 1989), 137.

Integration of Engineering Education and a Biblical Worldview

Is engineering education neutral with regards to a biblical worldview? It is not uncommon to hear of students within STEM (Science, Technology, Engineering, and Mathematics) disciplines being dissuaded by their professors from bringing their religious convictions to the classroom. While this is not a generalization amongst all STEM students, the view that science and faith are incompatible presents a strong case, not only within the classroom but also within churches. Such intellectual laziness is what Paul Bowers, in his 2008 Byang Kato memorial lecture, sought to respond to in retrieving Kato's "discipleship of the mind" which is, in Bower's words, "theologically vibrant, biblically sound, and sensitively suited to the contextual realities of modern Africa, including the modern African intellectual context."[9] Yet, given the scientific context that Africa finds itself in, there are different views on this science–faith topic and its implications for students in public universities. To illustrate the divergent views of faith and science amongst those who identify as evangelicals, note this survey among 10,000 US adults by the sociologist Elaine Howard Ecklund: "48 percent [of the respondents] view science and religion as complementary . . . 21 percent view the two worldviews as entirely independent of one another. About 30 percent see these worldviews in opposition."[10] By claiming that science and faith are "independent of one another," the 21 percent in the study are not clear whether this independence is contradictory or complementary. Further, the survey is based on a Western context, and parallels to the African context cannot be hastily made. A more robust integration of faith and science may be considered from an African Christian worldview. The science–faith dichotomy is a huge concern in the West. This may draw from the Platonic dualism recovered in the seventeenth and eighteenth centuries, which in the modern worldview continues to separate the empirical from the experiential. Paul Hiebert's life contribution to this pertinent topic of cultural worldviews has had a monumental impact on the theory and praxis of missions. He proposed the consideration of other cultural "schemas of reality" and how this transforms integration. An African approach to finding a solution to this false dichotomy can be found in the perspective of holism that is underpinned in the African worldview. This certainly means

9. Paul Bowers, "Christian Intellectual Responsibilities in Modern Africa," *Africa Journal of Evangelical Theology* 28, no. 2 (2009): 91–114.

10. Cathy Lynn Grossman, "70 Percent of Evangelicals Believe Religion and Science Are Not in Conflict," HuffPost, 16 March 2015, accessed 7 January 2017, https://www.huffingtonpost.com/2015/03/16/evangelicals-religion-science_n_6880356.html?guccounter=1.

that our theology must be rooted in the lived experience of a people group. Work and prayer can intermingle as much as human history and cosmic history should. Although some may see the faith–science dichotomy as rooted in the Western academy, the proliferation of new media means that it affects even the African context, necessitating the assessment of the same from a biblical worldview.

The above survey points to the effects of dichotomy in the academy when students are unable to relate their technical knowledge to their religious, and more specifically, biblical, convictions. Jame Schaefer and Paul Heidebrecht attempt an integration of technology and faith within Catholic institutions.[11] They affirm that the two disciplines can enrich each other, so that STEM practitioners may not only be technically astute but also have a well-rounded ethical and holistic outlook in their life and practice. A reformed outlook can also borrow from the doctrine of vocation in Martin Luther's and John Calvin's works. Timothy R. Tuinstra proposes that instilling vocational thinking in engineering students can help them see their profession as a sacred calling, for serving the community for the glory of Christ.[12] One might think that STEM disciplines are amoral, as they make use of first principles of logic and mathematics, yet their epistemological roots are embedded in the Judeo-Christian worldview.[13] In the absence of such biblical integration, STEM may be used to promote materialistic gains to maintain social mobility, critique the integration of good science with faith, and foster economic development without the deeper flourishing of the human person in Christ (see John 10:10).

Take, for instance, the medical strike in Kenya at the close of 2016 and beginning of 2017 that left many innocent people as casualties. The underlying issue seems to have been lack of justice extended to the healthcare industry in terms of better and sufficient equipment, requisite pay to facilitate healthcare professionalism, and the government keeping its word in being a crucial stakeholder in the process of healthcare delivery to Kenya's citizens. Yet while these issues did need to be resolved, it seems that the ethical dilemma of risking lives found neither empathy within the consciences of the doctors nor

---

11. Jame Schaefer and Paul C. Heidebrecht, "Pursuing Dialogue between Theologians and Engineers," in *Engineering Education and Practice: Embracing a Catholic Vision*, ed. James Heft and K. P. Hallinan (Notre Dame, IN: University of Notre Dame Press, 2012), 118–139.

12. Timothy R. Tuinstra, "Applying the Reformational Doctrine of Christian Vocation to Our Understanding of Engineering as a Sacred Calling," *Engineering and Computer Science Faculty Publications* 58 (2006): 85–92, http://digitalcommons.cedarville.edu/engineering_and_computer_science_publications/58.

13. Timothy R. Tuinstra, "God and the Engineer: An Integration Paper," *Faculty Integration Papers* 4 (2012): 1–11, http://digitalcommons.cedarville.edu/faculty_integration_papers/4.

agreement with the Hippocratic Oath that is central to the medical profession. In view of this, where was the moral compass among these STEM practitioners?

The compass can be drawn by theologians as they pursue the task of integration. Apart from exegeting the Word, they need to understand the methods, purposes, and limitations of certain technologies in order to better develop and apply their theology in the context of a scientifically driven world. Additionally, a proper theology of work that considers the following is crucial for such biblically based integration:

1. As we are imagers of God with the ability to know, science is created by God to aid in human flourishing that is in line with God's mandate.

2. The mandate to "have dominion" (Gen 1:26) implies not only a cultural mandate but also a mandate to Christian scientists to serve society for God's purposes.

3. The fall affects technological advancements when STEM practitioners seek to separate their work from God's providence. Separated from God, the STEM agenda may only be a contemporary form of idolatry.

4. Those who are redeemed by Jesus Christ can use their STEM disciplines and spheres of influence in the restoration of the cosmos, through gospel proclamation and practical mission.

This creation-fall-redemption-glorification model anchors STEM within God's mission for the world. If the theological enterprise itself uses scientific methods – for instance, by using the Bible and culture (to different extents within various traditions) as data for theologizing; and by using certain methodologies and propositional assumptions – why should we cast away science? Although one gets a hint that Augustine may have held to an incompatible faith–science view by preferring to call theology *sapienta* (wisdom) as opposed to *scientia* (knowledge), Thomas Aquinas's "Theology as the queen of the sciences" several decades after the theologian of Carthage speaks to a possible integration.[14] Yet it is necessary to observe that no one is neutral with regards to biblical convictions, not even in the context of the science–faith dialogue. Vern Poythress, a reformed theologian and mathematician, claims:

> We who are believers in Christ are already presupposing our loyalty to Christ and the truth about Christ presented in the Bible.

---

14. Millard J. Erickson, *Christian Theology* (Grand Rapids, MI: Baker, 1985), 33.

The involvement of presuppositions is not an intellectual game. It is not just an exercise in logic, in which someone proposes, "Let us explore in a disinterested way where various presuppositions lead." It is a requirement for Christian discipleship. A disciple, as we have observed . . . is *committed* . . . The whole person is involved. No one is religiously neutral.[15]

Although the scientific enterprise is a good of creation, the ramifications of the fall affect this exploration by reducing it to selfish aims, idolizing creation, and thus obliterating the creator–creature distinctions. Only through the redemption of Jesus Christ can this distinction be clarified and STEM professionals be enabled to use their gifts in restoring God's cosmic world. It is clear that an evangelical voice that takes seriously the role of the Bible in light of the STEM agenda should be heard in the cacophony of different voices. The Bible itself takes into account the scientific presuppositions undergirded by a providential God in Psalm 19 and Romans 1:18–32.

From these verses, it is clear that general revelation and the scientific enterprise that makes that clearer – for instance, in astronomy – point to the fact that there is intelligent design in creation, in agreement with the teleological view in Christian theology. Yet the fact that there are astronomers who dispute the fact of God's existence shows that no one is neutral. In this regard, special revelation is necessary for anyone to know God. Poythress argues that while general revelation may hint of a God who is there, the "verbal revelation" of the Scriptures is necessary for displaying to human beings God's power, providence, and plan for salvation.[16] He goes on: "because of the prestige of modern science, we experience a strong temptation to imagine either that we do not really need the Bible to understand the natural world, or that it plays at best a minor, incidental role."[17] A reclamation of the biblical worldview is fundamental to mission within the context of Kenyan public universities as well as theological institutions.

---

15. Foreword to John M. Frame, *Apologetics: A Justification of Christian Belief*, ed. Joseph E. Torres (Phillipsburg, NJ: P&R, 2015).

16. Vern S. Poythress, *Redeeming Science: A God-Centered Approach* (Wheaton, IL: Crossway, 2006), 38.

17. Poythress, *Redeeming Science*, 48.

Implications of Integrating Faith and STEM

Re-evaluating Theological Education and Curriculum

Quoting the classic theologian Thomas Oden, Kunhiyop elsewhere makes the case that retrieving the African contribution to Western theology can allow us to address afresh issues unique to the continent of Africa.[18] One of the areas that is pertinent in this matter is theological and ministerial education. In light of this, the author of this chapter suggests incorporation of technological issues or themes into theological curricula. A couple of factors inform this suggestion: First, according to a 2012 report, mobile phone penetration in the country sits at 75.4 percent.[19] Second, with the availability of such a resource comes ethical issues such as the ones we have experienced in the past few years, such as social media bullying, pornography, and gambling.

The author envisions the incorporation of units that tackle topics on technological issues within the African context. While most ministry training for lay and ordained leaders may not be in contexts that necessitate this, it should be a requirement for those working in urban contexts. Further sociologists have observed that the Internet is reshaping interpersonal relations as well as the idea of community, despite the fact that African scholars have long observed that individuality in Africa is a subset of the community. How do we then respond to the Scripture that reminds us: "And let us consider how to stir up one another to love and good works, not neglecting to meet together, as is the habit of some, but encouraging one another, and all the more as you see the Day drawing near" (Heb 10:24–25)? What implications does this have for the political, tribal, and ethical diatribes that have been synonymous with social media sites? What role do ministers and church leaders have to play in being "ambassadorial reconcilers," to use Paul's words in 2 Corinthians 5:11–21, in this context? In what ways can technology be used for evangelism and discipleship? Theological reflections in light of our technological context are both necessary and relevant.

---

18. Samuel W. Kunhiyop, "Challenges and Prospects of Teaching Theology in Africa," *Southern Baptist Journal of Theology* 15, no. 2 (2011): 64–76.

19. iHub Research and Research Solutions Africa, "Mobile Usage at the Base of the Pyramid in Kenya" (Nairobi: infoDev/The World Bank, 2012), accessed 25 January 2017, http://www.infodev.org/sites/default/files/final_kenya_bop_study_web_jan_02_2013_0.pdf.

Re-engaging the Public University

As the crucible in which students pursuing STEM courses are formed, public universities can be catalysts for such integration. First, undergraduate and postgraduate students can have units in theology and ethics as core courses – for instance, "Engineering as a Vocation." This will give students the ethical and vocational underpinnings for their life and practice. Second, societies such as the Africa Society of Evangelical Theology (ASET) can serve as a collaboration between the theoretical and practical exploration of theology and STEM disciplines by developing seminars and conferences that tackle the intersection of these topics. This would in a sense "redeem" science from the pitfalls of secular humanism and naturalistic worldviews that permeate scientific discourse. Apologetics Kenya has done just this through campus engagement in the public sphere, through quarterly lectures and fora.

Ian Barbour, the American scholar of science and religion, recognized in his Gifford Lectures that "our value priorities and our vision of the good life" would determine the types of technology we develop to deal with sustainable agriculture, renewable energy, and reforestation, themes that are as pertinent to the Majority World as much as they are at the locus of global development.[20] In sum, theologians can provide the theological resources to formulate curricula that can be useful for STEM students within public universities. By reclaiming a biblical worldview, these implications serve to deepen the impact of scientific knowledge and development for the cultivation of the world, as God's Eden being restored. This reclamation necessitates the collaboration of evangelicals and Christians within diverse disciplines for their mutual enrichment.

Conclusion

In summary, the author has used the example of the medical practitioners strikes to show that STEM education can no longer afford to be neutral, even with its distinguished role in Kenya's national development. Reclaiming a biblical worldview will give STEM students the ethical and salvific anchors that are crucial for their life and practice. Moreover, placing STEM within its proper place of a biblical worldview commends the gospel as the proper means of liberation and human flourishing in the lives of those whose work falls within STEM disciplines. Additionally, in reclaiming a holistic perspective on faith and science, the contribution of the African worldview cannot be ignored.

---

20. Ian Barbour, *Ethics in an Age of Technology*, Gifford Lectures 1990–1991(San Francisco: Harper, 1993).

The result is an enrichment of a theology of work, in which STEM practitioners see their work through the lens of the sustainability and restoration of the cosmos in the person of Jesus Christ.

Collaboration between theology and STEM disciplines can allow both theologians and other practitioners to enrich each other's work and ministries, in education, government, church, culture, and media, as part of God's redemptive purposes. At the very least, it would offer an apologetic against the argument of the incompatibility of faith and science that many students use as a crutch for their unbelief. In the long run, this may lead to the breaking down of barriers by increasing receptivity to the gospel message under the guidance of the Holy Spirit. To reclaim the biblical worldview for students of engineering within the Kenyan public universities would ultimately be reclaiming their lives for Jesus Christ, who has come to deal with their fallen nature, to renew their minds from distorted worldviews, and to offer abundance, in this life and the next. Integrating a biblical worldview and STEM in theological curricula is crucial to the flourishing of the church's ministry that is at once relevant, contextual, biblical, and balanced.

Bibliography

Barbour, Ian. *Ethics in an Age of Technology*. Gifford Lectures 1990–1991. San Francisco: Harper, 1993.

Bolt, John. *Bavinck on the Christian Life*. Wheaton, IL: Crossway, 2015.

Bowers, Paul. "Christian Intellectual Responsibilities in Modern Africa." *Africa Journal of Evangelical Theology* 28, no. 2 (2009): 91–114.

Erickson, Millard J. *Christian Theology*. Grand Rapids, MI: Baker, 1985.

Frame, John M. *Apologetics: A Justification of Christian Belief*, edited by Joseph E. Torres. Phillipsburg, NJ: P&R, 2015.

Grossman, Cathy Lynn. "70 Percent of Evangelicals Believe Religion and Science Are Not in Conflict." HuffPost, 16 March 2015. Accessed 7 January 2017. https://www. huffingtonpost.com/2015/03/16/evangelicals-religion-science_n_6880356.html.

Hiebert, Paul G. *Anthropological Reflections on Missiological Issues*. Grand Rapids, MI: Baker, 1994.

———. *The Gospel in Human Contexts: Anthropological Explorations for Contemporary Missions*. Grand Rapids, MI: Baker, 2009.

iHub Research and Research Solutions Africa. "Mobile Usage at the Base of the Pyramid in Kenya." Nairobi: infoDev/The World Bank, 2012. Accessed 25 January 2017. http://www.infodev.org/en/TopicPublications.34.html.

Kärkkäinen, Kiira, and Stéphan Vincent-Lancrin. "Sparking Innovation in STEM Education with Technology and Collaboration: A Case Study of the HP Catalyst

Initiative Centre." *OECD Education Working Papers* 91. Accessed 21 October 2016. http://dx.doi.org/10.1787/5k480sj9k442-en.

Kioko, Jackson Musyoka. "Causes of Building Failures in Africa: A Case Study on Collapsing Structures in Kenya." *IOSR Journal of Mechanical and Civil Engineering* 11, no. 3 (2014): 9–10.

Kunhiyop, Samuel Waje. "Challenges and Prospects of Teaching Theology in Africa." *Southern Baptist Journal of Theology* 15, no. 2 (2011): 64–76.

———. "Christian Relevance in Modern Africa." *Africa Journal of Evangelical Theology* 16, no. 1 (1997): 3–16.

Mbu, John. "Despite Headwinds, Africa's Economy Is Still Strong." World Economic Forum, 29 July 2016. Accessed 25 October 2016. https://www.weforum.org/agenda/2016/07/african-economic-situation-the-fundamentals-still-remain-strong/.

Moreland, J. P. *Christianity and the Nature of Science*. Grand Rapids, MI: Baker, 1989.

Naugle, David K. *Worldview: The History of a Concept*. Grand Rapids, MI: Eerdmans, 2002.

Ndereba, Kevin Muriithi. "Youth Worldviews among the De-churched in Nairobi and Implications for Ministry." Master's thesis, International Leadership University, 2015.

Noll, Mark. *The Scandal of the Evangelical Mind*. Grand Rapids, MI: Eerdmans, 1994.

Plantinga, Alvin. "On Christian Scholarship." In *Christian Scholarship in the Twenty First Century: Prospects and Perils*, eds. Thomas M. Crisp, Steve L. Porter and Gregg A. Ten Elshof, 18–33. Grand Rapids, MI: Eerdmans, 2014.

Poythress, Vern S. *Redeeming Science: A God-Centered Approach*. Wheaton, IL: Crossway, 2006.

Schaefer, Jame, and Paul C. Heidebrecht. "Pursuing Dialogue between Theologians and Engineers." In *Engineering Education and Practice: Embracing a Catholic Vision*, edited by James Heft and K. P. Hallinan, 118–139. Notre Dame, IN: University of Notre Dame Press, 2012.

Sire, James W. *The Universe Next Door: A Basic Worldview Catalog*. Downers Grove, IL: InterVarsity Press, 1997.

Smith, James K. A. *Desiring the Kingdom: Worship, Worldview and Cultural Formation*. Grand Rapids, MI: Baker Academic, 2009.

Tuinstra, Timothy R. "Applying the Reformational Doctrine of Christian Vocation to Our Understanding of Engineering as a Sacred Calling." *Engineering and Computer Science Faculty Publications* 58 (2006): 85–92. http://digitalcommons.cedarville.edu/engineering_and_computer_science_publications/58.

———. "God and the Engineer: An Integration Paper." *Faculty Integration Papers* 4 (2012): 1–11. http://digitalcommons.cedarville.edu/faculty_integration_papers/4.

Turaki, Yusufu. *African Traditional Religion and Worldview*. Nairobi: WordAlive, 2006.

8

Susanna Wesley: What Can She Teach Christian Educators in Africa?

Gregory Crofford
Dean of the School of Religion and Christian Ministry, Africa Nazarene University

Abstract

Susanna Wesley (1669–1742) is remembered primarily for being the mother of Methodism's co-founders, John and Charles Wesley. Methodism's matriarch grew up in an age when young girls were occupied primarily with keeping house. As such, they were rarely educated beyond the basic rudiments of reading and writing. Young Susanna, however, was shaped in the Puritan environment of her father Samuel Annesley's home, giving her a deep piety and a lifelong love of learning.

As the mother of nineteen children – only seven of whom lived to maturity – Susanna Wesley left an indelible imprint upon her progeny, both spiritually and educationally. Wesley read the writings of philosopher John Locke (1632–1704). In her 1732 letter "On Educating My Children," Wesley describes the methods she used to educate her children, methods that echo Locke's influential 1693 *Some Thoughts Concerning Education*. However, the author of this chapter observes that Wesley sometimes modified Locke's precepts in important ways, supplementing them with principles from her own Puritan upbringing, which resulted in an effective formula for Christian education. Notable among these modifications were her egalitarian views on the primary-level education of boys and girls, an aspect conspicuously absent from Locke's treatise. A devoted Christian, she also incorporated the memorization of Scripture into her lessons, providing a timeless model for the catechesis of young children.

The chapter closes with a brief application of Susanna Wesley's educational principles to twenty-first-century sub-Saharan Africa. Paramount is Wesley's conviction that children as young as age three are capable of understanding spiritual things and should be encouraged to memorize Scripture. Further, parents can teach children to read as early as age five, as practiced by Wesley. African families should feel free to adapt Wesley's practices to their own context, helping to build a strong foundation for the Christian education of young people.

Key words: Susanna Wesley, Puritan, Methodism, Christian education, Africa, Locke, memorization, Scripture

Introduction

Susanna Wesley (1669–1742) was the mother of John and Charles Wesley, the co-founders of Methodism. Though Mrs Wesley was theologically adept,[1] it was as the "Mother of Methodism" that Susanna made an enduring impact.[2] It is especially her methodology for educating young children that has drawn sustained attention. A number of studies have described those practices. However, this chapter will go further, interpreting Susanna Wesley's 1732 letter "On Educating My Children" through the lens of philosopher John Locke (1632–1704), specifically his influential 1693 *Some Thoughts Concerning Education*. The closing section of the chapter will draw lessons from Susanna Wesley's educational philosophy that are applicable in twenty-first-century Africa.

The Puritan Home as Church

To understand Susanna Wesley's educational practices, it is helpful to know something about the soil in which her faith and worldview took root. The

---

1. See Charles Wallace Jr., ed., *Susanna Wesley: The Complete Writings* (New York: Oxford University Press, 1997), where Susanna's theological acumen is apparent in letters and treatises. In a century more affirming of broader roles for women, she could have served as a pastor or university lecturer.

2. See, for example, Mabel R. Brailsford, *Susanna Wesley: The Mother of Methodism* (London: Epworth, 1938). The title is also used by Elizabeth Hart in "Finding the Real Susanna: Portraits of Susanna Wesley," *American Theological Library Association Summary of Proceedings* 45 (1991): 152–172; ATLA Religion Database with ATLASerials, EBSCOhost; accessed 14 February 2017.

daughter of Dr Samuel Annesley (1620–1696) – whom Richard Heitzenrater called "a noted nonconformist minister in London in the late 17th century"[3] – Susanna grew up as one of twenty-five children in a "spirited and lively family."[4] John Newton takes pains to debunk the myth that Puritan homes like that of the Annesleys would have been characterized by "unsmiling austerity." Yet he acknowledges that the Puritan ideal (as taught, for example, by Richard Baxter in his 1656 *The Reformed Pastor*) was that of the home as a community of faith. Newton explains: "If the Church was seen in terms of a home or family, then the converse was also true, and for the Puritan, the family was a microcosm of the Church. Home religion was quite central to Puritan piety, which was by no means focused solely on the pulpit."[5] In such a large family, Susanna would have come to know the comforting rhythms of Scripture reading and prayer, disciplines that she would one day inculcate in her own children as the wife of a Church of England priest in rural England.

From London to Epworth

Commenting on Susanna Wesley's education, Robert Monk observes: "The Annesley home was an outstanding example of a Puritan household where demanding educational standards accompanied disciplined devotional and moral training."[6] The Puritanism of her birth family shaped Susanna Wesley both spiritually and educationally. However, at age thirteen, she left the Nonconformist church of her father and joined the Church of England.[7] In 1688, she married Samuel Wesley, and following his brief service as a Navy chaplain and five years as rector in South Ormsby, Lincolnshire, the family (now with children) settled in 1695 in the isolated town of Epworth, where Samuel would serve as rector until his death in 1735.[8] The sometimes tumultuous relationship between the intelligent but mercurial clergyman and his gifted wife – which included a year-long separation over a political

---

3. Richard P. Heitzenrater, *John Wesley and the People Called Methodists*, 2nd ed. (Nashville: Abingdon, 2013), 28.

4. John A. Newton, *Susanna Wesley and the Puritan Tradition in Methodism*, 2nd ed. (London: Epworth, 2002), 43–44.

5. Newton, *Susanna Wesley*, 50.

6. Robert C. Monk, *John Wesley: His Puritan Heritage* (Nashville: Abingdon, 1966), 21.

7. Newton, *Susanna Wesley*, 57.

8. Henry Rack, *Reasonable Enthusiast: John Wesley and the Rise of Methodism*, 3rd ed. (London: Epworth, 2002), 47–48.

disagreement[9] – nevertheless resulted in nineteen children, of whom only four daughters and three sons reached maturity.[10] It was here that Susanna took up the task of providing a rudimentary education to her daughters and sons, a duty performed with love and zeal amidst the busy life of a country parish and managing the varied needs of a burgeoning household.

Qualifications for the Educational Task

Charles Wallace notes the educational disadvantage that girls faced at the time of Susanna Annesley's birth and how she was an outlier:

> Reading and writing, teaching and learning were not unknown among women of Susanna Wesley's generation, but quantitative studies confirm contemporary observations that female intellectual attainments lagged far behind those of males. Women had little access to formal education, were less literate than men, and their published writings were minuscule compared to the total output of the era. Susanna Wesley was therefore in the well-educated minority of women who could read and write and teach, albeit mostly within her own family.[11]

Wallace details the books that Susanna Wesley read, primarily from her access to the libraries of her father, Dr Samuel Annesley, and her husband, Samuel Wesley, Sr. These included an emphasis upon Puritan and Anglican divines such as Bishops Pearson and Beveridge, Henry Scougal, Jeremy Taylor, John Norris, Richard Lucas, and Richard Baxter. Thomas à Kempis's

---

9. Susanna considered King William III a "usurper" of the English throne that belonged by heredity to James II. When Susanna neglected to respond "amen" to Samuel's dinner-table prayer for King William III, and subsequent conversation revealed Susanna's thoughts on the matter, her husband concluded: "If we have two kings, we must have two beds." The rector soon left for London, where he remained for a year before he returned to Epworth and the couple was reconciled. See Newton, *Susanna Wesley*, 86–93. Patrick Oden concludes: "Yet, in their disagreement about all manner of topics, Susanna remained loyal to Samuel in public and in private." In Patrick Oden, "'Let Us Not Spend Our Time in Trifling': Susanna Wesley, A Mother to Her Sons," *Wesleyan Theological Journal* 48, no. 2 (September 2013): 118, ATLA Religion Database with ATLASerials, EBSCOhost, accessed 14 February 2017.

10. Rack, *Reasonable Enthusiast*, 48. John Wesley grew up in what Rack calls a "predominantly female household." For an account of the mostly unfortunate lives of Susanna's four daughters who lived to adulthood, see Samuel J. Rogal, "The Epworth Women: Susanna Wesley and Her Daughters," *Wesleyan Theological Journal* 18, no. 2 (September 1983): 80–89, ATLA Religion Database with ATLASerials, EBSCOhost, accessed 14 February 2017.

11. Charles Wallace, Jr., "'Some Stated Employment of Your Mind': Reading, Writing, and Religion in the Life of Susanna Wesley," *Church History* 58, no. 3 (September 1989): 355, ATLA Religion Database with ATLASerials, EBSCOhost, accessed 14 February 2017.

The Imitation of Christ and Lorenzo Scupoli's *Spiritual Combat* likewise were two Roman Catholic writings that influenced her, alongside Blaise Pascal's celebrated *Pensées*.[12]

However, most significant for our purposes is the influence that John Locke appears to have played in shaping Susanna Wesley's views on childrearing. Wallace observes: "Most notably, she read, quoted, and wrestled with the philosophical giant of the age, John Locke."[13]

Charles Wallace cautions that Susanna Wesley's reading of Pascal and Locke does not necessarily prove their impact upon her. Nonetheless, this chapter asserts the likelihood of John Locke's influence by comparing strands of thought contained in Locke's 1693 *Some Thoughts Concerning Education* with the educational methods employed by Wesley, especially as outlined in her 24 July 1732 letter "On Educating My Family."[14] The validity of this line of inquiry is further bolstered by Martha Bowden, who notes regarding the "regular method of living" referenced in Wesley's letter: "Given the importance of Lockean thought in eighteenth-century educational theories, we can assume an intended train of association, from the Rectory at Epworth, to the Holy Club at Oxford, to the ministry of the Wesleys throughout England and eventually to the colonies."[15] In light of Locke's general influence as affirmed by Wallace and Bowden, let us turn to an examination of Susanna Wesley's pedagogical methods. Our task will be to evaluate her educational precepts from the aforementioned 1693 Locke treatise as they are echoed, and sometimes modified, in Wesley's 1732 letter.

Susanna Wesley's 1732 Letter "On Educating My Children"

On 24 July 1732, Susanna Wesley penned a lengthy letter to her son, John.[16] She was responding to a request from John, who as an adult appreciated his

---

12. Wallace, "Some Stated Employment," 356–357.

13. Wallace, 357. Wallace adds: "She was particularly intrigued by the *Essay Concerning Human Understanding* and the way that Locke's theories could serve religion. From her point of view, Locke's empiricism might free Christians from the necessity of basing their religion on innate principles."

14. The letter appears in Wallace, *Susanna Wesley*, 369–376.

15. Martha F. Bowden, "Susanna Wesley's Educational Method," *Journal of the Canadian Church Historical Society* 44, no. 1 (2002): 53, ATLA Religion Database with ATLASerials, EBSCOhost, accessed 14 February 2017.

16. In *Susanna Wesley: The Complete Writings*, 369–376. Charles Wallace reproduces the 1 August 1742 letter from John Wesley, *The Works of John Wesley*, Vol. 19, *Journal and Diaries II (1738–42)*, ed. W. Reginald Ward and Richard P. Heitzenrater (Nashville: Abingdon, 1990), 462–464.

mother's earlier methods.[17] The resulting essay was what Charles Wallace calls "arguably the most influential of Susanna Wesley's writings."[18] The opening paragraph details Susanna's "regular method" as implemented from her children's birth:

> The children were always put into a regular method of living, in such things as they were capable of, from their birth: as in dressing, undressing, changing their linen, etc. The first quarter commonly passes in sleep. After that, they were, if possible, laid into their cradles awake and rocked to sleep; and so they were kept rocking till it was time for them to awake. This was done to bring them to a regular course of sleeping; which at first was three hours in the morning and three in the afternoon; afterwards two hours, till they needed none at all.[19]

"A Regular Method of Living"

Methodical regularity in all things is woven throughout the letter. This is seen in the careful scheduling of the day's activities, including set prayer times, mealtimes, and bedtimes. Susanna Wesley understood the importance of structure for the psychological well-being of a child. These boundaries extended to prohibitions against eating between meals or calling in a loud voice for food around the table. Wesley clarifies: "Instead, if they wanted aught they used to whisper to the maid which attended them, who came and spake to me."[20] This is a softening of John Locke's admonition in *Some Thoughts Concerning Education*, which allowed no such requests whatsoever: "I have seen children at a table, who, whatever was there, never asked for anything, but contentedly took what was given them; and at another place, I have seen others cry for every thing they saw, must be served out of every dish, and that first too. What made this vast difference, but this; that one was accustomed to have what they called or cried for, the other to go without it?"[21] Respecting the general

---

17. Elizabeth Hart, "Susanna Annesley Wesley: An Able Divine," *Touchstone* 6, no. 2 (May 1988): 10, ATLA Religion Database with ATLASerials, EBSCOhost, accessed 14 February 2017.

18. Hart, "Susanna Annesley Wesley," 367.

19. Hart, 369.

20. Hart, 369.

21. John Locke, in *Some Thoughts Concerning Education* (London: A&J Churchill, 1693), accessed 16 February 2017, http://www.sophia-project.org/uploads/1/3/9/5/13955288/locke_education.pdf.

principle from Locke, Wesley modified it in such a way that she maintained its value without slavishly following his advice to the letter.

"Conquering the Will"

A controversial element in the letter is what Susanna Wesley termed "conquering the will." She clarifies: "I insist upon conquering the will of children betimes, because this is the only strong and rational foundation of a religious education, without which both precept and example will be ineffectual." Later, she insists: "Break the will, if you would not damn the child." Citing David Naglee, Martha Bowden notes that "breaking the will" does not mean the "extinction of personality." Rather, it is the "elimination of selfishness."[22] Yet does this take into account the severe tone in parts of the five paragraphs allotted to the topic? In Wesley's view, a child from a year old must be taught to "fear the rod and cry softly." Indeed, to make a child obedient, it is better to "whip him ten times running" if necessary.[23] Maldwyn Edwards justifies the severity by noting that Mrs Wesley believed that a child who refused to be subject first to the will of the parent would not later be subject to the will of God.[24] Though the word is not used, what Wesley wrote in regard to conquering the will clearly addresses not routine childish antics but rebellion. As such, Wesley's method was a corrective to the rebellious child whose disobedience was a direct affront to parental authority.

The echo of John Locke's *Some Thoughts Concerning Education* is clear. On the one hand, Locke was critical of parents who overused the rod for routine correction, noting: "For I am very apt to think, that great severity of punishment does but very little good; nay, great harm in education: and I believe it will be found, that, *caeteris paribus* [all else being equal], those children who have been most chastised, seldom make the best men."[25] Since in Locke's view children are rational creatures, when confronted by their "lies" or other "ill-natured tricks," for example, he advised the use of shaming as an effective remedy.[26] On the other hand, he does allow for corporal punishment in the case of rebellion, or obstinacy. Locke clarifies:

---

22. Bowden, "Susanna Wesley's Educational Method," 60.

23. Charles Wallace, *Susanna Wesley*, 370.

24. Maldwyn Edwards, *Family Circle: A Study of the Epworth Household in Relation to John and Charles Wesley* (London: Epworth, 1961), 65.

25. Locke, *Some Thoughts Concerning Education*, paragraph 43.

26. Locke, paragraph 85.

But stubbornness and an obstinate disobedience must be mastered with force and blows: for this there is no other remedy. Whatever particular action you bid him do, or forbear, you must be sure to see yourself obeyed; no quarter in this case, no resistance. For when once it comes to be a trial of skill, a contest for mastery betwixt you, as it is, if you command, and he refuses, you must be sure to carry it, whatever blows it costs, if a nod or words will not prevail; unless, for ever after, you intend to live in obedience to your son.[27]

What Locke termed "obstinacy," Wesley called "self-will." Where Locke largely avoided religious terminology in *Some Thoughts Concerning Education*,[28] Susanna had no such compunction, calling self-will "the root of all sin and misery, so whatever cherishes this in children ensures their after-wretchedness and irreligion; whatever checks and mortifies it promotes their future happiness and piety."[29] Wesley viewed self-will as incipient rebellion and therefore was willing to employ what some may consider drastic measures to nip it in the bud.

"None of Them Was Taught to Read Till Five Years Old"

John Locke had advised: "When he can talk, 'tis time he should begin to learn to read."[30] Yet Susanna Wesley ignored the advice, in part because of a negative experience with her daughter, Kezzy. Having been "overruled," Susanna began teaching Kezzy to read at an unspecified earlier age. Susanna laments regarding her daughter: "She was more years learning than any of the rest had been months."[31] Summarizing the mother's method, John Tyson comments:

John and Charles Wesley first encountered and absorbed the Bible in the little school that their mother, Susanna Annsley [sic] Wesley (1669–1742), conducted in their home in Epworth, England. All of the Wesley children were home-schooled through the primary grades, due largely to financial necessity, and they were taught to read from the premier literary work in their house – the Bible. At

---

27. Locke, paragraph 78.

28. Only paragraph 137 addresses religion, under the heading of "God." The paragraph speaks in generic terms of God as the "Supreme Being," "Author," and "Maker," and the one "from whom we receive all good, who loves us and gives us all things."

29. Wallace, *Susanna Wesley*, 370.

30. Locke, *Some Thoughts Concerning Education*, paragraph 148.

31. Wallace, *Susanna Wesley*, 371.

the tender age of five, each child was taught to read, by beginning in Genesis and working their way through the Bible, under mother's watchful eye and encouraging instruction.[32]

To encourage youthful learning, Locke had advised: "There may be dice and play-things, with the letters on them, to teach children the alphabet by playing; and twenty other ways may be found, suitable to their particular tempers, to make this kind of learning a sport to them."[33] There is no evidence in Susanna Wesley's letter that she adopted Locke's creative suggestions when it came to teaching her children to read. Instead, within the space of six hours on a single day, her children were making their first faltering steps in reading, knowing all of their letters. Her son Samuel was reading verses from Genesis 1 on the next day.[34] In a bustling household where multiple children no doubt vied for the attention of their mother, one can surmise that Susanna's success was due in part to the child's anticipation of having dedicated time with a parent. The ability to read became a birthday present without monetary cost but of great worth.

Education for Both Boys and Girls

In John Locke's *Some Thoughts Concerning Education*, the language throughout the treatise speaks only of "he" and "him." Débora Barbosa Agra Junker notes: "In this work, Locke's primary concern is the education of gentlemen and members of the aristocracy . . . he ignores the existence of girls and fosters an unequal distribution of education where women and those who do not belong to the aristocracy would have limited access to education, or would be completely left out of the process altogether."[35]

Susanna Wesley was doubtless aware of this anti-female bias in childhood education. Her letter "On Educating My Family" ends with eight "bylaws" summarizing some of the fine points of the comportment she instilled in her offspring. The final bylaw is explicit:

---

32. John R. Tyson, *The Way of the Wesleys: A Short Introduction* (Grand Rapids, MI: Eerdmans, 2014), 1.

33. Locke, *Some Thoughts Concerning Education*, paragraph 148.

34. Wallace, *Susanna Wesley*, 371.

35. Débora B. Agra Junker, "Beyond the Domestication of Pedagogy: Envisioning New Perspectives on Education," *Encounter* 74, no. 3 (2014): 53, ATLA Religion Database with ATLASerials, EBSCOhost, accessed 18 February 2017.

8. That no girl be taught to work till she can read very well; and then that she be kept to her work with the same application, and for the same time, that she was held to reading. This rule is also much to be observed; for the putting children to learn sewing before they can read perfectly is the very reason why so few women can read fit to be heard, and never to be well understood.[36]

Unfortunately, this advocacy for educating young girls did not extend to higher education. Martha Bowden calls Susanna Wesley "of her own time in the sense that she did not protest against her daughters' exclusion from the universities, much less from preaching or ordination, but she did give them an education equal with her brothers at home."[37]

Catechesis as Education

Susanna Wesley was not merely an educator. Rather, she provided *Christian* education. In "On Educating My Family," she details the content of instruction: "The children of this family were taught, as soon as they could speak, the Lord's Prayer, which they were made to say at rising, and bedtime constantly; to which, as they grew bigger, were added a short prayer for their parents, and some collects; a short catechism, and some portion of Scripture, as their memory could bear."[38] While Wesley was not willing to follow John Locke's advice to teach children to read as soon as they could talk, she nevertheless proved that non-literate children are more than capable of memorization at such a tender age.

Richard Baxter's 1656 *The Reformed Pastor* includes a seventeen-point section on the duty of the pastor to catechize the children of the church.[39] By catechizing her own children at home, Susanna Wesley was fulfilling what many in her time considered a pastoral duty. Besides "On Educating My Children," Charles Wallace's collection includes Wesley's expositions on the Apostles' Creed and the Ten Commandments (both written to her daughter Susanna, or "Suky"), plus a question-and-answer treatise structured as a conversation with

---

36. Wallace, *Susanna Wesley*, 373.

37. Bowden, "Susanna Wesley's Educational Method," 61.

38. Wallace, *Susanna Wesley*, 371.

39. Richard Baxter, *The Reformed Pastor* (London: Epworth, 1656), 97–111; PDF version at Christian Classics Ethereal Library, accessed 19 February 2017, http://www.ccel.org/ccel/baxter/pastor.pdf.

her daughter Emilia, which today would be considered a work of apologetics.[40] Martha Bowden observes that the Lord's Prayer, the Ten Commandments, and the Apostles' Creed were the "three elements of faith outlined in the baptismal service for all those who would be confirmed."[41] Through the work of catechesis, Wesley maintained the Puritan concept of the home as a church and built a foundation of Christian faith for her children.

Lifelong Christian Educator

While Susanna Wesley's primary contribution to her children's Christian education was made during their early childhood, she maintained contact through writing letters to her grown sons Samuel, John, and Charles. Especially rich were her letters to John (whom she called "Jacky") when he was a student at Oxford. Among these, her 18 August 1725 letter on the nature of faith stands out. There, Susanna defined faith as "assent." Later in the same letter, she maintained that the doctrine of the "rigid Calvinists" was "shocking" and ended up making God the "author of sin."[42] No longer just a mother requiring a young boy to memorize precepts, she had moved to a new place in her relationship with her son, a discussion on virtually equal ground, together weighing theological ideas. Susanna seems to have understood her role as a Christian educator to be lifelong; it did only apply to small children under her charge. Rather, hers was equally to walk alongside her grown son as – to use the words of St Anselm – his faith sought understanding.[43]

Lessons for Twenty-First-Century African Christian Educators

Having seen the contours of Susanna Wesley's educational philosophy, especially as it compares with that of John Locke, let us briefly draw lessons for twenty-first-century African Christian educators. What does Wesley have to teach us?

---

40. See her 1709/10 "The Apostles' Creed Explicated in a Letter to Her Daughter Susanna," the 1709/10/11 "Obedience to the Laws of God," and the 1711/12 "A Religious Conference between Mother and Emilia," in Wallace, *Susanna Wesley*, 377–461.

41. Bowden, "Susanna Wesley's Educational Method," 54.

42. Wallace, *Susanna Wesley*, 112.

43. For more on Anselm's dictum, see Thomas Williams, "Saint Anselm," in *Stanford Encyclopedia of Philosophy*, accessed 19 February 2017, https://plato.stanford.edu/entries/anselm/.

First, Susanna Wesley is a reminder that *no child's age is too young to begin teaching him or her about Christian faith*. While – contra Locke – she insisted that a child attain the age of five before learning to read, a child need only know how to talk in order to begin memorizing key tenets of the faith. According to the American Academy of Pediatrics, for most children, language begins developing at twelve months, and by the end of the third year they "should speak well enough to be understood by those outside the family."[44] So a mere thirty-six months into their child's life, to follow the advice of Wesley, parents should intentionally be catechizing their child at home. In village settings in Africa where living happens communally within a walled courtyard, several families could carry out such efforts together, not only instilling Bible verses but recounting Bible stories. This would be an adaptation of Richard Baxter's home/church so successfully modeled first in the Samuel Annesley household in London, then later by Susanna Wesley in Epworth.

Second, Susanna Wesley's methods speak to the question of *gender parity in early childhood education*. What was an issue in eighteenth-century England remains an issue in many sub-Saharan African nations. According to a 2015 UNICEF report, 32 percent of girls living in West and Central Africa had dropped out before finishing primary school, as compared with 24 percent of boys.[45] In nine sub-Saharan nations, the dropout rate from primary school was over 10 percent higher for girls than for boys.[46] The report concludes: "While gaps in enrolment between girls and boys have decreased over the past two decades, girls are still more likely to face persistent barriers to their education than boys in many countries."[47] Wesley's commitment was to provide education with an emphasis upon Christian faith to both her sons *and* her daughters. As such, she is an inspiration for Christian parents and educators to make no discrimination based on gender when teaching our children. In the same way that she strongly recommended that girls be able to read well before they learned how to sew, it must be our commitment to resist the domestic demands that too often pull young girls away from school before they have had a chance to blossom educationally.

---

44. Richard Trubo, "Helping Your Late-Talking Children," WebMD, accessed 19 February 2017, https://www.webmd.com/baby/features/helping-your-late-talking-children#1.

45. UNICEF and UNESCO Institute for Statistics, *Fixing the Broken Promise of Education for All: Findings from the Global Initiative on Out-of-School Children* (Montreal: UNESCO Institute for Statistics, 2015), 25, accessed 19 February 2017, http://unesdoc.unesco.org/images/0023/002315/231508e.pdf.

46. UNICEF/UNESCO, *Fixing the Broken Promise*, 29. These nations were Angola, Cameroon, Central African Republic, Chad, Guinea, Niger, Nigeria, South Sudan, and Yemen.

47. UNICEF/UNESCO, 28.

Finally, the Susanna Wesley educational model underscores the *value of home education.* Following primary education at home, her sons Samuel, John, and Charles went on to pursue formal public schooling up through the university level. The foundation laid in those early childhood years served them well as preparation for more advanced education. To lower the dropout rates among both girls and boys in primary schools throughout Africa, widespread adoption of parts of the Susanna Wesley model – especially teaching five-year-olds to read – may prove useful as a way to prepare children for greater academic success in primary school, secondary school, and beyond.

Conclusion

Summarizing Susanna Wesley's impact as a Christian educator to her children, Maldwyn Edwards concludes: "She gave them not only knowledge but a zeal for more; no merely forced obedience could have accomplished that. She survived the acid test of a good teacher that when left to themselves, freed from her control, they still had a great love of sound learning."[48] Drawing upon ideas from both her own upbringing in a Puritan household and her reading in a variety of sources, but especially John Locke, Wesley adapted them to her own setting, engendering in her children a living Christian faith and the desire for knowledge. As we glean lessons from her example to be applied in twenty-first-century Africa, may those twin outcomes be realized for us as fully as they were for her.

Bibliography

Baxter, Richard. *The Reformed Pastor*. London: Epworth, 1656. PDF version at Christian Classics Ethereal Library. Accessed 19 February 2017. http://www.ccel.org/ccel/baxter/pastor.pdf.

Bowden, Martha F. "Susanna Wesley's Educational Method." *Journal of the Canadian Church Historical Society* 44, no. 1 (2002): 51–62. ATLA Religion Database with ATLASerials, EBSCOhost, accessed 14 February 2017.

Brailsford, Mabel R. *Susanna Wesley: The Mother of Methodism*. London: Epworth, 1938.

Edwards, Maldwyn. *Family Circle: A Study of the Epworth Household in Relation to John and Charles Wesley*. London: Epworth, 1949, 1961.

Hart, Elizabeth. "Finding the Real Susanna: Portraits of Susanna Wesley." *American Theological Library Association Summary of Proceedings* 45 (1991): 152–172. ATLA Religion Database with ATLASerials, EBSCOhost, accessed 14 February 2017.

---

48. Edwards, *Family Circle*, 67.

————. "Susanna Annesley Wesley: An Able Divine." *Touchstone* 6, no. 2 (May 1988): 4–12. ATLA Religion Database with ATLASerials, EBSCOhost, accessed 14 February 2017.

Heitzenrater, Richard P. *John Wesley and the People Called Methodists.* 2nd ed. Nashville: Abingdon, 2013.

Junker, Débora B. Agra. "Beyond the Domestication of Pedagogy: Envisioning New Perspectives on Education." *Encounter* 74, no. 3 (2014): 45–65. ATLA Religion Database with ATLASerials, EBSCOhost, accessed 18 February 2017.

Locke, John. *Some Thoughts Concerning Education.* London: A&J Churchill, 1693. Accessed 16 February 2017. http://www.sophia-project.org/uploads/1/3/9/5/13955288/locke_education.pdf. (This e-text is from the Sophia Project Philosophy Archives.)

Monk, Robert C. *John Wesley: His Puritan Heritage.* Nashville: Abingdon, 1966.

Newton, John A. *Susanna Wesley and the Puritan Tradition in Methodism.* 2nd ed. London: Epworth, 2002.

Oden, Patrick. "'Let Us Not Spend Our Time in Trifling': Susanna Wesley, a Mother to Her Sons." *Wesleyan Theological Journal* 48, no. 2 (September 2013): 112–125. ATLA Religion Database with ATLASerials, EBSCOhost, accessed 14 February 2017.

Rack, Henry. *Reasonable Enthusiast: John Wesley and the Rise of Methodism.* 3rd ed. London: Epworth, 2002.

Rogal, Samuel J. "The Epworth Women: Susanna Wesley and Her Daughters." *Wesleyan Theological Journal* 18, no. 2 (September 1983): 80–89. ATLA Religion Database with ATLASerials, EBSCOhost, accessed 14 February 2017.

Trubo, Richard. "Helping Your Late-Talking Children." WebMD. Accessed 19 February 2017. https://www.webmd.com/baby/features/helping-your-late-talking-children#1.

Tyson, John R. *The Way of the Wesleys: A Short Introduction.* Grand Rapids, MI: Eerdmans, 2014.

UNICEF and UNESCO Institute for Statistics. *Fixing the Broken Promise of Education for All: Findings from the Global Initiative on Out-of-School Children.* Montreal: UNESCO Institute for Statistics, 2015. Accessed 19 February 2017. http://unesdoc.unesco.org/images/0023/002315/231508e.pdf.

Wallace, Charles, Jr. "'Some Stated Employment of Your Mind': Reading, Writing, and Religion in the Life of Susanna Wesley." *Church History* 58, no. 3 (September 1989): 354–366. ATLA Religion Database with ATLASerials, EBSCOhost, accessed 14 February 2017.

————, ed. *Susanna Wesley: The Complete Writings.* New York: Oxford University Press, 1997.

Wesley, John. *The Works of John Wesley.* Bi-centennial ed. 35 vols, projected, edited by Frank Baker. Nashville: Abingdon, 1984–.

Williams, Thomas. "Saint Anselm." *Stanford Encyclopedia of Philosophy.* Accessed 19 February 2017. https://plato.stanford.edu/entries/anselm/.

9

Effects of the Transition of Theological Seminaries in Kenya to Universities on Their Evangelical Christian Identity: An Inquiry into Africa International University

Harriet Akugizibwe Caroline Kintu
Lecturer, International Leadership University

Abstract

A contemporary issue in theological education in Africa is the transitioning from theological seminaries to Christian universities. This restructuring has created a threat to the Christian identity of these institutions. History teaches that a number of institutions in the West that took this path experienced mission drift. The concern is that, unless institutions in Africa learn from history, the transition of these seminaries to universities may erode their evangelical Christian identity. This study therefore sought to investigate the effects of the transition of theological seminaries to universities on their evangelical Christian identity. This mixed methods study shows the effects of the transition of theological seminaries to universities on their evangelical Christian identity as revealed through the faculty and staff, students, campus ethos, and academic and non-academic programs at Africa International University in Nairobi, Kenya. Positive effects evidenced include a broadening of the Christian mission to include both evangelism and discipleship, both on campus and in society. However, there are also negative effects. The major concern is that the university is facing challenges in maintaining its evangelical Christian identity, even though measures have been put in place to preserve it. This study therefore makes recommendations that could be useful for Christian universities. It highlights the threat to the evangelical Christian identity of transitioned institutions and the likely loss of their influence in higher education, the church, and society at large. It is of practical value for further study and for formulation of effective measures to preserve and enhance evangelical Christian identity in Christian universities in Africa.

Key words: Christian higher education, theological education, evangelical Christian identity, institutional mission and vision

Introduction

Background to the Problem

Theological education in Africa in the past two decades has experienced a number of changes. One of the major changes has been the transition from theological seminaries to universities. Previously, most of these institutions were only accredited by Christian accrediting bodies like Association for Christian Theological Education in Africa (ACTEA). However, there is a growing need to educate not only for the ministry but also for the marketplace. A number of institutions in the West that took this path experienced mission drift. To meet accreditation requirements, certain compromises were necessary in the areas of curriculum and institutional ethos.[1]

The problem that arose from the acquisition of accreditation was the need to adhere to state and regional regulations and aspirations for academic respectability. The real challenge was to balance "academic integrity and credibility on the one hand and faithfulness to the Bible and the Great Commission on the other hand."[2] Unfortunately, some institutions were not able to find the balance and lost their original Christian vision and mission

---

1. Larry Poston, "The Role of Higher Education in the Christian World Mission: Past, Present and Future," *Alliance Academic Review 1999*, last modified 2006, accessed 31 October 2018, http://www.kneillfoster.com/aar/summary/index1999.html.

2. Poston, "The Role of Higher Education in the Christian World Mission."

in the name of academic respectability. This study investigated the effects of the transition of theological seminaries to universities on their evangelical Christian identity.

Problem Statement

Educational policies, the changing needs of the church and society, and internal institutional factors have impacted Christian institutions of higher learning in a number of significant ways. For instance, they have contributed to the need to pursue government accreditation and thus transition from theological seminaries to universities. This has led to the restructuring of these institutions and created a threat to their Christian identity. "The threat of becoming more and more secular is real and is growing as pluralistic, postmodern world and life views permeate our society."[3] This threat is not limited to the Western world; it is felt in many different parts of the world.

In Africa today, a growing number of theological institutions are transitioning to universities. There is need for evaluative research to find out how this transition has affected the evangelical Christian identity of these Christian institutions of higher learning in Africa.

The Purpose of the Study

The purpose of this research was to investigate the effects of the transition of theological seminaries in Kenya to universities on their evangelical Christian identity. This research focused on Africa International University (AIU)'s school of theology called Nairobi Evangelical Graduate School of Theology (NEGST). It is hoped that this research will make a contribution to Christian higher education in East Africa. The desired outcome of this work is the creation of a clear balance between achievement of academic respectability and preservation of the institutions' evangelical Christian identity.

Objectives of the Study

This study was guided by three objectives. This chapter is, however, a presentation only of objective number 3:

---

3. David S. Dockery and Gregory A. Thornbury, eds., *Shaping a Christian Worldview: The Foundations of Christian Higher Education* (Nashville: Broadman & Holman, 2002), 379.

1. To find out how theological seminaries described their identity before the transition.

2. To find out the factors that influenced the transition of theological seminaries to universities.

3. To find out the effects of the transition of theological seminaries to universities on their evangelical Christian identity.

Literature Review

There is a perceived contemporary threat to the evangelical Christian identity of Christian universities. Kromminga describes the basic threat as a shrinking God-concept. This, he says, "is the shrinking concept of God and His relevance to the world, which is so prevalent in modern thinking. This, it is contended, is the one all-pervasive threat to the Christian character of the Christian educational enterprise concept."[4] To compromise the evangelical Christian identity of an institution is to lose the vision and purpose of the institution.

Description of a Theological Seminary

This study's interest is in the transition of theological seminaries to universities. However, lessons are gleaned not only from theological seminaries but also from Bible colleges, Christian liberal arts universities, and other universities that have experienced mission drift. Ozan describes the transition from a college to university status as a change in organizational name, symbolizing the transition from a liberal arts mission to a comprehensive university mission.[5] In the case of this study, it is a transition from a theological seminary mindset to a liberal arts university mindset. The mission drift can be seen in different ways depending on the institution in question. The concern of this chapter is with the evangelical Christian identity of the institution.

Gangel defines a Christian college "as a post-secondary institution of learning that takes seriously an evangelical doctrinal statement, classes in Bible and Christian ministry, a distinctively Christian philosophy of education

---

4. J. H. Kromminga, "The Threats to the Christian Character of the Christian Institution," in *Christian Higher Education: The Contemporary Challenge* (Ontario: Wedge, 1976), 58.

5. Jaquette Ozan, "Why Do Colleges Become Universities? Mission Drift and the Enrolment Economy," *Research in Higher Education* 54, no. 5 (August 2013): 514–543, accessed 31 October 2018, https://doi.org/10.1007/s11162-013-9283-x.

and life, and the quality of spiritual life on campus."[6] Three different kinds of institutions can fit the above definition: theological seminaries, Christian liberal arts colleges, and Bible colleges. A theological seminary is a "graduate school for ministerial training generally offering a variety of master's degrees and possibly one or more doctoral programs. The basic degree of a seminary curriculum is a three-year Master of Divinity that is geared toward the graduate preparation of pastors and other professional church staff."[7] The transitioned seminaries are now more like Christian liberal arts colleges, except that most of them have several graduate programs.

To the general public, all Christian institutions appear to be the same, but this is not true. Some are simply Christian in background or name, while others are actively Christian at different levels. Even those that are actively Christian are varied in denomination and tradition. Benne, in his book *Quality with Soul*, discusses the major elements of the Christian tradition that must be explicitly and publicly relevant to any institution that identifies itself as evangelical. These include its vision, ethos, and persons.[8] This writer wishes to adopt Benne's components as central in defining an evangelical Christian university. In addition to Benne's components, the researcher also found in literature that curriculum and Christian tradition and background are crucial to the identity of an institution.[9] Space does not allow the elaboration of these components, but it is worth noting that they are clearly defined by biblical principles.

Christian Higher Education in Africa

Christian higher education in Africa started with the establishment of three theological centers at Alexandria, Carthage, and Hippo in the second century. It was revived in the eighteenth century in Freetown, Sierra Leone, following the abolition of the slave trade and the establishment of Fourah Bay College. Since

---

6. Kenneth Gangel, "Christian Higher Education and Lifelong Learning," in *Introduction to Biblical Christian Education*, ed. Werner Graendorf (Chicago: Moody, 1981), 333.

7. Kenneth Gangel and Warren S. Benson, *Christian Education: Its History and Philosophy* (Chicago: Moody, 1983), 361–362.

8. Robert Benne, *Quality with Soul: How Six Premier Colleges and Universities Keep Faith with Their Religious Traditions* (Grand Rapids, MI: Eerdmans, 2001), 6.

9. Stephen V. Monsma, "Christian Worldview in Academia," *Faculty Dialogue* 21 (Spring–Summer 1994): 139–147; Duane Litfin, *Conceiving the Christian College* (Grand Rapids, MI: Eerdmans, 2004); Gangel and Benson, *Christian Education*; Benne, *Quality with Soul*; Dockery and Thornbury, *Shaping a Christian Worldview*; Perry L. Glanzer et al., "Assessing the Denominational Identity of American Evangelical Colleges and Universities, Part I: Denominational Patronage and Institutional Policy," *Christian Higher Education* 12, no. 3 (2013): 181–202.

then the number of theological institutions has been on the increase. This is possibly due to the rapid growth of the Christian community in Africa and the corresponding urgent leadership training needs. The African church leadership also seems to value theological education more than before. The ACTEA directory statistics give an idea of the growth of theological education in Africa. The statistics show a rapid increase in the number of theological schools in Africa in recent years. According to the available data on the year of founding of 353 presently existing schools, 79 percent were begun since 1950; just under 63 percent since 1960; and nearly 40 percent since 1970.[10] While many of them were conservative, a major conflict arose between the secular authorities and missionary bodies in the twentieth century. This conflict was about the social relevance of Christian higher education. Modernity and development were presented as the benefits of science and the conquest of religion. It then became necessary to ponder the contribution of religion to national development. Many African educators have recognized the social relevance of the Christian religion and this has led to many institutions revisiting their objectives in higher education.[11] Today, many theological seminaries have transitioned into universities with the objective of training not only ministers for the church but also a workforce of integrity for the marketplace.

Many institutions that focused on the discipleship of students as the goal of education are now more evangelistic. As a result, they not only recruit born-again Christians as before, but they have adopted open recruitment whereby students of all faiths are admissible. These changes have implications for the evangelical Christian identity of the institutions.

Effects of the Transition of Theological Seminaries to Universities

There are positive and negative effects when a transition occurs in any institution. Evaluating the effects on the church-related colleges that modeled themselves after public universities and so changed their identities, DeJong states that "The simple growth in individual size of these colleges gave each of them more faculty members and students and provided a richer intellectual life . . . Better facilities and a better paid faculty helped to boost the academic

---

10. Paul Bowers, "New Light on Theological Education in Africa," *ACTEA Tools and Studies* 9 (1989), http://www.acteaweb.org/downloads/tools/Tools%20and%20Studies%2009.pdf.

11. International Association for the Promotion of Christian Higher Education, *Christian Education in the African Context: Proceedings of the African Regional Conference of IAPCHE, Harare, 4–9 March 1991* (Grand Rapids, MI: IAPCHE, 1992), 64–66.

programs of these colleges."[12] As seminaries become universities, they diversify by offering a variety of programs to attract students. Faculty numbers must then increase to meet the demand, and generally a richer intellectual life is expected. In Kenya, the Commission of University Education (CUE) demands certain standards. Thaver explains that "Kenya has very stringent regulations that need to be met in order for a private university to be established . . . stringent criteria include among others issues to do with admission requirements, program length, qualification levels, enrollments, competence of programs, minimum academic qualifications for staff, infrastructural facilities, and ethical standards governing staff members."[13] This leads to better facilities and better faculty, which help improve academic programs and the university as a whole. However, adhering to such stringent criteria has implications for the nature and mission of the institution.

This study focuses on the effects on the evangelical Christian identity of the institution. Longfield, in reference to the Midwestern region in the USA in the nineteenth century, points out that the effects on the Christian identity did not occur overnight. Rather the broad evangelical traditions of the institutions succumbed to liberalism and later to disestablishment of religion on campus.[14] This came in small doses as liberalism and later secularization infiltrated different aspects of the institutions. Previously, "The religious concerns of the schools were manifested in their staff, curriculum and religious activities."[15] As time went on, compromises were made as there was laxity on religious requirements in the hiring policy of administrators, faculty, and staff, and in student recruitment, to mention but a few. This is a common trend even in African Christian institutions. In describing private higher education in Africa, Thaver notes that not-for-profit institutions with a religious orientation strongly emphasize moral ideas and values. However, these institutions have consistently been challenged by the market-economy discourse prevalent in the for-profit institutions.[16] As a result, compromises are made that undermine the Christian values of the institution. The existing literature discusses the key

---

12. Arthur J. DeJong, *Reclaiming a Mission: New Direction for the Church-Related College* (Grand Rapids, MI: Eerdmans, 1990), 59.

13. Bev Thaver, "Private Higher Education in Africa: Six Country Case Studies," in *African Higher Education: An International Reference Handbook*, eds. Damtew Teferra and Philip G. Altbach (Indianapolis: Indiana University Press, 2003), 57.

14. George M. Marsden and Bradley J. Longfield, eds., *The Secularization of the Academy* (New York: Oxford University Press, 1992), 47.

15. Marsden and Longfield, *Secularization*, 47.

16. Thaver, "Private Higher Education," 53.

aspects of an institution that are affected by a change of mindset resulting in changes in the identity of the institution. These are presented below.

Christian Identity of Faculty and Staff

In most church-affiliated institutions, the teaching staff come largely from the sponsoring institution. Seminary training is often a prominent part of the curriculum. But with the revamping of Christian institutions, recruitment of faculty from a broader range is inevitable. New faculty recruitment patterns bring changes to the nature and mission of the already changing institution. For instance, in the mainline Protestant colleges in the USA, the change from Bible college to liberal arts university has given rise to an increase in student numbers and a higher demand for professors who were not readily available in Christian circles.[17] "Thus, into these changing, vulnerable colleges came bright young faculty members who brought with them the viewpoint and values of the large, urban, secular, research university."[18] Faculty members affect the identity of a university either positively or negatively. Where faculty are committed Christians, they influence their students in that regard, and the reverse is also true. This influence is reflected not only in life examples and teaching philosophy and practice, but more so in curriculum writing, administration, and policy and decision making. Christian institutions need to write curricula and make policies and decisions within the theoretical framework of their Christian tradition. Staff members and other stakeholders of the same theoretical framework should be identified, trained, and involved in writing curricula. This is applicable to any institution that is interested in preserving its traditions, beliefs, and convictions, whether Christian or not.

Furthermore, the introduction of new programs without the expansion of the financial base leads to academic staff challenges. On regulation in private higher education in Africa, Thaver found that in Africa, because of limited funds, private institutions often recruit from public universities, leading to moonlighting and its associated problems. For instance, he states that moonlighting staff are usually not bound by the same rules and loyalties as full-time staff.[19] There is a greater challenge for Christian universities who have a limited pool of Christian academics to recruit from, especially for non-theological/ministerial courses. Moreover, the professionals who evaluate

---

17. DeJong, *Reclaiming a Mission*, 61.

18. DeJong, 61.

19. Thaver, "Private Higher Education," 57.

programs for government accreditation are not necessarily Christian. All these issues have a direct impact on the Christian identity of seminaries that transition into universities.

Christian Identity of Students

DeJong explains how mainline Protestant colleges in the USA lost their leadership role in higher education when they adopted the public university model of education. In so doing they sacrificed their Christian distinctive and Christian influence on their students. "Instead of attempting to influence the total lives of their students as they had in the past, the church-related colleges adopted from the secular universities the concept of a 'value-free' approach to the educational process; as a result, the impact of the church-related colleges on the moral and spiritual dimension of students was greatly diminished."[20] The students an institution produces are a key revealer of institutional mission achievement. Suskie asserts that "the assessment of student learning is a major component of the assessment of institutional effectiveness."[21] However, the kind of students admitted also determines the identity of the institution. For instance, change in admission patterns affected the American mainline Protestant colleges' identity. "The influx of students on these campuses did not follow old patterns; and the homogeneity of many of the colleges was lost. The heterogeneity, welcomed though it was, came when the colleges were vulnerable. Thus, the changed student body in turn brought changes to these colleges."[22] The admissions criteria opened the door to all kinds of students, not just Christians, and that affected the Christian identity of the student body.

Academic Programs

After World War II, there was a rapid increase in urban public universities in the West that displaced Christian universities from their leadership role. Instead of Christian colleges being the influencers, they were now being influenced by the public universities. They started to model themselves after the large universities and in so doing they lost their uniqueness. One of the major areas affected was the structure of the universities. In public universities,

---

20. DeJong, *Reclaiming a Mission*, x.

21. Linda A. Suskie, *Assessing Student Learning: A Common-Sense Guide* (Bolton, MA: Anker, 2004), 9.

22. DeJong, *Reclaiming a Mission*, 60–61.

there is a distinct separation of the academic disciplines and of specializations in those disciplines. Christian colleges adopted this approach.[23] Lessons learnt from the experience of church-related colleges in the USA can be generalized in the African context. In the past two decades in Africa, there has been a rapid growth in the numbers of universities, and in the size and importance of university education, both public and private. This change in higher education has put pressure on seminaries to restructure and to reinvent their programs so as to be able to compete for students and faculty/staff, thus providing growth for the seminaries. This growth has had a significant effect on seminaries that have transitioned to universities and their evangelical Christian identity. In Kenya, the Commission of University Education governs all universities. As seminaries gain accreditation, they have to model themselves after other universities as approved by CUE. The impact of the original mission of Christian education is diminished as there is now a new approach and control over what can be included in the academic programs. Overall, there is a direct effect of the revised curriculum on the impact of education, on the quality and character of students, and on campus ethos.

Non-academic Programs

One of the major non-academic programs in Christian institutions of higher learning is chapel. It is one of the most important programs, one that reflects the Christian identity and the unique ethos and mission of a Christian university to the students and the world at large. This is one of the programs that get undermined as Christian institutions transition. DeJong says that in church-related colleges in the USA, chapel was affected mainly by the increased population of students and faculty. Because of this, chapel lost its effectiveness as a means for shaping and transmitting values. Even though this was not deliberate in many of these colleges, the Christian faith no longer maintained its unifying and energizing role and this opened the way to secularization of the institutions.[24] According to Longfield, in the Midwestern USA, chapel attendance requirements were relaxed due to logistical problems and student opposition. The major reason, though, was in relation to decisions made by administrators and faculty who believed that compulsory chapel was detrimental rather than beneficial to the cultivation of Christianity.[25] Sometimes

---

23. DeJong, 49–51.

24. DeJong, 60.

25. Marsden and Longfield, *Secularization*, 47.

chapel hour was maintained but was characterized by other programs that had nothing to do with spiritual matters.

Campus Ethos

The concern for many Christian educators is related to the mission and purpose of a Christian institution. Many Christian parents and students prefer a college environment with a strong Christian ethos and a strong Christian identity.[26] Administrators in Christian higher education should thus focus on features such as the integration of faith and learning, and providing spiritual mentors in the development of faith and character of students. Mulatu studied five institutions in East Africa that transitioned from theological institutions to universities. His study demonstrated that all five institutions changed their vision and mission statements as a result of the transition. Four of these institutions still declare publicly the relevance of their Christian vision; however, one of them does not, due to government regulations. Mulatu concludes that failure to declare the Christian vision and mission brings confusion regarding the ethos of the institution and undermines the ability to function as a distinctively Christian university.[27] This is a good example of how becoming a university can have a negative effect on the Christian identity of an institution.

Christian Tradition and the Background of the Institution

Benne carried out a study in six schools in the USA which he considered to have kept their faith. His study concluded that one of the major reasons why they kept their faith was because of their religious traditions and their continued active identification and connection with them. The schools were Calvin (Christian Reformed Church), Wheaton (evangelical), St Olaf and Valparaiso (Lutheran), Notre Dame (Catholic), and Baylor (Baptist). According to Benne, two things are apparent about these schools. First, they are academically excellent according to both religious and secular rankings.[28] And second, "The Christian account of life and reality is made visible and relevant in all facets of each school's activities – academic, extra-curricular, music and

---

26. Phil Davignon, "Factors Influencing College Choice and Satisfaction among Students at Christian Colleges and Universities," *Religion & Education* 43, no. 1 (2016): 77–94.

27. Semeon Mulatu, *Transitioning from a Theological College to a Christian University: A Multi-Case Study in the East African Context*, ICETE Series (Carlisle: Langham Global Library, 2017), 193.

28. Benne, *Quality with Soul*, 95.

the arts, worship, atmosphere, and self-definition. In other words, the schools have both quality and soul bound together."[29] However, it should be noted that Benne's study was published in 2001 and a more recent study may show different results. Nevertheless, it would be of great benefit to transitioned and transitioning institutions to learn from Benne's study how these institutions were able to maintain their identity. In East Africa, the five institutions studied by Mulatu were found to have maintained a close relationship with their sponsoring churches or denominations even after the transition. In fact, the churches and denominations supported the transition and have remained active in the governance of all five institutions.[30] It can be concluded that the continued active identification and connection with, and involvement of, the sponsoring churches, denominations, or organizations can help in preserving the Christian identity of a transitioned institution.

A Biblical Call to Preserve an Evangelical Christian Identity

The only constants in our world are God and Scripture. The immediate needs in our society are constantly in flux. Educationists jump from one trend to another. The drive to be contemporary is unending. A biblically informed philosophy of education will provide stability in the midst of change. A commitment to the biblical view of reality and the role of the church in history will give direction for the future. The Lord of the church is the Lord of history. And it is God who stands in the center of the universe. Not ourselves.[31]

In agreement with these words from Gangel and Benson, we argue that a Christian university should rely on God and the Bible in all its ventures in order to preserve its evangelical Christian identity. One may ask why it is necessary for a Christian university to be unapologetically Christian. The apostle Matthew gives us an answer in the very words of the Lord Jesus Christ in Matthew 5:13–16 (NIV):

You are the salt of the earth. But if the salt loses its saltiness, how can it be made salty again? It is no longer good for anything, except to be thrown out and trampled underfoot.

---

29. Benne, 95.

30. Mulatu, *Transitioning*, 195.

31. Gangel and Benson, *Christian Education*, 369.

> You are the light of the world. A town built on a hill cannot be
> hidden. Neither do people light a lamp and put it under a bowl.
> Instead they put it on its stand, and it gives light to everyone in
> the house. In the same way, let your light shine before others, that
> they may see your good deeds and glorify your Father in heaven.

This passage is an illustration of how true discipleship is lived out. True disciples of Jesus are known by their impact on others. Jesus used the salt and light metaphors to denote the proper way of life of his disciples. The salt metaphor highlights the negative or useless disciple, while the light metaphor signifies the positive influence on everyone. Both metaphors are used to emphasize the call for true discipleship to have an effect on other people.[32]

If salt loses its saltiness or its effectiveness, it cannot be made salty again. Jesus is making the ethical point that it is fatal for Christians to become useless to their mission. When salt loses its saltiness, it is no longer of any value and must be thrown away. "Jesus is saying that his disciples dare not allow the world to dilute their effectiveness, or they belong to the garbage heap. Such Christians will indeed be 'trampled' (implying judgment as in the parables of Matt 25) because they are ineffective and useless."[33] This is a stern warning to all Christians, and in this case Christian universities, to guard against becoming useless to their mission. Losing the evangelical Christian identity is losing saltiness and becoming of no value, thus not worth existence. Malik, in his book *A Christian Critique of the University*, asks sobering questions for Christian educators: "Can the university be recaptured for Christ? If Christ is going to be utterly effaced, what or who is going to replace him? In this fateful contest, who is going to win: Christ or Antichrist, the revolution or the myriad counterrevolutions since?"[34] It is depressing to imagine the worst.

In the phrase "You are the light," Jesus is referring to all his followers. God is light (1 John 1:5) and Jesus himself is the light (Matt 4:16), so Christians are to reflect Jesus so that the world may see him. In the same way a town on a hill cannot be hidden, the disciples must make their light visible. Osborne clarifies this, saying that "discipleship is as visible as light in the night, as a mountain in the flatlands. To flee into invisibility is to deny the call. Any community of Jesus which wants to be invisible is no longer a community that follows him."[35]

---

32. Grant R. Osborne, *Matthew*, Zondervan Exegetical Commentary on the New Testament, ed. Clinton E. Arnold (Grand Rapids, MI: Zondervan, 2010), 174.

33. Osborne, *Matthew*, 175.

34. Charles Habib Malik, *A Christian Critique of the University* (Downers Grove, IL: InterVarsity Press, 1982), 32.

35. Osborne, *Matthew*, 176.

Therefore, an institution that identifies itself as following Christ must display that. When people light a lamp, they do not hide it, but they put it on a stand so it can give light to everyone. What would be the point of lighting a lamp if you did not want to give light? Christians are called to be missionaries who carry God's light to the nations (v. 14). True discipleship is not passive; it is active. When it becomes inactive, it is useless.[36] Jesus concluded his teaching with an imperative and a reason for it in Matthew 5:16 (NIV): "Let your light shine before others, that they may see your good deeds and glorify your Father in heaven." The light must not be hidden or covered up. It must shine! That is how Jesus will be seen: when Christians let Jesus's light shine through them.

Therefore, the mission of a Christian university is both evangelism and discipleship, and unless the Christian institution maintains its evangelical Christian identity it cannot be effective in this mission. If it does not maintain its Christian identity, it loses its saltiness and cannot be made salty again, but rather has to be thrown out. Christian universities cannot afford to be naïve or passive. They have to participate actively to maintain saltiness and keep the light burning. Christian educators believe they are making a great impact in the world by providing a Christian education. Theological institutions are transitioning into universities as a way to broaden their impact in the world. It is, however, of paramount importance to take note of Osborne's caution: "The coming of God's kingdom is so much more than just being kind to others and performing good deeds. There is a demand to be different and act differently, that is, to be right with God and to act the way God demands, by following Jesus in countercultural directions. Change is the name of the game, and it must occur at the ontological level (who we are) and at the functional level (how we live and act)."[37] A Christian institution must be the light and the salt by preserving and living by its Christian identity.

The literature confirms that there is a real possibility of mission drift, liberalism, and secularization for institutions that seek government accreditation and transition to universities. Transitioning institutions should therefore make a commitment to stick to their Christian identity and lay down strategies on how to preserve it. Theological foundations in this study are presented as centered in God and his Word, which are the only constants in this world and the very reason for a Christian education. There is a biblical call to preserve an evangelical Christian identity as discussed from Matthew 5:13–16. The call is to all professing Christians to be salt and light in all their

---

36. Osborne, 176.

37. Osborne, 177.

endeavors. A Christian educator, therefore, should seek to reveal God through the education process.

Methodology

Research Design

This research employed the mixed methods approach to gather descriptive data. The sequential explanatory strategy was used. This involved the collection and analysis of quantitative data followed by the collection and analysis of qualitative data. The two methods were integrated during the interpretation phase of the study.[38] Likert types of questionnaires were used to gather quantitative data, while interviews and reviews of documents were used to gather qualitative data. Descriptive and inferential analysis was carried out.

Setting and Sampling Strategy

The target population for this study was Africa International University's students, faculty, and staff. The sample frame for this study was one of the schools in AIU. The school selected as a sample frame was Nairobi Evangelical Graduate School of Theology (NEGST). NEGST is the biggest of the four schools at AIU, with its student population being about half of the total population of the university. The number of students in NEGST was about 500, and the number of teaching faculty was about seventeen. There were an estimated fifty PhD/DMin students, 150 master's students, 200 bachelor's students, seventy diploma students, and thirty certificate students at NEGST. Students, faculty, and staff members from the selected school participated in the study. Students were selected using random sampling from master's and PhD/DMin degree level. Faculty members were selected using the purposive sampling method. The selected students, faculty, and staff were requested to fill in a questionnaire for quantitative data and to be interviewed for qualitative data. Sixty-two questionnaires were filled in, and twenty-two interviews were carried out.

---

38. John W. Creswell, *Research Design: Qualitative, Quantitative and Mixed Methods Approaches*, 2nd ed. (London: Sage, 2003), 215.

Data Collection Techniques

Data collection was conducted by the researcher herself. A permissions letter was presented to the relevant authorities in order to access institutional documents. Quantitative data was collected first by using questionnaires. After hearing an explanation of the research and signing the letter of consent, the participants were handed a questionnaire and requested to fill it in while the researcher waited. Qualitative data was collected next using review of documents and interviews.

Data Analysis

Descriptive and inferential data analysis was carried out in this research. SPSS software was used to analyze quantitative data, while NVivo was used to analyze qualitative data. Descriptive responses, frequency tables, and charts were constructed to show findings for each of the three research questions. In order to infer the results from samples to population, hypothesis testing was carried out. A chi-square test was used to test the hypotheses. The level of significance was 0.05, which gives a 95 percent confidence level.

Research Findings and Discussion

Effects of the Transition from a Theological Seminary to a University on the Evangelical Christian Identity of the Institution

This chapter focuses on the effects of the transition of a theological seminary to a university on its evangelical Christian identity. According to quantitative data, a cumulative percentage of 69.4 percent affirmed that the transition had an effect on the evangelical Christian identity of the university. Both quantitative and qualitative data revealed that there were positive and negative effects of the transition on the evangelical Christian identity of the university. The effects identified were in regard to academic programs, student admissions criteria, the hiring policy of faculty and staff, the quality and character of students, faculty, and staff, extra-curricular programs, the campus ethos, and the Christian mission of the university.

A comparison was made of the opinions of staff and students concerning the effects of the transition of NEGST to AIU on its evangelical Christian identity to test hypothesis 4. Hypothesis 4 stated that the transition from a theological seminary to a university has had no significant effect on the evangelical Christian identity of AIU. We were unable to reject the null hypothesis that there was no significant effect of the transition from a seminary to a university on its evangelical Christian identity. This is because $p = .092$, which is greater than the 0.05 level of significance. Results from the interviews showed thirty-four references in relation to the effect of the transition on the evangelical identity. In summary, the effects were said to be mostly negative, but positive effects were also mentioned. Participants indicated a drift from the evangelical Christian identity evidenced by a shift from the original mission, moral deterioration, "lukewarmness," secularism, and clash of faiths. On a positive note, the transition was seen as having created an opportunity for evangelism, discipleship, and mentoring – opportunities that would enhance the evangelical Christian identity.

As seen from the literature review, people are the bearers of an institution's identity. This research therefore sought to find out about the Christian identity of faculty and staff before and after the transition. Half of the respondents to the questionnaires (50%) believed that the transition of this seminary to a university had affected the quality of faculty and staff. When asked whether the hiring policy had changed, 37.1 percent of the respondents were non-committal, as they were not conversant with the hiring policy. A comparison of the curriculum written in 2003 with the one written in 2015 gives us an insight into this matter. The first one, written before the transition, emphasizes the requirements in regard to commitment to the Christian faith and says nothing about academic qualifications.[39] The one written after the transition does the opposite: the emphasis is put on academic qualifications and nothing is said about Christian faith requirements. The curriculum written in 2015 states that all faculty members have earned the required credentials in their fields to allow them to teach at the appropriate levels of instruction in the university. The appendix lists the names of the teaching staff, their ranks, their academic qualifications and areas of specialization, the number of years in university teaching, their professional experiences, and their research and publications.[40] Nothing is mentioned about their Christian faith, nor is there any indication that this is required. The document's silence on this issue speaks volumes.

It is well understood that transition from a theological seminary to a university requires the introduction of new programs. Introduction of new programs without the expansion of the financial base leads to academic staff challenges. Mulatu's study of five institutions in East Africa that transitioned

---

39. Nairobi Evangelical Graduate School of Theology, "Curriculum," presented to the Kenya Commission for Higher Education, December 2003.

40. Africa International University, "Curriculum for Bachelor of Science in Information Technology," submitted to the Commission for University Education, November 2015.

confirms that: "Before their transitions, all the five institutions in this study had a policy of hiring Christians only. However, four out of the five institutions have indicated that they have hired non-Christians or nominal Christians as part-time faculty members because they could not find enough committed Christians who could teach all the courses they offer."[41] Poe emphasizes the role of the faculty as a critical factor in preserving the Christian identity of an institution when he refers to two similar pieces of research: one conducted at Baylor and one by Burtchaell – one being quantitative and the other narrative. He concludes that "More than the formal ties to a denomination, the policies of the board or the initiatives of the president, the extent to which students ever see a relationship between God and what they study depends upon the faculty."[42] Faculty and staff members pass on to students what they come with, whether they purpose to or not.

A total of 64.5 percent of respondents affirmed that the transition from a theological seminary to a university had had a significant effect on the academic programs at the institution. This was in terms of the introduction of non-theological courses. This led to changes in student enrolment criteria. According to the curriculum written in 2003, the institution admitted only students who had evidence of a mature Christian character and a divine call to the Christian ministry. The curriculum written in 2015, after getting a government charter, does not make this a requirement for applicants except for those applying for theological courses. This was confirmed by a cumulative percentage of 72.6 percent that affirmed that there had been a change in the admissions criteria. Interview respondents gave details about the nature of the change, all of them indicating that admission was now open to all. The advantage seen in this was the opportunity to influence students of other faiths with the gospel and Christian values. The concern, however, was the fear of increasing numbers of non-believers on campus who might compromise the evangelical Christian identity of the institution. This is expected to continue, especially as the government is expected to send more students every year whom the university has no opportunity to select but must willingly receive.[43]

41. Mulatu, *Transitioning*, 194.

42. Harry L. Poe, *Christianity in the Academy: Teaching at the Intersection of Faith and Learning* (Grand Rapids, MI: Baker Academic, 2004), 49.

43. Kenya Universities and Colleges Central Placement Services, "Admission of 10,000 Government Sponsored Students to Degree Courses in Private Universities," accessed 7 May 2017, http://kuccps.net/?q=content/admission-10000-government-sponsored-students-degree-courses-private-universities.

Regarding the quality and character of students, a cumulative percentage of 77.4 affirmative responses led to the conclusion that the transition had had a major impact on the quality and character of students. A prevalent theme in interviews was moral deterioration. All twenty-two people interviewed made a comment about moral deterioration, evidenced by reports of cases like "theft," "drunkenness," "bad dressing code," "immorality," "expulsion of students on character grounds," and "lack of interest in and/or some resistance to spiritual things like chapel and theological university core courses." Such cases were unheard of before the transition. This was seen as a negative effect of the transition which had allowed the admission of non-believers.

In relation to the above, similar sentiments were expressed as to how the transition from a theological seminary to a university had affected campus ethos. A total of 74.2 percent indicated that the transition had had a significant impact on the campus ethos. The most prevalent themes from interviewees had to do with age, behavior, and the presence of non-Christian students. The student population is now much younger than before the transition. The behavior is immature, probably due to younger (even underage) students and/or the fact that there are non-believers on campus. Student respondent MA012 expressed frustration as a result of tensions and conflicts arising from having to share dorms with young students. "Can you imagine the difficulty of mixing grownups with young people in the dorm?" he asked. On the other hand, a faculty member (SS002) expressed that "People are adjusting to relating with young people. There is a need to be sensitive." In this we see a challenge and an opportunity. While ongoing unresolved conflicts between mature Christian students and young students may seem to be a negative effect on the Christian identity of the institution, they also provide a great opportunity for mature Christians to let their light shine as they mentor and influence these young people for the sake of Christ.

In terms of non-academic programs, a cumulative percentage of 54.8 percent had noticed changes. Interview respondents explained the changes observed in non-academic programs as follows: "a lot of young people-related activities like sports," "intervarsity sports," "drama," "internal and external outreaches or missions," "Christian Union," "more dynamic and lively chapels to suit young people," and "maintained programs like chapel and small group meetings that were there before." This was a positive effect, as a good number of programs had been put in place to meet not only the felt needs of the young students, but also their spiritual needs – a mission pursued by all those who identify themselves as evangelical Christians.

Quantitative data showed a 33.8 percent disagreement as to the existence of benefits of the transition to the Christian identity; 37.1 percent agreement; and 29.0 percent unsure. A benefit that was mentioned by all twenty-two interview participants was the opportunity for Christian ministry – evangelism on campus and Christian impact on the society. This is a sign that the Christian mission has broadened. The focus was not only to train pastors and church ministers, but also to train laypeople who would go out into the marketplace and impact the world for Christ.

However, regarding whether there were disadvantages in transitioning from a seminary to a university in relation to the Christian mission of this institution, the responses received revealed a high cumulative percentage of 71.0 percent in the affirmative. Interview respondents described the effect on the mission in both negative and positive terms. Negatively, there were themes of moral deterioration, compromise of the Christian mission, mission drift, clash of faiths, and lack of focus. In view of all this, it can be concluded that there are negative effects of the transition from a theological seminary to a university on the Christian identity of the university.

On the other hand, some did not consider the effect to be a loss of mission but a broadening of the mission. Respondent MA0011 stated: "We now have an opportunity for ministry right here on campus, besides Christians who will change the world will not remain in a box." Both views (positive and negative) seem to have a similar underlying concern: to maintain the Christian mission. However, the disadvantages seem to outweigh the advantages. The study results revealed that a high cumulative percentage of 71.0 percent "strongly agreed" and "agreed" that there were disadvantages in transitioning from a seminary to a university in relation to the Christian mission of this institution. Only 9.75 percent "disagreed," while 4.8 percent "strongly disagreed" with this. In view of these findings, it seems conclusive that the transition of the seminary to a university has negatively affected the Christian mission of this institution. In summary, examples of issues raised include mission drift, compromise of Christian mission, moral deterioration, and a threat to possible future loss of Christian identity. Being aware of the threat will help combat it. As the institution transitions, there is a need to safeguard the Christian mission of the institution.

Furthermore, 67.7 percent of the respondents were of the view that the university was experiencing challenges in relation to maintaining its evangelical Christian identity. Among the challenges stated were the loss of control over the kinds of students admitted, thus accepting students of different faiths, like Muslims, and the corresponding challenge of enforcing Christian values;

unethical and unchristian behavior; the increasing number of secular programs and thus the increasing number of non-Christian students; adherence to a non-Christian accrediting body (CUE) and the corresponding preoccupation with the image of the university in order to please CUE; and ensuring that the institution stays focused on the Christian mission.

On a positive note, the research also showed that the university had put in place measures to ensure that the evangelical Christian identity of the institution was preserved, as indicated by 59.7 percent of the respondents who attested to this. Some measures already existed but were now being emphasized, while more measures had been introduced. Interview respondents listed the measures in place that they conceived as being helpful in maintaining the evangelical Christian identity. They included the following: integration of faith and learning, theological university core courses, making chapel and small-group meetings a requirement, on-campus evangelistic missions, Christian Union meetings, mentoring programs, ensuring the curriculum and the faculty were Christ-centered, focusing on the core values, and ongoing communication of the vision and mission of the institution.

Implications and Recommendations of the Study

The purpose of this study was to investigate the effects of the transition of theological seminaries to universities on their evangelical Christian identity. It is hoped that this research will make a contribution to Christian higher education in East Africa, especially in terms of encouraging Christian universities to remain committed and preserve their evangelical Christian identity. Onwu, concluding his topic "The Challenge of the African Context for Higher Education" at the African Regional Conference, stated the commitment of Christian higher education in Africa to maintain an evangelical Christian identity in spite of the challenges involved:

> Therefore, being committed to Christ, we endeavor to be meaningfully involved in the world. Christian higher education as our ministry of witness is to be carried out in the context of the struggles and aspirations of the African peoples in the midst of the diversity of faiths and ideologies. With this in mind, we seek to train people to be spiritually committed, biblically competent and professionally qualified. Thus, we attempt to provide a theological education that is thoroughly biblical, genuinely contextual and wholesomely evangelical. It is in this kind of commitment that

Christian educators can become agents of change in contemporary Africa.[44]

This commitment to preserve Christian identity should be pursued at all costs. Unfortunately, in history, many institutions lost the battle. There were a number of precipitating factors to this loss. For instance, when Christian institutions welcomed faculty from public universities with their "value-free points of view," they did not realize what effect that would have on their core values. But it affected their academic and non-academic programs, the quality and character of students and staff, the campus ethos, and eventually their purpose and mission. DeJong adds that "The inroads the value-free point of view had made into both the church and affiliated colleges contributed to weakening ties between the two."[45] These institutions not only lost their faith, which was a unifying and energizing influence, but they "also lost their historic touch stone – the church – so there was little to call them back to their unique identity and mission."[46] Operating in this vacuum with no accountability, against the background of the secular winds blowing in the USA, Christian institutions could hardly hold on to their evangelical Christian identity and so lost their influence, not only in the church but also in higher education and society at large. This research has showed a potential loophole in the hiring policy of faculty and staff at AIU. Current policy documents need to emphasize above all else the Christian faith and commitment of faculty and staff. There should be no compromise in this matter, as it will determine the future of the institution in every way.

Benne, in his book *Quality with Soul*, gives important suggestions on how to keep the faith – in other words, strategies to preserve the Christian identity. Among them he suggests the importance of the sponsoring religious traditions supplying people with the vision of the school; the maintenance of the connection with the sponsors, especially in governance issues; and the critical mass being intensely committed to and educated about the sponsoring tradition, mission, vision, and ethos of the school. The selection of the board, administrative staff, faculty, and students should be guided primarily by their religious convictions. The religious vision should organize and direct the identity, mission, and ethos of the school.[47] Benne concluded, "The careful attention given to persons, ethos and vision has made our six

---

44. International Association for the Promotion of Christian Higher Education, 70.

45. DeJong, *Reclaiming a Mission*, 78.

46. DeJong, 79.

47. Benne, *Quality with Soul*, 177–206.

schools identifiably Christian in all the major facets of their lives. The strategies they have employed have flowed from the fundamental convictions that the Christian religious account is comprehensive, unsurpassable, and central."[48] In Rine's study, "denominational identity was emphasized across many facets of institutional life, including campus ethos, curriculum, corporate worship, institutional governance, and public rhetoric."[49] There is a lot that can be learnt from these studies and recommendations. Further recommendations guided by this research's findings are discussed below to support the university under study and other transitioned or transitioning Christian universities in East Africa and beyond. It is hoped that their governing bodies, program developers, curriculum policy makers, sponsors, educational and Christian researchers, students, the church in Africa, and other interested external agencies will find these recommendations helpful.

Christian universities need to be aware of the possible threat to their Christian identity and make an unwavering commitment to guard it. This should not just be in policy documents, a Bible course here and there, or weekly chapels, but it should also be in the willingness to stand against and challenge powers that threaten their identity. That means all persons related to the university should be sensitized to live for Christ, advocate for him, and even be willing to suffer loss for the sake of Christ. As Peter said, "Judge for yourselves whether it is right in God's sight to listen to you rather than God. For we cannot stop speaking about what we have seen and heard" (Acts 4:19b–20, BSB).

Since the Commission of University Education (CUE) in Kenya has much control not only over public universities but also over private Christian universities that are accredited by the government, some of its requirements may not be supportive of evangelical Christian identity. Therefore, Christian universities should work together so that they can have a voice to advocate for their rights. For instance, it is understood that student enrolment criteria must remain open and non-discriminatory, as per CUE regulations. However, if at any point there are more non-Christian students than Christian students, that will be a clear indicator of the fading of the Christian identity. Therefore, universities should work together with churches and intensify recruitment efforts among Christians so that the population of Christians remains dominant in all Christian universities. Furthermore, a maximum percentage of non-

---

48. Benne, 177–206.

49. P. Jesse Rine, Perry L. Glanzer and Phil Davignon, "Assessing the Denominational Identity of American Evangelical Colleges and Universities, Part II: Faculty Perspectives and Practices," *Christian Higher Education* 12, no. 4 (2013): 243–265. DOI: 10.1080/15363759.2013.805996.

Christian students should be agreed on and adhered to, in spite of the need to increase student enrolment.

In relation to the above, the Christian university should maintain close contact and relationships with its founding body, sponsors, and the church of Christ at large. This is important for accountability and support purposes. Since the quality of faculty and staff members has an impact on the quality of students, and together they reflect the identity of the university, there should not be laxity in the hiring policy. The hiring policy should be thorough and restrictive so that only committed evangelical Christians can be hired and they can be held accountable. The sponsoring organization and the church at large should be involved in supplying faithful workers in the field of education.

The Christian campus ethos should be guarded by putting measures in place to support it. Leaders, administrators, faculty, and all staff should show enthusiasm and set an example for one another, and more especially for the students. These programs should be geared not just to the students but to the whole community. Chapel time should be used only for spiritual purposes and not for other agendas. Small groups should be well planned with goals and objectives so that they are not perceived merely as social events. Mentoring programs and other such activities should be put in place in such a way that every individual in the community will feel loved, cared for, and supported. Persons are the major bearers of an institution's identity. A Christian education must therefore aim for the human heart and rely on the Bible in its attempt to expand, contextualize, and integrate faith and learning.

Conclusion

The transition of theological seminaries to universities seems to have been inevitable. Educational policies, financial challenges, low student enrolment, and other market factors in the church and society have precipitated the change. The transition has both positive and negative effects to the evangelical Christian identity in terms of academic programs, campus ethos, and the Christian identity of faculty and students. This study was limited by the fact that it focused on only one institution. Another study involving several universities is recommended. There is also a need to further investigate the threat to evangelical Christian identity and to come up with solutions. This could include formulation of an assessment tool that would help Christian universities to gauge or evaluate their commitment and faithfulness to the evangelical Christian identity. Internal criteria to measure faithfulness to the evangelical Christian identity would serve as a tool in preserving that identity.

Ultimately, the desire is that evangelical Christian identity will be preserved in all Christian institutions. Therefore, it is of paramount importance that further study be carried out that will lead to formulation of effective measures to preserve and enhance the evangelical Christian identity in Christian universities applicable in the African context.

Bibliography

Africa International University. "Curriculum for Bachelor of Science in Information Technology." Submitted to the Commission for University Education, November 2015.

Astley, Jeff. *The Philosophy of Christian Religious Education*. Birmingham, AL: Religious Education Press, 1994.

Benne, Robert. *Quality with Soul: How Six Premier Colleges and Universities Keep Faith with Their Religious Traditions*. Grand Rapids, MI: Eerdmans, 2001.

Bowers, Paul. "New Light on Theological Education in Africa." *ACTEA Tools and Studies* 9 (1989). http://www.acteaweb.org/downloads/tools/Tools%20and%20Studies%2009.pdf.

Business Dictionary. "Organization Theory." *BusinessDictionary*. http://www.businessdictionary.com/definition/organization-theory.html.

Chandran, Emil. *Research Methods: A Quantitative Approach with Illustrations from Christian Ministries*. Nairobi: Daystar University, 2004.

Cohen, Louis Lawrence M., and Keith Morrison. *Research Methods in Education*. London: Routledge, 2007.

Corthial, Pierre. "The Threats to the Christian Character of the Christian Institution." In *Christian Higher Education: The Contemporary Challenge*. Ontario: Wedge Publishing Foundation, 1976.

Creswell, John W. *Research Design: Qualitative, Quantitative and Mixed Methods Approaches*. 2nd ed. London: Sage, 2003.

Dacin, M. Tina, Jerry Goodstein, and Scott W. Richard. "Institutional Theory and Institutional Change: Introduction to the Special Research Forum." *Academy of Management Journal* 45, no. 1 (February 2002): 45–56. Accessed October 2018. https://www.jstor.org/stable/3069284.

Davignon, Phil. "Factors Influencing College Choice and Satisfaction among Students at Christian Colleges and Universities." *Religion & Education* 43, no. 1 (2016): 77–94.

———. "Faith-Based Higher Education and the Religiosity of Christian College Students." PhD diss., Baylor University, 2014.

DeJong, Arthur J. *Reclaiming a Mission: New Direction for the Church-Related College*. Grand Rapids, MI: Eerdmans, 1990.

Dockery, David S., and Gregory Alan Thornbury, eds. *Shaping a Christian Worldview: The Foundations of Christian Higher Education*. Nashville: Broadman & Holman, 2002.

Gall, Joyce P., M. D. Gall, and R. Walter Borg. *Educational Research Methods: An Introduction*. 8th ed. Boston: Pearson, 2007.

Gangel, Kenneth. "Christian Higher Education and Lifelong Learning." In *Introduction to Biblical Christian Education*, edited by Werner Graendorf, 332–346. Chicago: Moody, 1981.

Gangel, Kenneth O., and Warren S. Benson. *Christian Education: Its History and Philosophy*. Chicago: Moody, 1983.

Glanzer, Perry L., P. Jesse Rine, and Phil Davignon. "Assessing the Denominational Identity of American Evangelical Colleges and Universities, Part I: Denominational Patronage and Institutional Policy." *Christian Higher Education* 12, no. 3 (2013): 181–202. Accessed 31 October 2018. DOI: 10.1080/15363759.2013.785871.

Henry, Douglas V., and Bob R. Agee, eds. *Faithful Learning and the Christian Scholarly Vocation*. Grand Rapids, MI: Eerdmans, 2003.

Holmes, F. Arthur. *The Idea of a Christian College*. Grand Rapids, MI: Eerdmans, 1975.

Hughes, Richard T. *The Vocation of a Christian Scholar: How Christian Faith Can Sustain the Life of the Mind*. Grand Rapids, MI: Eerdmans, 2005.

Institute for the Advancement of Calvinism. *Christian Higher Education: The Contemporary Challenge*. Transvaal: Potchefstroom Herald, 1976.

International Association for the Promotion of Christian Higher Education. *Christian Education in the African Context: Proceedings of the African Regional Conference of IAPCHE, Harare, 4–9 March 1991*. Grand Rapids, MI: IAPCHE, 1992.

InterUniversity Council of East Africa Directory. East African Universities and Higher Education in Partnership with Inter University Council of East Africa Directory 2015/2016.

Kenya Universities and Colleges Central Placement Services. "Admission of 10,000 Government Sponsored Students to Degree Courses in Private Universities." Accessed 7 May 2017. http://kuccps.net/?q=content/admission-10000-government-sponsored-students-degree-courses-private-universities.

Kothari, C. R., and Gaurav Garg. *Research Methodology: Methods and Techniques*. 3rd ed. New Delhi: New Age International, 2014.

Kromminga, J. H. "The Threats to the Christian Character of the Christian Institution." In *Christian Higher Education: The Contemporary Challenge*. Ontario: Wedge, 1976.

Litfin, Duane. *Conceiving the Christian College*. Grand Rapids, MI: Eerdmans, 2004.

Malik, Charles Habib. *A Christian Critique of the University*. Downers Grove, IL: InterVarsity Press, 1982.

Marsden, George M., and Bradley J. Longfield, eds. *The Secularization of the Academy*. New York: Oxford University Press, 1992.

Marvin, Taylor, ed. *Foundations for Christian Education in an Era of Change*. Nashville: Abingdon, 1976.

Monroe, Kelly, ed. *Finding God at Harvard: Spiritual Journeys of Thinking Christians.* Grand Rapids, MI: Zondervan, 1996.

Monsma, Stephen V. "Christian Worldview in Academia." *Faculty Dialogue* 21 (Spring–Summer 1994): 139–147.

Mugenda, Abel Gitau. *Social Science Research: Theory and Principles.* Nairobi: Applied Research and Training, 2008.

Mugenda, Olive M., and Abel G. Mugenda. *Research Methods: Quantitative and Qualitative Approaches.* Nairobi: African Centre for Technology Studies, 2003.

Mulatu, Semeon. "Transitioning from a Theological Christian University to a Christian University in East African Context: A Multi-Case Study." PhD diss., Southern Baptist Theological Seminary, 2012. ProQuest LLC, 2012. ERIC, EBSCOhost. Accessed 2 February 2016.

———. *Transitioning from a Theological College to a Christian University: A Multi-Case Study in the East African Context.* ICETE Series. Carlisle: Langham Global Library, 2017.

Nairobi Evangelical Graduate School of Theology. "Curriculum." Presented to the Kenya Commission for Higher Education, December 2003.

Ogunji, James A. "Fostering the Identity and Mission of Christian Education in Africa." *Journal of Research on Christian Education* 21, no. 1 (1 January 2012): 46–61. ERIC, EBSCOhost. Accessed 22 February 2016.

Osborne, Grant R. *Matthew.* Zondervan Exegetical Commentary on the New Testament. Edited by Clinton E. Arnold. Grand Rapids, MI: Zondervan, 2010.

Ozan, Jaquette. "Why Do Colleges Become Universities? Mission Drift and the Enrolment Economy." *Research in Higher Education* 54, no. 5 (August 2013): 514–543. Accessed 31 October 2018. https://doi.org/10.1007/s11162-013-9283-x.

Poe, Harry L. *Christianity in the Academy: Teaching at the Intersection of Faith and Learning.* Grand Rapids, MI: Baker Academic, 2004.

Poston, Larry. "The Role of Higher Education in the Christian World Mission: Past, Present and Future." *Alliance Academic Review 1999,* last modified 2006, accessed 31 October 2018. http://www.kneillfoster.com/aar/summary/index1999.html.

Rine, P. Jesse, Perry L. Glanzer, and Phil Davignon. "Assessing the Denominational Identity of American Evangelical Colleges and Universities, Part II: Faculty Perspectives and Practices." *Christian Higher Education* 12, no. 4, (2013): 243–265. DOI: 10.1080/15363759.2013.805996.

Ringenberg, William C. *The Christian College: A History of Protestant Higher Education in America.* Grand Rapids, MI: Eerdmans, 1984.

Suskie, Linda A. *Assessing Student Learning: A Common-Sense Guide.* Bolton, MA: Anker, 2004.

Swezey, James A., and T. Christopher Ross. "Balancing Religious Identity and Academic Reputation at a Christian University." *Christian Higher Education* 11, no. 2 (1 January 2012): 94–114. ERIC, EBSCOhost. Accessed 22 February 2016.

Thaver, Bev. "Private Higher Education in Africa: Six Country Case Studies." In *African Higher Education: An International Reference Handbook*, edited by Damtew Teferra and Philip G. Altbach, 53–60. Indianapolis: Indiana University Press, 2003.

Wolterstorff, Nicholas. *Educating for Shalom: Essays in Christian Higher Education.* Edited by Clarence W. Joldersma and Gloria Goris Stronks. Grand Rapids, MI: Eerdmans, 2004.

10

Educational Liturgy: Towards Innovation, Creativity, and Devotion

Robert D. Falconer

Programme Coordinator for MTh and PhD Research, South Africa Theological Seminary

Abstract

This paper explores the benefits of liturgical ritual in Christian educational institutions. As evangelicals, we all too often neglect liturgy and ritual at the expense of what may well be a fruitful and liberating experience, especially for education. To begin, I argue, along with James K. A. Smith and Peter Leithart, that we are *liturgical creatures* and that all of us participate in secular liturgies. I highlight the formation of the students' desires and the development of habit. It will be proposed that the university (or school) is a liturgical space. At a very fundamental level, the university is already a place of liturgy and ritual. After observing features of the *already* existing liturgical fabric of an educational institution, suggestions are offered in the way of further possibilities for experiencing education as liturgy, namely, habits and practices, and baptism as reformation and reshaping. This leads on to the necessity for such an educational liturgy, its beauty, as well as its benefits. I propose how purposeful liturgy in education may facilitate innovation and creativity, and, more importantly, how it leads the student towards devotion to Christ. Educational Liturgy is about formation, over and above *in*formation.

Key words: Christian education, educational liturgy, educational habits, secular liturgies, rituals, liturgical creatures, Christian creativity, Christian devotion

Introduction

The word "liturgy" conjures up images of incense, bells, vestments, sacraments, prayers, chanting, and so on. This is true of many forms of traditional Christian liturgy, especially in the Roman Catholic, Orthodox, and High Anglican ecclesiastical traditions. More generally, Christian liturgy might refer to any regular pattern of worship of a congregation prescribed for public worship. It is, therefore, true that liturgy exists in every Christian church, whether it be formal and rich or informal and shallow.[1] Liturgy may also be found outside the church's masonry walls. The Christian philosopher James K. A. Smith has identified liturgy not only in the home, but also in shopping malls and sports stadiums, and even in the universities and schools.[2] One might call these "secular liturgies."

Wolterstorff describes liturgy as like music whereby "one acquires some particular liturgical know-how by being inducted into a social practice for the exercise of this know-how."[3] He continues to explain how this know-how is shared from those who know to those who do not have the know-how, and how, in this way, it is handed down. I imagine it is like learning a cultural dance from a foreign community, learned by awkward imitation.

This chapter explores *educational liturgy*, and how students might be liberated by liturgical rituals in the classroom and education, moving students towards innovation, creativity, and Christian devotion. While some introductory thoughts have been given towards a definition of liturgy, the next discussion will offer a detailed definition, followed by a discussion on the formation of desires. After that, I will examine the university as a liturgical space, followed by suggestions for a methodology for experiencing education as liturgy. Some thoughts on purposeful liturgical education will then be offered, followed by a conclusion.

---

1. By "informal and shallow," I do not necessarily mean that an informal liturgy *is* shallow, even though this is often the case, but rather I use "formal and rich or informal and shallow" to signify the two extremes. Naturally, there exists everything in between, even an informal liturgy that could be said to be rich.

2. James K. A. Smith, *Desiring the Kingdom: Worship, Worldview, and Cultural Formation*, Cultural Liturgies (Grand Rapids, MI: Baker Academic, 2009), Kindle.

3. Nicholas Wolterstorff, *The God We Worship: An Exploration of Liturgical Theology*, Kantzer Lectures in Revealed Theology (Grand Rapids, MI: Eerdmans, 2015), Kindle.

Definition of Liturgy

Pickstock explains that etymologically, "liturgy" means "the work of the people," and for a liturgical culture, all activities are in one way or another a liturgical enactment. Liturgy may be considered as a subcategory of ritual. Ritual becomes liturgy when the participation in a ritual assists in a divine act, or is itself a divine act.[4] This is true of ecclesiastical liturgy. If we considered the meaning of liturgy in even broader terms, we might say that it is a body of rites, a fixed set of rituals and words said, or even a collection of ideas and habits (or observances).

Unfortunately, for many people, the term "ritual" has negative connotations, referring to religious, superstitious activities irrelevant to modern life.[5] This kind of response is understandable, especially when ritual signifies repetition, sometimes without a narrative of reason. A liturgy, on the other hand, assumes that the ritual is a type of signifying structure "possible only in terms of its organization around some privileged transcendent signifier, even if this remains mysterious in character and open to interpretation," says Pickstock.[6] The transcendent or the divine is not, however, necessary for secular liturgies, but as we will see, they are substituted by secular desires.

Ratzinger (Pope Benedict XVI Emeritus) develops a detailed discussion on liturgy, albeit the Roman Catholic liturgy, in his book *The Spirit of the Liturgy*. Although he would not limit liturgy to "a kind of anticipation," he affirms that it includes being "a kind of anticipation, a kind of rehearsal, a prelude for the life to come, for eternal life." In part, he believes that liturgy allows for the rediscovery within us for true childhood, an "openness to a greatness still to come, which is still unfulfilled in adult life."[7] While an evangelical Christian may not wish to endorse all that Ratzinger says about liturgy, his description is no doubt, at least for me, much more attractive than meaningless ritual. It would be helpful to keep in mind this description for the discussions which follow.

---

4. Catherine Pickstock, "Liturgy, Art and Politics," *Modern Theology* 16, no. 2 (2000): 163; Wolterstorff, *God We Worship*, understands the theology of liturgy as that place where theologians arrive at a self-understanding of the liturgical theology, both implicit and explicit. The goal of liturgical theology, he believes, is not self-examination by the church of its liturgy, but rather "self-understanding by the church of the theology implicit and explicit in its liturgy." In this way, liturgical theology is like creedal theology.

5. Andrea McCloskey, "The Promise of Ritual: A Lens for Understanding Persistent Practices in Mathematics Classrooms," *Educational Studies in Mathematics* 86, no. 1 (2014): 24.

6. Pickstock, "Liturgy, Art and Politics," 159.

7. Joseph Ratzinger, *The Spirit of the Liturgy*, trans. J. Saward (San Francisco: Ignatius, 2000), 14.

Formation of Desires

Liturgical Creatures and Secular Liturgies

Not all rituals and liturgies are religious, and while "rituals constitute the very core of every religion," rituals become "religious as soon as they implicate a transcendent reality," according to Altena and Hermans.[8] Warnick argues that we ought not to think of rituals as existing only in religious ceremonies, but rather recognize them "as something that permeates everyday life."[9] Therefore, we take up liturgical practices every day, and in turn, these practices shape our desires. Leithart tells us that "our lives are formed out of habits and rituals."[10] Human beings are by nature "liturgical creatures";[11] we cannot help but *worship*, and therefore we are formed fundamentally by worship-type practices or liturgies. Whether such liturgies are "secular" or Christian, they nonetheless shape what we love, says Smith.[12] Währisch-Oblau, referring to Smith's description of human beings as "embodied actors rather than merely thinking things," understands the identity of the human as located in the "affective motivations and concerns." This is because humans are "desiring, imaginative animals, lovers whose deepest desire is the good life."[13] Whether we are aware of it or not, we all participate meaningfully in secular liturgies; for example, shopping malls and sports stadiums are liturgical spaces:

The shopping mall (1) is usually located in the prime position in the city, as churches once were; (2) "secular icons" remind us of the object of our devotion (advertising); (3) sweet and savory smells draw us into restaurants and coffee shops; (4) shop assistants assist us like church stewards might; (5) tellers help us "tithe" to the secular liturgical space; (6) secular music can be heard in the background;[14] (7) the entrance(s) to shopping malls are grand; (8) secular

---

8. Patrick Altena and Chris A. M. Hermans, "Ritual Education in a Pluralistic Society," *International Journal of Education & Religion* 4, no. 2 (2003): 111.

9. Bryan R. Warnick, "Ritual, Imitation and Education in R. S. Peters," *Journal of Philosophy of Education* 43, no. s1 (2009): 57.

10. Peter J. Leithart, "Habit-Forming: Liturgies of Education," First Things Lecture, 14 December 2015, https://www.firstthings.com/media/habit-forming-liturgies-of-education.

11. Likewise, Pickstock, "Liturgy, Art and Politics," 160, argues that the human life is fundamentally ritual – it is liturgical in character – in the same way that the human is linguistic and social.

12. James K. A. Smith, *Imagining the Kingdom: How Worship Works*, Cultural Liturgies (Grand Rapids, MI: Baker Academic, 2013), Kindle.

13. Claudia Währisch-Oblau, "Evangelism and Popular Culture," *International Review of Mission* 103, no. 2 (2014): 222.

14. In the Majority World it is often religious music.

evangelism calls for our devotion (television commercials, billboards, and advertisements act as a kind of "secular evangelism").[15]

On the other hand, the liturgy of a *sports stadium*[16] is marked by the following: (1) Mascots remind us of the team we are devoted to; (2) songs affirm our devotion to the nation or to the team we support; (3) processions exhibit the object of our devotion; (4) visuals in the way of "sponsorship signage" advertise in the hope of acquiring our devotion; (5) attending a sports event in a stadium is often patriotic; (6) spectating at a sports event (or even a music concert) in a stadium forms our love for a particular sport (or music band) and nation.[17]

Währisch-Oblau points out that Protestant worship seems to be more focused on the cognitive, with few affective and sensual elements and little bodily involvement, at least in traditional congregations of the West. Such a liturgy is limited to Scripture reading, the expository sermon, and the Lord's Supper. Secular liturgies, on the other hand, have a strong physical element which allows space for emotion, providing "thick practices that really shape people's lives and beliefs."[18] Engaging with Smith's work on secular liturgy, Währisch-Oblau writes:

> Smith posits that liturgies – whether "sacred" or "secular" – shape and constitute our identities by forming our most fundamental desires and our most basic attunement to the world. He suggests reading culture through the lens of worship, exegeting practices as liturgies that function as pedagogies of desire, and analyzing what vision of human flourishing is implicit in this or that practice. We may then see, for example, that consumer capitalism aims to redirect the desires for wholeness, healing and belonging toward the consumption of material goods.[19]

Therefore, while there is nothing wrong with visiting shopping malls and attending sports or music events at sports stadiums, or even enjoying them,

---

15. James K. A. Smith, *You Are What You Love: The Spiritual Power of Habit* (Grand Rapids, MI: Brazos, 2016), Kindle.

16. Währisch-Oblau, in "Evangelism and Popular Culture," 221, tells how "certain expressions of popular culture function like religion: football, with its rituals, ecstasy and community."

17. Smith, *You Are What You Love*.

18. Währisch-Oblau, "Evangelism and Popular Culture," 223. Some Pentecostal and charismatic liturgies embody many of the positive attributes of secular liturgies, even if such liturgies are not always theologically rich.

19. Währisch-Oblau, 222.

we should be aware of the secular liturgies in place and that they compete for our devotion. Smith explains that these rituals grab hold of our hearts and direct them towards a secular devotion, promoting the good life and promises of happiness. Students have, therefore, already been shaped by such secular liturgies by the time they go to their universities and schools.[20]

Desire

I suggest that Christian education should be a liturgy, a body of rituals that, most importantly, directs the students' desires towards a Christ-centered devotion and then also provides opportunities to students to discover their loves and passions, whether in the arts, creative writing, the sciences, languages, mathematics, and so on, exposing to them what it is they love and desire. Accordingly, Willard reminds us that "love is an emotional response aroused in the will by visions of the good"; love can only exist in a vision of the "beloved."[21]

Considering this, it is not surprising that "liturgical enjoyment is sustainable enjoyment," despite the efforts and disciplines that are required, as Pickstock rightly put it. She continues by offering a striking thought: "only the liturgical offers a vision of an alternative that can nonetheless be regarded as a real possibility, a pleasure that we might work for in the heart of our lives."[22]

Habits

Students, however, can rarely tell what their desires are from an instant of exposure to a certain subject or discipline. They need frequent exposure to different subjects and disciplines by the formation of habits. An example of frequent exposure in an English class might be that students begin each lesson with ten minutes of writing a short impromptu poem. Such a habit may inspire the creativity and devotion of a future African poet.

For many people, the word "rite" or "ritual" is usually viewed negatively, with suspicion; it "suggests rigidity, a restriction to prescribed forms," Ratzinger tells us. He continues by saying that it is often viewed "in opposition to that creativity and dynamism of inculturation by which, so people say, we get a really living liturgy, in which each community can express itself."[23] But such

---

20. Smith, *You Are What You Love*.

21. Dallas Willard, *The Divine Conspiracy: Rediscovering Our Hidden Life in God* (London: Harper Collins, 1998), 354.

22. Pickstock, "Liturgy, Art and Politics," 163.

23. Ratzinger, *Spirit of the Liturgy*, 159.

a negative attitude need not be. Could liturgy, its rites and rituals, not be the very engine of creativity and dynamism? This chapter argues for such a lively liturgy in education.

Bruton recommends that rituals that run every day thinking ought to be let go of for the development of innovative ideas and imaginative processes. This, he believes, helps students "move beyond their normal thinking into an imaginative world of response to inner visions."[24] Considering my previous argument, I am at odds with Bruton; I argue that liturgy and its rituals undergird and stimulate creative thinking and imagination.

Formation

We are liturgical creatures who are partners with God in this world; we are in liturgical dialogue with him, responding to his Word and empowered by his divine speech.[25] On the other hand, as Smith proclaims, the mission of Christian education is not simply about imparting information to the students (though it is that too), but it is more importantly and fundamentally an exercise in formation.[26] Authentic Christian education should offer an education that is both holistic and formative. While it should provide knowledge and skill, it should also shape the students' fundamental orientation to the world.

It becomes clear, then, that students' formation in Christian education ought to be a liturgical partner with God, empowered by his divine speech to be orientated towards the world in such a way as to communicate this divine speech effectively in word and deed. Altena and Hermans continue this theme, explaining that rites "occur because people have certain reasons for performing them because they cherish certain expectations regarding the effects of the ritual act"; these effects, they believe, "may be understood in terms of communication."[27]

Liturgy and its rites are among the spiritual disciplines, the purpose of which is the transformation and formation of the person. Foster explains that these disciplines "aim at replacing old destructive habits of thought with new life-giving habits."[28] Horton agrees and says that "*Being* disciples involves a

---

24. Dean Bruton, "Learning Creativity and Design for Innovation," *International Journal of Technology & Design Education* 21, no. 3 (2011): 324.

25. Leithart, "Habit-Forming."

26. Smith, *Imagining the Kingdom.*

27. Altena and Hermans, "Ritual Education in a Pluralistic Society," 109.

28. Richard Foster, *Celebration of Discipline: The Path to Spiritual Growth* (London: Hodder & Stoughton, 2008), 78.

whole formation of life, with new choices, habits, and virtues that exhibit new character."[29]

University as Liturgical Space

Earlier we looked at two secular liturgies, namely, shopping malls and sports stadiums. In this discussion, I want to consider the university (or a school or college) as a liturgical space.

Already, the university is fundamentally a place of liturgy and ritual. As Leithart highlights,[30] this is evident in the following ways: (1) The classroom is the space for a formative liturgical dialogue between the teacher and students – that is, the teacher speaks, perhaps with a question, and the students respond. (2) The ritualized rhythm is also evident in the assignment (or paper) writing: The student reads, studies, and writes, and then the professor evaluates. (3) There is a meeting of old and young (there is a difference in maturity in terms of mastering content). (4) Professors and teachers take on the function of "priests of knowledge," evident at graduation when such "priests" walk in procession in their brightly colored "vestments." (5) The professor or teacher enacts the "mystical ritual," both evoking the traditions of the past and reaching forward into the future in foresight and equipping students for their future. (6) The students, on the other hand, with the help of the professor, reach back into the past, acquiring and studying the traditions of the past for their academic disciplines. (7) No doubt, in universities a more general sense of traditional heritage also exists. (8) As with ecclesiastical liturgies, a pursuit of truth is evident in universities, along with certain devotion(s) and commitment(s).

Warnick explains that rituals serve as a stage for imitative learning, but they are also an invitation, pointing "students to social practices rather than just to individual examples." Students usually undervalue the practiced ritual until they have considerable experience in it. Such liturgical rituals become "useful when a student has to be internal to the practice to appreciate what it has to offer." When students enter more deeply into a practice, and if it is successful, they will see its inherent worth.[31]

Evidently, the university (or place of learning) *is* a formative liturgical institution whereby liturgies and rituals have established a pedagogy of desire.

---

29. Michael Horton, *The Gospel Commission: Recovering God's Strategy for Making Disciples* (Grand Rapids, MI: Baker, 2011), 141.

30. Leithart, "Habit-Forming."

31. Warnick, "Ritual, Imitation and Education," 62.

Christian education, and to some extent all education, is for lovers; it is for desirers. I argue that any place of education is not ultimately about imparting knowledge, but, like secular liturgies, it seeks to grab hold of our hearts, our desires, and our imagination, making us certain kinds of people. Similarly, St Augustine wrote in the *City of God* that people are an assembly of reasonable beings joined together by a common or collective agreement as to the objects of their love (desire). Therefore, if we are to discover the character of a people, we need only observe what they love. They are "bound together by higher interests."[32]

Perhaps the most dramatic evidence of the university as a liturgical space may be found in the architecture of some of the greatest universities – the University of Oxford, the University of Cambridge, the University of Sydney, and so on – which were often designed in the Gothic tradition, towering like medieval Gothic cathedrals. Could these be the "Cathedrals of Learning," fully furnished with liturgical expression?[33]

Methodology: Experiencing Education as Liturgy

Habits and Practices

Having observed features of the existing liturgical fabric of educational spaces, I wish to offer a further reflection on additional methodology or possibilities for experiencing education as liturgy.

Leithart mentions how God himself is a divine liturgist, speaking forth creative speech in a way that is repetitive and ritualized. It goes without saying that we were created in the image of God and thus we too are liturgical. And as liturgical creatures, habits are formed,[34] obviously by instruction, although primarily by practice. This is true of sportsmen and musicians, for example. Leithart continues, "In the church, the liturgy is one of the Spirit's instruments for shaping godly persons and communities, and the same is true in education."[35]

Habits are formed by means of practices that train our desires by giving fuel to our imaginations through real-life rituals.[36] So, when we consider particularly Christian education – not simply Christian beliefs (those are

---

32. Augustine, *The City of God*, trans. Marcus Dods (Peabody, MA: Hendrickson, 2014), book 19, ch. 24.

33. Smith, *Desiring the Kingdom*.

34. Cf. Ratzinger, *Spirit of the Liturgy*, 160.

35. Leithart, "Habit-Forming."

36. Smith, *Desiring the Kingdom*.

important too), but Christian practice – we need to ask ourselves what this might look like in terms of methodology and experience. The following are some ideas for experiencing education as liturgy.

Marrying Church and Classroom in Chapel

The chapel offers space for the community of the Christian university to gather and engage in liturgical practices that not only demonstrate the kingdom of God but also form our imaginations. As I have argued, Christian education is formation, and such formation begins in the practice of Christian worship. Therefore, worship is the prerequisite of Christian education. This is vital when Christian students begin to engage with the world. The chapel also acts as a type of mediation between the church and the university, whereby it extends Sunday worship into daily worship and liturgical practices that are meaningful.[37]

Connecting the Classroom with the Neighborhood

Intentional apprenticeship to Jesus provides connections between faith in Christ Jesus and the life of obedience and fulfillment in his kingdom. Those who have found their way into this kingdom and are apprenticed to Jesus will certainly want to share the new reality. Naturally, when people discover something great, they want all those whom they care about to be a part of it as well. And Jesus's apprentices are called to love their neighbors.[38]

Smith offers the following suggestions for the Christian university and its students who consider themselves apprentices of Jesus: They could see their neighborhood and wider environment as a place for nurturing Christian practices and intentional communities. This does not just mean having Bible studies (though that's not a bad idea), but that students engage in varied Christian practices – for example, sharing meals, observing the Sabbath together, doing acts of kindness and generosity, the faculty extending acts of hospitality to the students, and even students demonstrating hospitality to those outside the walls of the university, worshiping together, and embarking on a humanitarian project. Such practices might contribute towards a "rich fabric of formation that would nourish the imagination and prime the community for thinking Christianly in their learning and scholarship."[39]

---

37. Smith.

38. Cf. Matt 5:13, 43–48; 19:19; 22:36–40; Mark 12:29–31; Luke 6:27; 10:25–37; Willard, *Divine Conspiracy*, 328.

39. Smith, *Desiring the Kingdom*.

Embodied Learning

Students ought to be encouraged to connect their minds with their bodies when learning. Willard says it well when he proclaims the irony that "*all* of the 'spiritual' disciplines are, or essentially involve, bodily behaviors," and he is right that this "makes perfect sense," because "the body is the first field of energy beyond our thoughts that we have direction over, and all else we influence is due to our power over it."[40] Educational liturgy would do well to adopt an embodied approach to learning that deliberately unthinks and undoes our dualistic legacy.[41]

Stolz points out the significance of embodied learning in how we think and learn, and that a recent movement called "embodied cognition" draws from several traditions in philosophy, psychology, and cognitive science. Proponents of embodied cognition begin, as their starting point, not with a disembodied "mind working on abstract problems, but a body that requires the mind to make it function."[42] The phenomenology of embodied learning, therefore, requires a profound connection between intellect, perception, and action, learning as unified persons instead of Cartesian entities.[43] Stolz explains: "If every experience embodies reaction and interaction of the whole organism to and with his or her environment, the experience cannot be just 'physical' or 'mental' because such views continue to perpetuate unaltered dualistic views and prejudices that are unsatisfactory theories of perception."[44] Embodied learning that is liturgically informed should discover ways of creating learning environments that invigorate such practices that enliven the imagination and form the students' characters.[45]

Demonstrating the Kingdom of God

Währisch-Oblau proclaims that Christian worship ought to be "lived and understood as 'practicing (for) the Kingdom.'"[46] This might be done in part by forming a series of rituals demonstrating the kingdom of God in the following

---

40. Willard, *Divine Conspiracy*, 387.

41. Pickstock, "Liturgy, Art and Politics," 162.

42. Steven A. Stolz, "Embodied Learning," *Educational Philosophy & Theory* 47, no. 5 (2015): 475.

43. Cf. Stolz, "Embodied Learning," 478–482.

44. Stolz, 478–479.

45. Cf. Smith, *Desiring the Kingdom*.

46. Währisch-Oblau, "Evangelism and Popular Culture," 223.

ways:[47] (1) *Know God's story.* Spend time each week learning about Christ through the Gospels. (2) *Celebrate.* Make God the center of your celebrations and invite people to them (e.g. graduations, reunions, anniversaries). (3) *Listen.* Listen to other people and to the people in your community; listen to their concerns and fears, their hopes and desires. Sow the love of Christ by listening. (4) *Bless others.* Bless those within and outside of your university community. (5) *Re-create.* Allow time for leisure, but also to design and to create beauty. (6) *Become people of peace.* Work alongside people of peace, receive people and welcome them, serve people. Contribute to your community. (7) *Practice hospitality.* Eat with others, Christians and non-Christians. Jesus often did this! Invite people. Open your home or your dorm. (8) *Share your faith as a Christian in culturally relevant ways.* Invite people to become a part of the gospel story. Demonstrate and proclaim the gospel in a way that people can understand.[48]

Baptism: Reformation and Reshaping

Another way of experiencing education as liturgy is the concept of the liturgical act of baptism. The students' baptism is the renunciation of all secular liturgies.[49] It is not that students should never participate in them, but that they are to put secular liturgies into perspective. Baptism acts as a political statement, vying for the students' unaltered devotion and allegiance to Christ, allowing for these *strange* Christian liturgies to grab hold of the students' hearts, desires, and imaginations. If the Christian university can harness this, it will, as Smith says, "be much stranger than many of our existing Christian colleges, but its strangeness would stem from the fact that it is a space for the formation of a peculiar people."[50] Leithart comments further that baptism, and in turn, discipleship, calls us out of the liturgies of the world and directs our attention

---

47. Most of the following points are not originally mine, but are taken from notes made from a variety of sources now lost to me.

48. Michael Frost's little book *Surprise the World: The Five Habits of Highly Missional People* (Colorado Springs: NavPress, 2015) offers similar suggestions.

49. In his book *Surprised by Hope: Rethinking Heaven, the Resurrection, and the Mission of the Church* (New York: HarperOne, 2008), 272, N. T. Wright alludes to a similar idea, using different language, when he writes, "The important thing, then, is that in the simple but powerful action of plunging someone into the water in the name of the triune God, there is *a real dying to the old creation and a real rising into the new* – with all the dangerous privileges and responsibilities that then accompany the new life as it sets out in the as-yet-unredeemed world. Baptism is not magic, a conjuring trick with water. But neither is it simply a visual aid. It is one of the points, established by Jesus himself, where heaven and earth interlock, where new creation, resurrection life, appears within the midst of the old" (emphasis mine).

50. Smith, *Desiring the Kingdom*.

to the cosmic liturgist.[51] With that in mind, I will now explore how purposeful liturgy in education directs the student towards innovation, creativity, and devotion to Christ.

Purposeful Liturgical Education

Purposeful Liturgy in Ritual and Practice: Towards Innovation and Creativity

Education trains students in the basic skills of reading, writing, mathematics, science, art, and so on. And in the university, education trains the students in their professions. Yet, more importantly, education offers opportunities to students, exposing to them their desires, their loves.

Innovation and creativity happen when ritualized actions are put in place. Such "actions free us and form us to love certain things."[52] Take, for instance, training for football, learning a new language, or learning a musical instrument: the same exercise is done repeatedly until it becomes instinctive. None of it is spontaneous until the mind and body have trained and practiced certain ritualized actions.[53] It is only when we are liberated by such rituals to play the game well, to speak the new language fluently, or to play great music without thinking too much about it that it becomes part of our lives.[54] It takes liturgical practice. Consequently, liturgy gives birth to innovation and creativity. Learning liturgy in ritual and practice, then, is not merely "information acquisition; it's more like inscribing something into the very fiber of your being."[55] In this way, "*We exhibit excellence in our everyday creativity . . .* we become masters of creativity in endeavors arising from our distant gifts, talents, and calling. We are emboldened to believe that God has called us to build a glorious culture by reflecting His image, and we will devote our days to intelligently and imaginatively creating a life and a culture that reflects God's creativity and excellence."[56] I believe that if Christian education takes liturgy in

---

51. Leithart, "Habit-Forming."

52. Leithart.

53. Cf. Stolz, "Embodied Learning," 478–484.

54. Horton, *Gospel Commission*, 147, and Willard, *Divine Conspiracy*, 386.

55. Smith, *You Are What You Love.*

56. Dick Staub, *The Culturally Savvy Christian: A Manifesto for Deepening Faith and Enriching Popular Culture in an Age of Christianity-Lite* (San Francisco: Jossey-Bass, 2007), 109; italics original. In Staub, *Culturally Savvy Christian*, 108–109, these words are used slightly differently. He argues that, as one of five steps, "with God's glory as our goal and guide, we seek to become fully human in the following ways: . . . *We exhibit excellence in our everyday creativity*," etc.

ritual and practice seriously and is purposeful in its implementation, education will experience progression towards a greater expression of innovation and creativity.

Purposeful Liturgy in Worship and Education: Towards Devotion to Christ

Staub articulates "worship" as "the practice (or may I say, 'habit' or 'ritual') of adoring, reverencing, and honoring." The Christian "knows that God is central and worships God as a way of life."[57] Foster explains worship as to experience "reality, to touch Life. It is to know, to feel, to experience the resurrected Christ in the midst of the gathered community."[58] Piper takes a different approach, consistent with his "Christian hedonism." He believes that worship is not an end in itself; rather, "happiness in God is the end of all our seeking." There is nothing, he says, that can be sought that is beyond this higher goal.[59] Further, Piper understands that "the quickening of the heart's affections" transforms the outward ritual into worship that is authentic,[60] and I think this ought to be affirmed. It is not that there should be no rituals or liturgy, but rather that they serve a purpose: they transform into authentic worship and lead to heartfelt devotion to Christ. Wolterstorff, who advocates liturgical practices more than Piper does, writes, "When the church assembles for communal worship, she does what she was called into existence to do. The church exists to worship God in Christ. It is in this sense that, in enacting the liturgy, she actualizes herself; and in actualizing herself, she manifests herself."[61] The invitation is for both the church and the educational institution to enact their liturgical practices or rituals and so actualize themselves. In this way they become expressions of mission, calling us to action, to Christian practices. If this is so, could the edges of church, chapel, and classroom be blurred to facilitate Christian practices?

Obviously, the church and the educational institution are different, and the university chapel mediates between the two; yet they ought to share the same goal: to draw people into fellowship with Jesus Christ, to equip, shape, and form them so that they may be meaningful and effective doers of the Word.[62] Leithart

---

57. Staub, *Culturally Savvy Christian*, 107.

58. Foster, *Celebration of Discipline*, 197.

59. Piper's "Christian hedonist theology" is controversial and not accepted by all, not even within his own theological tradition.

60. John Piper, *Desiring God: Meditations of a Christian Hedonist* (Colorado Springs: Multnomah, 2003), 90.

61. Wolterstorff, *God We Worship*.

62. Cf. Smith, *Imagining the Kingdom*.

agrees: "Liturgy should be a central part of the school. It's the central part that brings education together – it forms the students' devotion to Jesus Christ."[63]

Ratzinger[64] once said, "Christianity is not an intellectual system, a collection of dogmas, or a moralism. Christianity is instead an encounter, a love story."[65] May this be true of Christian education as well!

Conclusion

In this chapter, I have explored educational liturgy and argued how students might be liberated by liturgical rituals in education that move students towards innovation, creativity, and Christian devotion. To that end, I began by defining liturgy and ritual, and then offered a discussion on the formation of desires. After that, I examined the university as a liturgical space, and then gave suggestions for a methodology for experiencing education as liturgy. I provided some thoughts on purposeful liturgy in ritual and practice, exploring innovation and creativity. Lastly, some thoughts on purposeful liturgy in worship and education with an emphasis on devotion to Christ were offered.

In conclusion, the main idea in this chapter is that educational liturgy is formation over and above *in*formation and that Christian education should be a pedagogy of desire, directing the students towards innovation, creativity, and devotion to Christ.

Bibliography

Altena, Patrick, and Chris A. M. Hermans. "Ritual Education in a Pluralistic Society." *International Journal of Education & Religion* 4, no. 2 (2003): 105–127.

Augustine. *The City of God*. Translated by Marcus Dods. Peabody, MA: Hendrickson, 2014.

Bruton, Dean. "Learning Creativity and Design for Innovation." *International Journal of Technology & Design Education* 21, no. 3 (2011): 321–333. DOI: 10.1007/s10798-010-9122-8.

Foster, Richard. *Celebration of Discipline: The Path to Spiritual Growth*. London: Hodder & Stoughton, 2008.

Frost, Michael. *Surprise the World: The Five Habits of Highly Missional People*. Colorado Springs: NavPress, 2015.

---

63. Leithart, "Habit-Forming."

64. A.k.a. Pope Benedict XVI Emeritus.

65. Joseph Ratzinger, "Funeral Homily for Msgr. Luigi Giussani," 2004, http://www.communio-icr.com/files/ratzinger31-4.pdf.

Horton, Michael. *The Gospel Commission: Recovering God's Strategy for Making Disciples*. Grand Rapids, MI: Baker, 2011.

Leithart, Peter J. "Habit-Forming: Liturgies of Education, 2015." First Things Lecture, 14 December 2015. https://www.firstthings.com/media/habit-forming-liturgies-of-education.

McCloskey, Andrea. "The Promise of Ritual: A Lens for Understanding Persistent Practices in Mathematics Classrooms." *Educational Studies in Mathematics* 86, no. 1 (2014): 19–38. DOI: 10.1007/s10649-013-9520-4.

Pickstock, Catherine. "Liturgy, Art and Politics." *Modern Theology* 16, no. 2 (2000): 159–180.

Piper, John. *Desiring God: Meditations of a Christian Hedonist*. Colorado Springs: Multnomah, 2003.

Ratzinger, Joseph. "Funeral Homily for Msgr. Luigi Giussani." 2004. http://www.communio-icr.com/files/ratzinger31-4.pdf.

———. *The Spirit of the Liturgy*. Translated by J. Saward. San Francisco: Ignatius, 2000.

Smith, James K. A. *Desiring the Kingdom: Worship, Worldview, and Cultural Formation*. Cultural Liturgies. Grand Rapids, MI: Baker Academic, 2009. Kindle.

———. *Imagining the Kingdom: How Worship Works*. Cultural Liturgies. Grand Rapids, MI: Baker Academic, 2013. Kindle.

———. *You Are What You Love: The Spiritual Power of Habit*. Grand Rapids, MI: Brazos, 2016. Kindle.

Staub, Dick. *The Culturally Savvy Christian: A Manifesto for Deepening Faith and Enriching Popular Culture in an Age of Christianity-Lite*. San Francisco: Jossey-Bass, 2007.

Stolz, Steven A. "Embodied Learning." *Educational Philosophy & Theory* 47, no. 5 (2015): 474–487. DOI: 10.1080/00131857.2013.879694.

Währisch-Oblau, Claudia. "Evangelism and Popular Culture." *International Review of Mission* 103, no. 2 (2014): 215–226.

Warnick, Bryan R. "Ritual, Imitation and Education in R. S. Peters." *Journal of Philosophy of Education* 43, no. s1 (2009): 57–74. DOI: 1467-9752.2009.00735.x.

Willard, Dallas. *The Divine Conspiracy: Rediscovering Our Hidden Life in God*. London: Harper Collins, 1998.

Wolterstorff, Nicholas. *The God We Worship: An Exploration of Liturgical Theology*. Kantzer Lectures in Revealed Theology (KLRT). Grand Rapids, MI: Eerdmans, 2015. Kindle.

Wright, N. T. *Surprised by Hope: Rethinking Heaven, the Resurrection, and the Mission of the Church*. New York: HarperOne, 2008.

11

The Strengths and Weaknesses of Christian Higher Education in Africa

Rodney L. Reed

Deputy Vice Chancellor of Academic Affairs, Africa Nazarene University

Abstract

This essay examines the strengths and weaknesses of Christian higher education in Africa. The strengths that have been identified include God himself, a worldview that is convincing, a clear sense of the mission and vision of Christian higher education institutions, a highly committed staff, networks among CHEIs. The weaknesses that have been identified are anti-intellectualism, a shallow pietism, an ethnic subservience, and a propensity toward uncritical Westernization. Christian higher education institutions in Africa that maximize these strengths and beware of these weaknesses will stand a good chance of negotiating the perilous waters of higher education in Africa in the twenty-first century.

Key words: Christian, higher education, Africa, universities, worldview, SWOT analysis, holistic, mission, vision, anti-intellectualism, pietism, Westernization

Introduction

It goes almost without saying that these are turbulent times in higher education across the continent of Africa. Explosive growth in the numbers of students qualifying for higher education; the corresponding rapid rise in the number of universities,[1] with the claims of both "massification"[2] and dilution of university education; the lack of qualified academic staff and the sensitive issues surrounding staff development policies and their implementation; the inadequacy of government resources to fund the higher education sector, and hence the rise of private university education, with some of it being "for-profit";[3] the lack of resources of many families to afford private university education alongside, on the other hand, a growing upper and middle class with much higher expectations; "turf wars" between government accreditors and other regulatory bodies with ever-new and sometimes conflicting expectations; universities and colleges being targets for terrorism; student and staff unrest; the placement of government-sponsored students into private universities; calls for free university education; and crackdowns on exam cheating in the national exams at the end of secondary school, which affects the number of students qualifying for university education: these are just some of the factors that make sailing on the waters of higher education institutional management in Africa such a perilous endeavor today.

This is all the more so for educational institutions that are grounded in Christian faith. In addition to all of the above, they have the added complications of insufficient funding, denominational attachments, maintaining a special kind of image and ethos, and the need to maintain theological orthodoxy, among others. Truly, the task of guiding a Christian higher education institution into the future is a daunting one, and the need for some "navigational tools" for this journey is critical.

One such tool commonly employed by organizations in their strategic management is a review of their current situation, called a "SWOT analysis." SWOT, of course, is an acronym for Strengths, Weaknesses, Opportunities, and Threats. The first two refer to the strengths and weaknesses *internal* to the organization, while the latter two refer to the opportunities and threats that

---

1. For the rapid increase in numbers of universities in sub-Saharan Africa, see Michael J. Schultheis, "Head in the Clouds and Feet in the Mud: The Role of Private Universities in the Integration of Christian Mission and Transformational Development," *Transformation* 22, no. 2 (April 2005): 100.

2. For evidence of massification of higher education in Africa see Perry L. Glanzer, Joel A. Carpenter, and Nick Lantinga, "Looking for God in the University: Examining Trends in Christian Higher Education," *Higher Education* 61, no. 6 (2011): 730, DOI: 10.1007/s10734-010-9359-x; and Goolam Mohamedbhai, "Massification in Higher Education Institutions in Africa: Causes, Consequences, and Responses," *International Journal of African Higher Education* 1, no. 1 (2014): 59–83.

3. Schultheis, "Head in the Clouds," 101.

are presented to the organization by its *external* environment.[4] This chapter examines the strengths and weaknesses of the Christian higher education (hereafter referred to as "CHE") sector in Africa in a humble attempt to aid those who are collectively responsible for its future development.[5]

Such an exercise is not without its dangers and limitations, and the reader should be made aware of them. These dangers and limitations revolve around the uniqueness of each Christian higher education institution (hereafter referred to as "CHEI"). First, CHEIs find uniqueness in relation to both their external and internal environments. Externally, there are significant differences in political systems, economic development, and technological infrastructure available to CHEIs in the various locations and countries where they operate. Internally, CHEIs vary in that some are focused on the training of clergy for the ministry of the church (e.g. seminaries and Bible colleges), while others are educating persons for a broader range of professions and careers (e.g. colleges and universities). This chapter primarily addresses the context of Christian universities, but to a lesser extent also Bible colleges and seminaries.

Second, the doctrinal and denominational variations within Christianity itself also lend uniqueness to CHEIs. Without going into details, the bottom line is that theology and church polity make a difference in how a CHEI articulates its mission and does its work, and these differences must be factored into any institution's strategic management. More will be said on this later.

With all of these factors of the uniqueness of CHEIs to consider, some will question the advisability of attempting to do SWOT analysis for the entire CHE sector. In other words, if every institution is different, isn't doing a strategic analysis for the entire sector an exercise in futility? Notwithstanding these disclaimers, there are some common characteristics across the CHE sector in Africa that may prove such an exercise valuable for those leading and working within CHEIs. Nevertheless, each institution should do its own homework and not rely solely on the generalizations made here.

Because the purpose of this research is more to inspire and encourage than to dissect and analyze, what follows will focus less on statistical data and case studies of CHEIs and more on general observation. Its tone is less technical and more aspirational. Readers who are hoping for extensive data collection

---

4. Marilyn M. Helms and Judy Nixon, "Exploring SWOT Analysis: Where Are We Now? A Review of Academic Research from the Last Decade," *Journal of Strategy and Management* 3, no. 3 (2010): 215–251, accessed 25 February 2017, http://dx.doi.org/10.1108/17554251011064837.

5. SWOT analysis normally includes an entire range of data collection techniques, including market research, stakeholder surveys, etc. While those would indeed be valuable and should be done, this research will consist primarily of secondary data based on relevant literature.

on the CHE sector in Africa will likely be disappointed. The intention of this research is to offer some direction to those responsible for the well-being of CEIs across the continent.

So let's begin our analysis of the strengths and weaknesses of the CHE sector. But as we do this, it is imperative to note that we cannot hope to go into detail regarding each and every strength and weakness. What is offered here is merely an overview of some of the more significant strengths and weaknesses that may affect Christian higher education in the years ahead.

Strengths

Strengths refer to the advantages or assets internal to the organization that can be leveraged to move the organization forward in the accomplishment of its mission.

God

Without question, the single most important strength that Christian institutions of higher learning have is God! Christians believe that God exists and is actively involved in our world. God is not sitting on the sidelines or up in the grandstands merely watching what is happening in this world.[6] Christian theism traditionally holds that though God remains transcendent from the world, God is, nevertheless, actively engaged with it through the ongoing work of his Holy Spirit.

What this means for CHEIs is that they are not alone in the noble task of Christian education. God is with them. In fact, ultimately, Christian education is part of God's mission and we are joining God in his saving activity here on earth. So God is there to enlighten, to provide wisdom and knowledge for the tasks at hand, to guide, direct, encourage and strengthen, and all of this for administrators, faculty, staff, and students alike. What a tremendous asset!

Yet so many CHEIs operate on a day-to-day basis as though God were not a player in what they are doing. In fact, to even mention God as a factor in a SWOT analysis or as an active agent in HE in a research paper of this nature may seem problematic to some because even many persons working in the CHE sector have become accustomed to concerning themselves only with what they can statistically measure and empirically verify. CHEIs should be encouraged to intentionally solicit God's activity on their campuses and in the

---

6. That is what is typically called "deism."

decisions that are made. Everything that is done should be carried out with the assurance that God is at work in it.

A Convincing Worldview

According to various authors, a worldview is:

- A comprehensive life system that answers all of life's age-old questions.[7]
- Our beliefs and assumptions about how the world fits together.[8]
- The umbrella of meaning under which all facets of life and learning are gathered and interpreted.[9]
- A perspective of the world that results in a set of beliefs about the most important issues in life.[10]

In this chapter, the working definition of a worldview is: A way of understanding and making sense of the world around us and our place in it. It is the interpretive grid through which we filter the knowledge that comes to us and our experiences in life. Christian apologist Israel Wayne writes about the importance of one's worldview,

Everyone has a worldview. Whether or not we realize it, we all have certain presuppositions and biases that affect the way we view all of life and reality. A worldview is like a set of lenses which taint our vision or alter the way we perceive the world around us. Our worldview is formed by our education, our upbringing, the culture we live in, the books we read, the media and movies we absorb, etc. For many people, their worldview is simply something they have absorbed by osmosis from their surrounding cultural influences. They have never thought strategically about what they

---

7. Charles Colson, *How Now Shall We Live?*, eds. Judith Markham and Lynn Vanderzalm (Carol Stream, IL: Tyndale House, 1999), xi. See also 3–40.

8. Steve Wilkins, *Beyond Bumper Sticker Ethics: An Introduction to Theories of Right and Wrong* (Downers Grove, IL: InterVarsity Press, 1995), 19.

9. Robert Benne, *Quality with Soul: How Six Premier Colleges and Universities Keep Faith with Their Religious Traditions* (Grand Rapids, MI: Eerdmans, 2001). Benne's term of preference is "vision" rather than "worldview," but he is essentially describing the same thing.

10. Jonathan Morrow, *Welcome to College: A Christ-Follower's Guide for the Journey* (Grand Rapids, MI: Kregel, 2008), 26.

believe and wouldn't be able to give a rational defense of their beliefs to others.[11]

There are many options today in terms of worldviews. Some are religious in nature, some are economic, and some are social-scientific. Without trying to sound arrogant, Christians have a worldview that "sells" – that is, a worldview that effectively makes sense of the world and the place of humanity in it. It is not possible here to present a full apology for the Christian worldview. Suffice it to say that Christians believe in a Creator who has imbued the created order with purpose. Life has meaning; history has an end toward which it is moving; the creation – in particular, humanity – is accountable to more than just itself. We may call this "cosmic purpose." In the Christian worldview, the entire universe is stamped with this purpose, given to it by God. Many young people today are looking for this kind of meaning and purpose in life. They want to know that they are part of something bigger than themselves. Many secular or public universities today are held captive to the worldview of scientific naturalism which suffers from an inability to provide that meaning and purpose for life.[12] This failure is epitomized in the words of prominent evolutionary biologist at Oxford University Richard Dawkins, whose recent writings on atheism have become very popular: "there is [in the universe] at bottom, no design, no purpose, no evil, no good – nothing but blind, pitiless indifference."[13]

---

11. Israel Wayne, "What Is a Christian Worldview?," Biblical Worldview, accessed 4 December 2016, http://www.christianworldview.net.

12. See Anita Fitzgerald Henk, "Walking the Tightrope: Christian Colleges and Universities in a Time of Change," *Christian Higher Education* 10, no. 3–4 (2011): 203, DOI: 10.1080/15363759.2011.577711, who argues that "by the 21st century, the general concept that the college president is the keeper and disseminator of moral values seems unusual, archaic, or even conflicted to most members of higher education communities *writ large*." See also Dickson K. Nkonge, "Theological Education Institutions in Kenya and the Future of the Church: An Anglican Case Study," *Journal of Adult Theological Education* 10, no. 2 (November 2013): 150, whose research into Anglican theological education institutions in Kenya led him to conclude that the "Athens" model of theological training which emphasizes mentorship and character formation is more preferable for the Anglican Church of Kenya to adopt than the "Berlin" model which is more focused on research and university-style education.

13. Cited in Alister E. McGrath, "Has Science Eliminated God? Richard Dawkins and the Meaning of Life," *Science and Christian Belief* 17, no. 2 (October 2005): 115–135, ATLA Religion Database with ATLASerials, EBSCOhost, accessed 25 February 2017; and Jeffery C. Davis and Philip G. Ryken, "Theological Convictions," in *Liberal Arts for the Christian Life*, eds. Jeffery C. Davis and Philip G. Ryken (Wheaton, IL: Crossway, 2012), 67. For additional literature on the failure of the modern university to provide meaning and purpose in life, see, for example, David Sloan, "Faith and Knowledge: Religion and the Modern University," in *The Future of Religious Colleges: The Proceedings of the Harvard Conference on the Future of Religious Colleges, October 6–7, 2000*, ed. Paul J. Dovre (Grand Rapids, MI: Eerdmans, 2002), 3–7; Neil Postman, *The End of Education: Redefining the Value of School* (New York: Vintage, 1996), 19; Arthur E. Holmes, *The Idea of a Christian College*, rev. ed. (Grand Rapids, MI: Eerdmans, 1987).

If a worldview is like a lens, then the Christian worldview enables the problems of the world to be seen with less distortion and with greater focus, so as to provide better responses to the problems facing the world today. Let us take the example of corruption. Many African countries are beset with high levels of corruption. The worldview of scientific naturalism seems to suggest that the best response to this corruption is through the use of managerial systems and technology that will make it more and more difficult for corrupt practices to take place. In Nairobi, the Kenyan government has installed CCTV cameras along most of the major roads to monitor traffic and capture traffic offenders on camera. Those who park their vehicles on city streets must pay for the parking by mobile phone money transfers, rather than by giving cash to the city parking officers. More and more regulations are being put in place to guide procurement and tendering practices. More and more businesses are insisting that monetary transactions be done through electronic transfers from bank account to bank account, rather than through cash transactions between people. All of this is in an effort to "reduce the human element" in corruption. The more automated and regulated the process is, the less opportunity there will be for corruption to flourish, it is believed.

As helpful as they are, none of these technological or managerial solutions can address the heart of the matter! They simply make it more difficult for those who are corrupt to carry out corruption. They do not change corrupt people themselves; they deal with the practice of corruption, rather than the person. In fact, if society does not deal with the heart of the problem, it is only a matter of time before a new, more technologically sophisticated means of corruption will enter the scene to bypass the current technological barriers and managerial systems that have been set up.

CHEIs know what is the true illness of humanity. In fact, CHEIs understand that humans themselves are humanity's deepest problem and that any education which fails to address the "inner" issues of spiritual and character formation of the human person is seriously deficient and in danger of only treating the symptoms rather than offering a true cure. Thus, while not neglecting the need for and role of technological and managerial solutions, Christian universities have a special mandate to shape the character of their students through chapel services, strong Christian Unions, Bible studies, and small groups and through the integration of faith in the classroom. This leads to the next strength of CHEIs.

The Clarity of the Mission and Vision of a Christian University

The word "university" derives from the Latin *universitas*, meaning "the whole." By implication, one could say that a university was meant to be a place where one word – a final, comprehensive, integrated word – could be said about something after considering it from all points of view. Universities were intended to be places where the whole body of knowledge about something could be explored and where knowledge across disciplines would be harmonized and integrated into a unified whole. This unified knowledge would then provide insight into the meaning of life for all humanity and the purpose of education.[14]

The modern secular university has moved far from that ideal and, in some cases, has become almost the anti-type of it. Within their academic "silos," schools and departments of such universities with their research agendas and academic programs exist in virtual isolation from one another, oblivious to the knowledge being created in other departments of the university. Very little effort is made at integrating knowledge across disciplines.[15] Where departments are aware of one another, due to "conflicting" philosophies of knowledge, truth claims, and methods of data collection, they often find themselves at war with one another, rather than working together to create an integrated, unified body of knowledge.[16]

Furthermore, the dominant market demand in higher education today continues to be toward ever-increasing specialization, graduates who are often taught only a relatively narrow body of knowledge in a particular field and who

---

14. See Davis and Ryken, "Theological Convictions," 40.

15. For a discussion of the fragmentation of knowledge and the lack of interrelatedness of the disciplines within the modern university, see David S. Dockery, "The Great Commandment as a Paradigm for Christian Higher Education," in *The Future of Christian Higher Education*, eds. David S. Dockery and David P. Gushee (Nashville: Broadman & Holman, 1999), 12; Rick Ostrander, "The Distinctive of a Christian College: An Historical Perspective," in *The Soul of a Christian University: A Field Guide for Educators*, ed. Stephen T. Beers (Abilene, TX: Abilene Christian University Press, 2008), 45–46. The realization that a "silo-mentality" has existed in universities and hence the need to recapture this original ideal of the university as a place of integrated knowledge is being seen now in research grant criteria that favor cross-disciplinary teams of researchers rather than teams from a single discipline, or from a single institution, or single researchers in one discipline.

16. In fact, on a theoretical level, with the rise of postmodern skepticism about attaining knowledge that is universal and not limited by one's perspective, the whole notion of arriving at a unified, integrated body of knowledge has now come seriously into question in many circles of higher education. Indeed, on many secular university campuses, knowledge has become "tribal"! On a practical level, the conflicts between the various schools of thought within a university often reveal themselves in discussions about the relative merits of pure science, social science, and arts and humanities programs, and in the budgetary decisions made by university funding boards for these programs.

enter the job market with a limited skill set.[17] The result of this emphasis on specialization is that these graduates find it difficult to move laterally in their career progression. Such an education is not truly a "university education" in the best sense of the phrase. It is really only a hyped-up, white-collar version of vocational/technical training.

Worse still, because of the preoccupation with being industry-ready, these graduates are often ill-prepared to negotiate the non-career challenges of life. As the saying goes, they are able to make a successful living, but not a successful life. The literature documenting the failure of universities to address the deeper issues of life is large and ever-growing. This will be explored more later, but for now, let this point be underscored with a lengthy quote from Darryl Tippens:

> Complaints against the academy are not new, of course. . . . In the late 1990s, Ernie Boyer described "a growing feeling in [the United States] that higher education is, in fact, part of the problem rather than the solution . . ." Nathan Hatch, president of Wake Forrest University, describes the "rising tide of criticism, wave upon wave" that is eroding "the esteem once accorded the academy." Anthony Kronman argues eloquently that our society is in desperate need of universities that will address the question of life's meaning and purpose. Yet, he maintains, the modern university is unwilling or unable to deal with such urgent matters. In the halls of Congress and in the media we hear a chorus of complaints, Universities are too expensive, too arrogant, too easy, too politicized, too unaccountable or too out of touch. . . . *The Chronicle of Higher Education* reports that "[u]ndergraduate education in the research university is a project in ruins." Harry Lewis, former dean of Harvard College, says that Harvard's undergraduate curriculum is a "total disunity." David L. Kirp notes an incoherence and uncertainty "about what knowledge matters most." C. John Summerville, professor emeritus of English history, the University of Florida in a recent book, *The Decline of the Secular University*, maintains that universities today cannot or will not address the most urgent questions that face us, because to do so would require some attention to matters of faith and values – and universities just

---

17. Joel A. Carpenter, "New Christian Universities and the Conversion of Cultures," *Evangelical Review of Theology* 36, no. 1 (January 2012): 17–18, Religion and Philosophy Collection, EBSCOhost, accessed 30 January 2016.

cannot go there. "Universities are not really looking for answers to our life questions."[18]

While Christian universities and other CHEIs are certainly not immune from the "silo-mentality," market forces demanding more specialization, and the temptation to view education only for its utility in securing jobs and careers, CHEIs and other colleges and universities in the liberal arts tradition have a long history of offering a truly holistic education – one that addresses the whole person and that seeks to integrate knowledge across disciplines.[19] Many CHEIs have affirmations of holistic education embedded in their mission and vision statements or educational philosophies.[20]

The reason why CHEIs are more likely to take up the challenge of a holistic and integrated education is because CHEIs typically claim that God is the source of all knowledge and, therefore, all knowledge must be holistic in nature. To affirm any less would be to imply that God's own nature is somehow divided. When the Bible says in Colossians 1:17 (NIV) that "in him [Christ] all things hold together," and this in the immediate context of all things being created in Christ (v. 16), CHEIs insist that this becomes both the foundation and the *telos* for all education. The coherence of all things in Christ is the basic assumption of CHE, and the understanding of that coherence, resulting in the glory and peace (shalom) of God, is the goal toward which CHE aspires. One of the

---

18. Darryl Tippens, "Scholars and Witnesses: The Christian University Difference," in Beers, *Soul of a Christian University*, 22–23 (the author's footnotes within the quoted text have been removed). Admittedly, this is evident from the American context. This research is assuming that it is true or becoming increasingly true in the African context as well. But research needs to be done to substantiate this assumption. Interestingly, T. Derrick Mashau, "A Reformed Missional Perspective on Secularism and Pluralism in Africa: Their Impact on African Christianity and the Revival of Traditional Religion," *Calvin Theological Journal* 44, no. 1 (2009): 109, argues that the process of secularization in South Africa has precipitated a reaction to it which has ironically led to a revival of African traditional religious expression.

19. See Jim Harries, "Does Faith in Secularism Undermine Mission and Development in Africa?," *Evangelical Review of Theology* 40, no. 2 (2016): 109, who argues that the African worldview is more naturally holistic because it lacks the bifurcation between the "religious" and the "secular" found in the West. He goes on to argue that for that reason Western aid agencies err when they try to deliver aid to Africa's poor in a purely secular manner. In an analogous way, African CHEIs have a double reason then to emphasize holistic education that is not so segmented along disciplinary lines: its Christian worldview and its African heritage.

20. See, for example, the following: Trevecca Nazarene University (www.trevecca.edu/about/holistic-education), Africa Nazarene University (https://www.anu.ac.ke/mission-vision/), Kenya Methodist University (http://kemu.ac.ke/index.php/about-kemu/about-us-kemu/our-values), and Daystar University (https://www.daystar.ac.ke/about-us.html).

greatest strengths of CHEIs is this fundamental principle that all knowledge has both its source and its end in God.[21]

This fundamental principle is the basis for the oft-mentioned quest for the integration of faith and learning in CHEIs.[22] CHEIs demand that their faculty seek new, creative, and more comprehensive ways to "bring God into the curriculum and the classroom." Contrast this with many public universities, where God and matters of faith tend to be marginalized so that a religiously inclusive environment prevails in the classroom.[23] The integration of faith and learning in CHEIs, then, provides the freedom for faculty and students to explore the deeper issues of life – issues that go far beyond merely preparing for a career.

Furthermore, it provides a clear reason for the core functions of a university and its faculty: teaching/learning, research, and community engagement. All of these are conducted as expressions of the Great Commandment: to love God and to love our fellow human beings.[24] The faculty members of Christian universities are urged not to view teaching as a time-consuming distraction in the pursuit of their research agenda or, worse yet, their paychecks. They are more naturally enabled to see their research, not in terms of how it can make a name for themselves, but in terms of how much genuine good it can do for society. And the same is true for their community engagements. In fact, according to Jacobsen and Jacobsen, "Scholarship is . . . a communal activity."

---

21. See Leland Ryken, "The Student's Calling" (1984), reprinted in Davis and Ryken, *Liberal Arts for the Christian Life*, 17–18; Holmes, *Idea of a Christian College*, 17–27, 36; R. T. Hughes, "Christian Faith and the Life of the Mind," in *Faithful Learning and the Christian Scholarly Vocation*, eds. Douglas V. Henry and Bob R. Agee (Grand Rapids, MI: Eerdmans, 2003), 6; B. J. van der Walt, "The Challenge of Christian Higher Education on the African Continent in the Twenty-First Century," *Christian Higher Education* 1, nos. 2–3 (2002): 206, 214.

22. It should be noted that the language of "integration" has been criticized by some Christian scholars who claim that it shares a theological affinity with the Reformed theological tradition and does not fit as well with other theological traditions and some postmodern notions. For example, see some of the contributions to Douglas Jacobsen and Rhonda Hustedt Jacobsen, eds., *Scholarship and Christian Faith: Enlarging the Conversation* (New York: Oxford University Press, 2004), 15–44. However, for my purposes, the language of integration will be used to represent all attempts to engage in the process of education from a distinctly Christian perspective.

23. James A. Ogunji, "Fostering the Identity and Mission of Christian Education in Africa," *Journal of Research on Christian Education* 21, no. 1 (2012): 52–53, DOI: 10.1080/10656219.2012.659611.

24. For the centrality of the Great Commandment to the mission of Christian higher education, see Dockery, "Great Commandment," 8–9; and Duane Litfin, "Loving God as the Key to a Christian Liberal Arts Education," in Davis and Ryken, *Liberal Arts for the Christian Life*, 101–109.

Christian scholars have a special responsibility with regard to this communal dimension of scholarship because the core Christian values of love and reconciliation are communally oriented. This means that while Christian scholarship will often follow the lines of division that exist within the academy as a whole, Christian scholars should feel a special responsibility to frame their work in a way that really does contribute to the overall good of the world and to the benefit of the academy as a whole.[25]

Another dimension of the strength that CHEIs have in relation to their mission is in their understanding of the teaching and learning process itself and the faculty/student relationship. For CHEIs it is not about merely the transmission of knowledge. It is about the transformation of a life, not just through the impact of new knowledge, deep as that impact can sometimes be, but through the mediation of the grace of God in the life of the student in the classroom and in the total university experience. The faculty member is more than a "sage on the stage," being called to be a mentor-figure who participates in channeling that grace of God into the life of the student. The student is more than a mere learner but is rather a disciple or at least a potential disciple (taking into account the large number of non-Christians and nominal Christians who are students in CHEIs). The goal of a Christian university is not just to produce well-trained graduates, but to produce faithful disciples who will think Christianly about how to address the problems of the world around them. This is a great strength of CHEIs.

A Highly Committed Staff

CHEIs are generally blessed with staff, both teaching and non-teaching, who are highly committed and believe in the mission and vision of the CHEI.[26] It is no secret that most CHEIs cannot adequately compensate their staff. Yet many non-teaching staff members of CHEIs are highly trained in their areas and

---

25. Jacobsen and Jacobsen, *Scholarship and Christian Faith*, xii.

26. Interestingly, a study of staff members in evangelical HEIs found a negative correlation between workplace climate and commitment to the workplace. See John Charles Thomas, "Administrative, Faculty, and Staff Perceptions of Organizational Climate and Commitment in Christian Higher Education," *Christian Higher Education* 7, no. 3 (July 2008): 226–252, Academic Search Premier, EBSCOhost, accessed 30 December 2015. The author (240) suggests various reasons for this, one of which hints at potentially uniquely high levels of commitment of staff in CHEIs: "[P]erhaps a negative correlation does exist given the unique nature of Christian higher education employees . . . It is possible that such employees maintain employment for reasons other than those assessed by the [Organizational Commitment Questionnaire]."

many CHEI faculty members have advanced degrees and are well-established scholars in their academic fields. In both cases, these staff members could likely earn more money if they were to take their credentials and experience elsewhere. However, many remain with the CHEI because they are committed and loyal staff members who have bought into the vision of Christian higher education, who genuinely want to see the institution prosper, and who want to do their work within the context of a Christian ethos. They love their students and want to contribute to the holistic transformation of those students. This is one of the hallmarks of CHEIs.

Networks among CHEIs

Another strength of CHEIs is the natural network of relationships that exists among them due to their common mission, vision, and values. Sometimes these networks take the shape of organizations that facilitate their cooperation and mutual objectives, like the Council for Christian Colleges and Universities in the US (www.cccu.org) or the Kenya Association of Private Universities. Sometimes they take the shape of professional societies for the promotion of research, publication, and conferencing, like the Africa Society of Evangelical Theology. In other cases, they exist in the form of informal networking between administrators, researchers, and students from various CHEIs. Whatever form these networks take, they are a great source of strength for CHEIs.

For example, the above-mentioned Africa Society of Evangelical Theology (ASET) began when a group of religious scholars from various institutions in Kenya concluded that there existed no cost-effective way for Christian theologians and scholars of religion in much of Africa to conference together and to present and publish research. Most of those kinds of opportunities were available only to those who could travel to the US or Europe. ASET was created to provide such a forum in the African context. After just six years, at its 2016 conference, twenty-six papers were presented from scholars working in over a dozen institutions in at least five countries. The research of ASET scholars is already being published and is thereby contributing to the pool of scholarly knowledge about Christianity in Africa.

These networks should be nurtured. CHEIs should further organize to promote and advocate for their mutual agendas within their local, national, and even international settings. There is great potential for collaboration and working together for their mutual benefit. Individual institutions may lack the capacity to accomplish something or may be easily ignored in the larger society. But by working together, CHEIs can make a bigger mark.

These – God, a worldview, a clear mission and vision, a highly committed staff, and networks among CHEIs – are a few (not all) of the strengths that CHEIs have as they face an uncertain future in higher education provision. Indeed, they are significant. However, these strengths have tended to be undermined by some inherent weaknesses. We now turn to a discussion of a few of the representative weaknesses of CHEIs in Africa.

Weaknesses

While CHEIs have some formidable strengths, they also have weaknesses which can diminish their effectiveness in the accomplishment of their mission.

Anti-Intellectualism

One of those weaknesses that is actually more prevalent in Christian churches generally but can also infect CHEIs is anti-intellectualism. Over twenty years ago, Mark Noll wrote a seminal book entitled *The Scandal of the Evangelical Mind*. He opened the first chapter with the provocative statement, "The scandal of the evangelical mind is that there is not much of an evangelical mind."[27] He continued,

> Despite dynamic success at a popular level, modern American evangelicals have failed notably in sustaining serious intellectual life. They have nourished millions of believers in the simple verities of the gospel but have largely abandoned the universities, the arts, and the other realms of "high" culture. . . . Evangelicals sponsor dozens of theological seminaries, scores of colleges, hundreds of radio stations and thousands of unbelievably diverse parachurch agencies – but not a single research university or a single periodical devoted to in-depth interaction with modern culture.[28]

Noll points the finger at anti-intellectualism and a misplaced intellectualism (e.g. pseudo-science) as the primary culprits in the lack of intellectual rigor among American evangelicals.[29]

---

27. Mark A. Noll, *The Scandal of the Evangelical Mind* (Grand Rapids, MI: Eerdmans, 1994), 3.

28. Noll, *Scandal of the Evangelical Mind*.

29. Noll, 3–28; see also Alister E. McGrath, "The Lord Is My Light: On the Discipleship of the Mind," *Evangelical Quarterly* 83, no. 2 (April 2011): 133–145, Academic Search Premier, EBSCOhost, accessed 31 December 2015.

One version of this anti-intellectualism comes about quite naturally as a result of the process of human development and education, especially university education. University education generally takes place at the time when, according to Erikson's Life Cycle theory of human development,[30] young people are going through their own "identity crisis," seeking to understand what they believe and value in distinction from the belief and value systems inherited from their parents/communities. This period of a young person's life is often characterized by rebellion and/or rejection of parental values and belief systems, as they seek to discern their own identity and way in life. Many times this happens at the very time the young person is away for higher education. Quite naturally, the young person returns home to the family/community a changed person with new and sometimes "foreign" perspectives on things. In many instances, this change in the young person seems hostile to values and beliefs held dear by the family/community. The family may come to believe that the university education has "ruined" their child because he or she no longer fits in well in the community. In such cases, a distrust of higher education can arise.[31]

A second version of this anti-intellectualism is historically traceable at least as far back as the rise of the Enlightenment and the scientific method. Since at least the time of Galileo, persons of science have occasionally been labeled as heretics because it seemed as though what they had discovered through the use of the scientific method was at odds with revealed faith. Indeed, there are some Christians (and some atheists and agnostics) who seem to think that any advance in scientific knowledge comes at the expense of Christian faith. These Christians are, therefore, suspicious of the whole academic enterprise and often allege that a battle between science and religion is underway. Oddly, one would then think that the best way to win the battle would be to be better than your opponent in your application of the rules of the game – in this case, to be better scientists than the scientists who are allegedly hostile to Christian faith. However, in this instance, Christian anti-intellectualism seems to employ the strategy of abandoning the battlefield altogether and retreating to its "fortress of

---

30. Saul A. McLeod, "Erik Erikson's Stages of Psychosocial Development," SimplyPsychology, accessed 30 January 2015, www.simplypsychology.org/Erik-Erikson.html.

31. Ironically, this kind of suspicion of higher education can even apply to theological education. Many denominational and local church leaders harbor such suspicions of recent seminary or university religion department graduates who are returning "home" to serve in ministry.

faith," issuing statements condemning modern science but offering no rebuttal using credible methods the scientist would use in his or her craft.[32]

Similarly, in a secular educational setting, the prospects of our impressionable young people being taught by faculty who are religious skeptics or even atheists and make fun of them for their "naïve" religious beliefs, the lack of teaching on moral values, and the positively immoral lifestyles that are prevalent on many university campuses are all seen as corrupting influences on the young. In such cases, the educational process seems to many Christians to be inexorably hostile to Christian faith. They therefore seek to insulate their young people from these corrupting influences by creating their own sectarian (but "safe") educational subculture. They establish their own educational institutions for the purpose of screening out knowledge that is deemed dangerous and providing a safe atmosphere in which to learn.

Surely, one of the best reasons to send young people to a Christian university is so that they can learn in a morally and spiritually safe or "faith-friendly" environment, rather than one that is hostile to Christian faith. However, there is a difference between desiring a Christian-friendly environment for learning and an anti-intellectualism that narrowly censors what students can be exposed to. The anti-intellectualism referred to here unduly restricts freedom of inquiry and engages in unjustified "heresy hunting," sometimes among its own faculty, to "purge" the university of ideas and teachings deemed to be dangerous.

Surely CHEIs are falling short of fulfilling their mission and vision if they only isolate and insulate young people from perceived "worldly" ideas. If CHEIs are supposed to be places where an understanding is being sought of how all things cohere in Christ, then CHEIs must be places of open-minded discovery[33] rather than narrow-minded intellectual bigotry. They ought to be places where the wagons of learning are moving forward into uncharted territory, rather than circled up in a defensive posture for fear of attack. They must be places

---

32. There may be a third strand of Christian anti-intellectualism that is more homegrown in Africa. I recall when I was asked to speak at a denominational gathering of an African indigenous church in Kenya that was founded largely by Kenyans opposed to British colonial rule and to some of the impositions of the missionary-controlled churches (e.g. opposition to female genital mutilation). I was there speaking as part of the launch of this church's first Bible training center for ministers. I was told that the church, which was founded in the 1920s, had, until the time of the launch of this Bible training center, opposed the formal education of its ministers because they wanted their ministers to rely on the Holy Spirit and because, in their early years, they associated formal education with their missionary and colonial oppressors. Philip Jenkins, *The Next Christendom: The Coming of Global Christianity* (New York: Oxford University Press, 2003), 72–91, sees this transition from skepticism toward formal education to acceptance of it as part of Africa's version of the classical transition from a sect to a church.

33. Tippens, "Scholars and Witnesses," 29–30.

where claims to truth are freely discussed and assessed. Unfortunately, there are many topics of scientific inquiry or of social, moral, or religious significance that are "off limits" at some CHEIs or cannot be discussed in an unbiased and objective manner.[34] Surely CHEI students, at the right stage in their educational development, need to be allowed to read, for example, atheists like Marx and Nietzsche – and not simply a biased secondhand reading of them through the lenses of their hostile critics. Rather, they should be exposed to views potentially hostile to Christian faith in the most objective and compelling manner, and only then be provided an even more compelling rebuttal from an informed Christian perspective. Unprejudiced exposure to other viewpoints is an essential element of a good education, and being able to process evidence presented in that fashion is the essence of what it means to be a truly educated and discerning person.

Unfortunately, this kind of anti-intellectualism is all too common within CHEIs. In some instances, the faculty themselves see their role as being the preservers of undefiled truth and on the front lines in the war against a "godless view of science" or some other perceived enemy of the faith. In other cases, the faculty may be open toward some of the discoveries of modern science, but the institution's administration either holds a hostile attitude toward academic freedom or is beholden to the interests of its denominational or other stakeholders who bear this anti-intellectualism. In the United States, in particular, many seminaries and CHEIs have been battlegrounds between so-called "Fundamentalists" and "Liberals" or "Moderates," each fighting for a controlling interest in the school. Interestingly, in many such instances, both the Fundamentalists and the Liberals suffer from the same closed-mindedness.[35] But our concern here is primarily with the fundamentalist mentality that permeates many Christian denominations and CHEIs and which undermines the ability of the CHEI to engage in serious academic inquiry. Indeed, Noll has described the influence of the fundamentalist movement on evangelical Christianity as "an intellectual disaster."[36] Os Guinness describes this anti-intellectualism as sinful and a denial of the Great Commandment of Christ, to love God with our entire mind: "Evangelicals have been deeply sinful in being anti-intellectual ever since the 1820s and 1830s. For the longest time, we

---

34. Dan Boone, *A Charitable Discourse: Talking about the Things That Divide Us* (Kansas City, MO: Beacon Hill, 2010), devotes the entire book to probing such "off-limits" topics.

35. For the closed-mindedness of liberal higher education in America, see Allan Bloom, *The Closing of the American Mind: How Higher Education Has Failed Democracy and Impoverished the Souls of Today's Students* (1987; New York: Simon & Schuster, 2012).

36. Noll, *Scandal of the Evangelical Mind*, 109.

didn't pay the cultural price for that because we had the numbers, the social zeal, and the spiritual passion for the gospel. But today we are beginning to pay the cultural price."[37]

Part of that price is a self-imposed exile from the top levels of academic discourse; being marginalized in many of the higher education institutions which were actually founded by Christians of earlier generations but have now essentially gone secular; and an inability to influence modern society with their ideas.

Pietistic Experiential Religion

Even where there is not a hostile attitude toward education and scientific discovery, there is across a wide swath of Christianity around the world a kind of shallow pietism that lacks intellectual excellence and rigor. The word "pietism" has a historical background that may prove useful here. The Pietist movement of the seventeenth and eighteenth centuries, in contradistinction to the rigid Protestant Scholasticism of the sixteenth century, called attention to the fact that Christian faith was not found in holding the right beliefs, but in having a vital relationship with God. This emphasis on vital religious experience has characterized much of Christianity, especially in American evangelical churches and the churches in Africa and elsewhere with an American missionary heritage.[38]

This emphasis on religious experience unfortunately fostered a benign neglect of intellectual pursuits. Faith stopped seeking understanding. Christianity became characterized by seeking God with one's heart, rather than with one's mind. Salvation became narrowed down to an individual soul being "born again," as opposed to that personal salvation being understood in the larger context of cosmic salvation. And with the rise of a premillennial eschatology, a pessimism regarding the salvation of the world set in across much of evangelical Christianity, further diminishing the perceived need to understand the world around us ("because it is all going to be destroyed by fire anyway!"). Some denominations eschewed university education and instead established only Bible colleges in the belief that, because the time is so short (before the end of time), we must focus our energies on saving souls. As true as

---

37. Cited in Noll, 23.

38. This includes a wide variety of forms of Christianity: Pentecostalism, Holiness, and, in much of Africa, even mainline denominations are very "pietistic" in nature.

this may be, it is far from fulfilling our CHE mandate of seeking to understand how *all things* cohere in Christ!

Pietistic experiential Christianity has been hugely successful in Africa. Most of the population of sub-Saharan Africa now embraces some form of this type of Christianity. Yet despite this success, already the most prestigious HEIs in Africa are modeling the progressively secularizing trend of HEIs in other parts of the world. Why? In part, it is because of pietistic Christianity's neglect of serious intellectual pursuits. There are more than enough Christians teaching in those institutions to influence them but, because of this neglect, many of those Christians are not grounded sufficiently or don't actually believe in the viability of their Christian worldview.

It is vital that African Christianity in general, and CHEIs in particular, find this proper balance between being a religion of the heart and of the mind. If it cannot, more and more of the young people raised in churches across Africa will go on to public universities and return home only to find that they are "intellectual strangers" in the very churches that raised them and nurtured them in the faith. If CHEIs do not find that balance, the same thing will happen at another level: the brightest of our Christian youth who did undergraduate degrees at our CHEIs and who go on to a master's or PhD in prestigious graduate schools will return to teach at our CHEIs, only to find themselves to be "intellectual strangers" within their own alma maters.

Ethnic or Political Subservience

Still another weakness inherent in CHEIs in many parts of Africa is their tendency to be subservient to ethnic or political interests. What began as a well-intentioned strategy by the denominational missionary agencies to allocate the missionary outreach of particular ethnic groups to specific denominations so as to avoid competition and maximize impact had the unintended consequence of making whole denominations in some African countries little more than tribal enclaves. In Kenya, for example, one can almost assume that if you are from Meru, you are Methodist, and if you are from Kisii, you are Seventh Day Adventist. This, in turn, has often led the church to be captive to the political kingpins who rule those ethnic groups.[39]

---

39. See Barasa Kundu Nyukuri, "Impact of Past and Potential Ethnic Conflicts on Kenyan's Stability and Development" (paper prepared for the USAID conference on conflict resolution in the Greater Horn of Africa, June 1997), 32, accessed 30 January 2016, http://citeseerx.ist. psu.edu/viewdoc/download?doi=10.1.1.596.7855&rep=rep1&type=pdf, who argues that the

And as the church has gone, so too have some of its educational institutions. In fact, higher education, in general, has been ethnicized and politicized to an alarming degree.[40] After citing John Dewey's theory that social problem solving and "continuous, graded, economic improvement and social rectification" should be a key benefit of education to a society, Joseph Kahiga notes that instead of solving this problem in Kenya, higher education has capitulated to it. He writes, "Tribalism has unfortunately infiltrated the very high learning institutions in Kenya. This is deadly, terribly destructive to the minds of the young being molded for universal service in the world society."[41]

Uncritical Westernization

Another weakness of African societies in general and also of African CHEIs is the temptation to mimic the West and to import Western society's culture (and problems) into Africa. The pressure upon the rest of the world to Westernize is very significant. Sometimes this pressure comes covertly via the entertainment industry and other media outlets; sometimes it comes more directly when Western governments and donor agencies try to impose certain values on African societies and organizations.[42]

Unfortunately, this gets brought into the church and CHEIs. Many churches and CHEIs have roots in Western mission organizations and so it is quite natural and expected to see some of that "family resemblance." However, some churches in Africa merely imitate what they see on Western Christian broadcasting networks. Western Christianity has its own problems and Christians in Africa and African-based CHEIs should guard against importing the negative "baggage" of the Western church. Liberal versus conservative, ordination of gay and lesbian clergy, the split between "sacred and secular" spheres of life: these may be key issues for the church to struggle with elsewhere in the world at this moment in time. However, they may not be as relevant in Africa. Furthermore, some of those issues presuppose a Western culture that

---

less socially active churches were dominant in the areas of Kenya that experienced the fiercest effects of its pre-1997 election-related violence.

40. Van der Walt, "Challenge of Christian Higher Education," 203–204.

41. Joseph K. Kahiga, "Education for Transformation: A Focus on the Post-election Violence in Kenya," *African Ecclesial Review* 51, no. 4 (2009): 490, ATLA Religion Database with ATLASerials, EBSCOhost, accessed 5 February 2018.

42. The 2015 visit of US President Barak Obama to three African nations is a case in point. President Obama was not hesitant about advocating for greater acceptance of homosexuality in African countries, despite the fact that homosexual practice is taboo in virtually all, if not all, African cultures.

contains ideas and traditions that are alien to African Christianity. Here is where African Christianity and especially African CHEIs must guard what is good in our African heritage and resist the temptation to uncritically accept what is being peddled from the West.[43]

Conclusion

The primary purpose of this research is to contribute meaningfully to the discourse about the present and future of Christian higher education in Africa by outlining some of the strengths and weaknesses of the CHEI sector in Africa today. The strengths that have been identified include God himself, a worldview that is convincing, a clear sense of the mission and vision of Christian higher education institutions, a highly committed staff, networks among CHEIs. We have also identified weaknesses: anti-intellectualism, a shallow pietism, ethnic or political subservience, and a propensity toward uncritical Westernization. Surely there is more that could be said about each of these strengths and weaknesses, and there are still other strengths and weaknesses that could be identified. But this will have to suffice.

As noted at the beginning of this study, these are amazingly challenging times in Christian higher education in many parts of Africa. One could not blame CHEI administrators for feeling as though the seas are raging around them and threatening their institutions in many respects. It is hoped that this research can in some small way serve as a beacon of light in that stormy environment to guide those ships in the night away from the rocky reefs that could do them harm. Christian higher education institutions in Africa that maximize these strengths and beware of these weaknesses will stand a good chance of navigating the perilous waters of higher education in Africa in the twenty-first century.

Bibliography

Beers, Stephen T., ed. *The Soul of a Christian University: A Field Guide for Educators*. Abilene, TX: Abilene Christian University Press, 2008.

Benne, Robert. *Quality with Soul: How Six Premier Colleges and Universities Keep Faith with Their Religious Traditions*. Grand Rapids, MI: Eerdmans, 2001.

---

43. Benjamin Kiriswa's article is a good example of the literature on the need for proper contextualization or inculturation: "Interaction between African and Christian Moral Values: The Ongoing Youth Christian Education in Modern Kenya," *AFER* 29, no. 6 (December 1987): 361–371, ATLA Religion Database with ATLASerials, EBSCOhost, accessed 30 January 2016.

Bloom, Allan. *The Closing of the American Mind: How Higher Education Has Failed Democracy and Impoverished the Souls of Today's Students*. New York: Simon & Schuster, 2012.

Boone, Dan. *A Charitable Discourse: Talking about the Things That Divide Us*. Kansas City, MO: Beacon Hill, 2010.

Carpenter, Joel A. "New Christian Universities and the Conversion of Cultures." *Evangelical Review of Theology* 36, no. 1 (January 2012): 17–18. Religion and Philosophy Collection, EBSCOhost. Accessed 30 January 2016.

Colson, Charles. *How Now Shall We Live?* Edited by Judith Markham and Lynn Vanderzalm, Carol Stream, IL: Tyndale House, 1999.

Davis, Jeffery C., and Philip G. Ryken, eds. *Liberal Arts for the Christian Life*. Wheaton, IL: Crossway, 2012.

Dockery, David S., and David P. Gushee, eds. *The Future of Christian Higher Education*. Nashville: Broadman & Holman, 1999.

Dovre, Paul J., ed. *The Future of Religious Colleges: The Proceedings of the Harvard Conference on the Future of Religious Colleges, October 6–7, 2000*. Grand Rapids, MI: Eerdmans, 2002.

Glanzer, Perry L., Joel A. Carpenter, and Nick Lantinga. "Looking for God in the University: Examining Trends in Christian Higher Education." *Higher Education* 61 no. 6 (2011): 721–755. DOI: 10.1007/s10734-010-9359-x.

Harries, Jim. "Does Faith in Secularism Undermine Mission and Development in Africa?" *Evangelical Review of Theology* 40, no. 2 (2016): 100–110.

Helms, Marilyn M., and Judy Nixon. "Exploring SWOT Analysis: Where Are We Now? A Review of Academic Research from the Last Decade." *Journal of Strategy and Management* 3, no. 3 (2010): 215–251. Accessed 25 February 2017. http://dx.doi.org/10.1108/17554251011064837.

Henk, Anita Fitzgerald. "Walking the Tightrope: Christian Colleges and Universities in a Time of Change." *Christian Higher Education* 10, no. 3–4 (2011): 196–214. DOI: 10.1080/15363759.2011.577711.

Henry, Douglas V., and Bob R. Agee, eds. *Faithful Learning and the Christian Scholarly Vocation*. Grand Rapids, MI: Eerdmans, 2003.

Hittenberger, Jeffery S. "Globalization, 'Marketization,' and the Mission of Pentecostal Higher Education in Africa." *Pneuma: The Journal of the Society for Pentecostal Studies* 26, no. 2 (2004): 191–194. Religion and Philosophy Collection, EBSCOhost. Accessed 30 January 2016.

Holmes, Arthur E. *The Idea of a Christian College*. Rev. ed. Grand Rapids, MI: Eerdmans, 1987.

Hughes, R. T. "Christian Faith and the Life of the Mind." In *Faithful Learning and the Christian Scholarly Vocation*, edited by D. V. Henry and B. R. Agee, 3–25. Grand Rapids, MI: Eerdmans, 2003.

Jacobsen, Douglas, and Rhonda Hustedt Jacobsen, eds. *Scholarship and Christian Faith: Enlarging the Conversation*. New York: Oxford University Press, 2004.

Jenkins, Phillip. *The Next Christendom: The Coming of Global Christianity.* Oxford/ New York: Oxford University Press, 2003.

Kahiga, Joseph K. "Education for Transformation: A Focus on the Post-election Violence in Kenya." *African Ecclesial Review* 51, no. 4 (2009): 484–492. ATLA Religion Database with ATLASerials, EBSCOhost. Accessed 5 February 2018.

Kiriswa, Benjamin. "Interaction between African and Christian Moral Values: The Ongoing Youth Christian Education in Modern Kenya." *AFER* 29, no. 6 (December 1987): 361–371. ATLA Religion Database with ATLASerials, EBSCOhost. Accessed 30 January 2016.

Mashau, T. Derrick. "A Reformed Missional Perspective on Secularism and Pluralism in Africa: Their Impact on African Christianity and the Revival of Traditional Religion." *Calvin Theological Journal* 44 (2009): 108–126.

McGrath, Alister E. "Has Science Eliminated God? Richard Dawkins and the Meaning of Life." *Science and Christian Belief* 17, no. 2 (October 2005): 115–135. ATLA Religion Database with ATLASerials, EBSCOhost. Accessed 25 February 2017.

———. "The Lord Is My Light: On the Discipleship of the Mind." *Evangelical Quarterly* 83, no. 2 (April 2011): 133–145. Academic Search Premier, EBSCOhost. Accessed 31 December 2015.

McLeod, Saul A. "Erik Erikson's Stages of Psychosocial Development." SimplyPsychology. Accessed 30 January 2015. www.simplypsychology.org/Erik-Erikson.html.

Mohamedbhai, Goolam. "Massification in Higher Education Institutions in Africa: Causes, Consequences, and Responses." *International Journal of African Higher Education* 1, no. 1 (2014): 59–83.

Morrow, Jonathan. *Welcome to College: A Christ-Follower's Guide for the Journey.* Grand Rapids, MI: Kregel, 2008.

Murillo, Nelly Garcia. "Christian Higher Education in a Global Context: Implications for Curriculum, Pedagogy, and Administration." *Evangelical Review of Theology* 36, no. 1 (2012): 4–13.

Nkonge, Dickson K. "Theological Education Institutions in Kenya and the Future of the Church: An Anglican Case Study." *Journal of Adult Theological Education* 10, no. 2 (November 2013): 147–161.

Noll, Mark A. *The Scandal of the Evangelical Mind.* Grand Rapids, MI: Eerdmans, 1994.

Nyukuri, Barasa Kundu. "Impact of Past and Potential Ethnic Conflicts on Kenyans' Stability and Development." Paper prepared for the USAID conference on conflict resolution in the Greater Horn of Africa, June 1997. Accessed 30 January 2016. http://citeseerx.ist.psu.edu/viewdoc/download?doi=10.1.1.596.7855&rep=rep1&type=pdf.

Ogunji, James A. "Fostering the Identity and Mission of Christian Education in Africa." *Journal of Research on Christian Education* 21, no. 1 (2012): 46–61. DOI: 10.1080/10656219.2012.659611.

Postman, Neil. *The End of Education: Redefining the Value of School.* New York: Vintage, 1996.

Schultheis, Michael J. "Head in the Clouds and Feet in the Mud: The Role of Private Universities in the Integration of Christian Mission and Transformational Development." *Transformation* 22, no. 2 (April 2005): 97–105.

Thomas, John Charles. "Administrative, Faculty, and Staff Perceptions of Organizational Climate and Commitment in Christian Higher Education." *Christian Higher Education* 7, no. 3 (July 2008): 226–252. Academic Search Premier, EBSCOhost. Accessed 30 December 2015.

Van der Walt, B. J. "The Challenge of Christian Higher Education on the African Continent in the Twenty-First Century." *Christian Higher Education* 1, nos. 2–3 (2002): 195–227. DOI: 10.1080/15363750213811.

Wayne, Israel. "What Is a Christian Worldview?" Biblical Worldview. Accessed 4 December 2016. http://www.christianworldview.net.

Wilkins, Steve. *Beyond Bumper Sticker Ethics: An Introduction to Theories of Right and Wrong.* Downers Grove, IL: InterVarsity Press, 1995.

List of Contributors

David Bawks is an ordained minister with Nairobi Chapel, having served in Kenya since 2008. He graduated from Wheaton College (Illinois, USA) with a bachelor of arts in Biblical/Theological Studies and History, then went on to complete a master of divinity at Africa International University. Previously, he taught at Carlile College and led the Nairobi Chapel Tyrannus Hall training ministry. Currently, he leads a new church plant at Nairobi Chapel Karen.

Elkanah Cheboi is a PhD candidate at Africa International University studying Biblical Studies. He is a licensed pastor with the Africa Inland Church Kenya. He teaches in several colleges in Kenya and Rwanda on a part-time basis. In the past he served for five years as a local church pastor and as a chaplain in a mission hospital and nursing college.

J. Gregory Crofford is in his third decade of missionary service, having worked in educational and church development roles in four sub-Saharan African nations and Haiti. Currently, he is Dean of the School of Religion and Christian Ministry at Africa Nazarene University, where he is also Coordinator of the PhD (Religion) program. Dr Crofford received his PhD (Theology) from the University of Manchester (UK) with a focus on Wesleyan theology. He is an ordained elder in the Church of the Nazarene.

Robert Falconer (PhD) holds degrees in Architecture and Theology. He practiced architecture for seven years, after which he went to Kenya for three years as a missionary. He currently works at the South African Theological Seminary as the program coordinator for MTh and PhD research and takes a mentorship approach to student research concept development and supervision. His primary research interests are architecture and theology, soteriology, eschatology, and African theology.

Harriet Akugizibwe Caroline Kintu has been a missionary with Campus Crusade for Christ International (Cru) since 1996. She is currently a lecturer at International Leadership University, formerly known as Nairobi International School of Theology (NIST). Harriet is a PhD candidate (Education Curriculum and Instruction) at Africa International University. She holds a master of education (Curriculum and Instruction) from Africa International University, a master of arts in Biblical Counseling from Nairobi International School of

Theology, and a bachelor of arts with education from Makerere University Kampala. Before joining NIST in 2000, Harriet trained and mentored new Cru staff for the Southern and Eastern Africa region. She is married to Moses Kintu (PhD) and they have three teenage sons.

Paul M. Mbandi is the Executive Director of Missions Afield Leadership Development Africa (MALDA) and the leader of the PhD in Theological Studies program at International Leadership University in Nairobi, Kenya. He holds a PhD in Theological Studies from Trinity International University.

Elizabeth Mburu is the regional coordinator of Langham Literature in Africa. She also serves as an adjunct associate professor of New Testament and Greek at International Leadership University, Africa International University, and Pan Africa Christian University. She pursued her doctoral studies at Southeastern Baptist Theological Seminary in Wake Forest, North Carolina, USA, earning a PhD in Biblical Studies – New Testament. Currently she teaches Greek, New Testament Studies, Hermeneutics, and Worldview Studies. She serves on the editorial teams of the Africa Bible Commentary (as coordinator and New Testament editor) and the Africa Society for Evangelical Theology, and is a curriculum evaluator for the Association of Christian Theological Education in Africa (ACTEA).

Kyama Mugambi is an associate researcher with the Centre for World Christianity at the Africa International University (AIU). He also serves as the Editorial Manager of the African Theological Network Press (ATNP). Prior to this he was the director of Africa-wide church-planting initiatives at the Mavuno Church. His PhD from AIU is in World Christianity, focusing on leadership in African Christian revitalization movements. His research interests include African Pentecostalism, current issues in African Christianity, and the role of faith in public life.

Kevin Muriithi serves two congregations in Loresho Parish as a youth pastor in the Presbyterian Church. Having studied and worked as an electrical engineer in energy and power systems, he was awarded an MA in Biblical and Theological Studies at the International Leadership University with highest honors. As a co-founder of Apologetics Kenya, he has presented and written papers for several institutions and publications, including the *Africa Bible Commentary*, in addition to his book *A Curious Faith: Love, Loss and Living*. He is also an adjunct lecturer at the Pan Africa Christian University. He is married to Jessica Murugi Muriithi and they reside in Nairobi.

David K. Ngaruiya is an associate professor at the International Leadership University where he has served in various capacities, such as Deputy Vice Chancellor for Research, Extension, and Development. He holds a PhD in Intercultural Studies from Trinity Evangelical Divinity School. He served as chair of the Africa Society of Evangelical Theology (2015–2016). He has published journal and book articles and served as co-editor and contributor to the book *Communities of Faith in Africa and African Diaspora* (Pickwick Publications, 2013). He also served as one of the directors of the Africa Leadership Study published by Orbis in New York and is currently the Director of PhD in Theological Studies at the International Leadership University.

Samuel Otieno Oketch has been the Nazarene Compassionate Ministries Africa East Field Coordinator since March 2012. He previously served in the HIV and AIDS department in the same ministry from November 2004. Oketch attended Africa Nazarene University between 1999 and 2003, and attained a bachelor's degree in Theology. In 2005, he graduated with a master of arts in Religion from the same university, and is currently a student in the doctor of ministry program at Africa Nazarene University. Oketch is an ordained minister in the Church of the Nazarene.

Rodney L. Reed is a missionary educator who has served at Africa Nazarene University in Nairobi, Kenya, since 2001. Currently, he is the Deputy Vice-Chancellor of Academic Affairs, a position he has held since 2010. Prior to that he served as the Chair of the Department of Religion for nine years. He holds a PhD in Theological Ethics from Drew University and is an ordained minister in the Church of the Nazarene.

Langham Partnership is a global fellowship working in pursuit of the vision God entrusted to its founder John Stott –

> *to facilitate the growth of the church in maturity and Christ-likeness through raising the standards of biblical preaching and teaching.*

Our vision is to see churches in the majority world equipped for mission and growing to maturity in Christ through the ministry of pastors and leaders who believe, teach and live by the Word of God.

Our mission is to strengthen the ministry of the Word of God through:
• nurturing national movements for biblical preaching
• fostering the creation and distribution of evangelical literature
• enhancing evangelical theological education
especially in countries where churches are under-resourced.

Our ministry

Langham Preaching partners with national leaders to nurture indigenous biblical preaching movements for pastors and lay preachers all around the world. With the support of a team of trainers from many countries, a multi-level programme of seminars provides practical training, and is followed by a programme for training local facilitators. Local preachers' groups and national and regional networks ensure continuity and ongoing development, seeking to build vigorous movements committed to Bible exposition.

Langham Literature provides majority world preachers, scholars and seminary libraries with evangelical books and electronic resources through publishing and distribution, grants and discounts. The programme also fosters the creation of indigenous evangelical books in many languages, through writer's grants, strengthening local evangelical publishing houses, and investment in major regional literature projects, such as one volume Bible commentaries like *The Africa Bible Commentary* and *The South Asia Bible Commentary*.

Langham Scholars provides financial support for evangelical doctoral students from the majority world so that, when they return home, they may train pastors and other Christian leaders with sound, biblical and theological teaching. This programme equips those who equip others. Langham Scholars also works in partnership with majority world seminaries in strengthening evangelical theological education. A growing number of Langham Scholars study in high quality doctoral programmes in the majority world itself. As well as teaching the next generation of pastors, graduated Langham Scholars exercise significant influence through their writing and leadership.

To learn more about Langham Partnership and the work we do visit **langham.org**

Lightning Source UK Ltd.
Milton Keynes UK
UKHW010935230219
337623UK00004B/80/P